BEV & WINDY
HOPE THAT YOU ENJOY
THE BOOK. THANKS FOR
OUR SUPPORT FOR THE NEXT
NEW CITY OF DUNWOODY.

Oliver

CREATING THE NEW CITY OF SANDY SPRINGS

THE 21ST CENTURY PARADIGM: PRIVATE INDUSTRY

Oliver W. Porter

Bloomington, IN  Milton Keynes, UK
authorHOUSE®

AuthorHouse™
1663 Liberty Drive, Suite 200
Bloomington, IN 47403
www.authorhouse.com
Phone: 1-800-839-8640

AuthorHouse™ UK Ltd.
500 Avebury Boulevard
Central Milton Keynes, MK9 2BE
www.authorhouse.co.uk
Phone: 08001974150

This book is a work of non-fiction. Unless otherwise noted, the author and the publisher make no explicit guarantees as to the accuracy of the information contained in this book and in some cases, names of people and places have been altered to protect their privacy.

First published by AuthorHouse 8/7/2006

ISBN: 1-4259-5437-5 (sc)
ISBN: 1-4259-5436-7 (dj)

Library of Congress Control Number: 2006907041

Printed in the United States of America
Bloomington, Indiana

This book is printed on acid-free paper.

ACKNOWLEDGEMENTS

The following individuals are acknowledged for their contribution in editing and proof-reading the manuscript.

Teara Joy Collins, Senior, University of Georgia, School of Journalism for proofing and commenting on the book, and for assistance with my cranky computer.

Bernard Kearse, Attorney, Author, and co-chair of the Human Resources Task Force, for very helpful suggestions on the book.

Brent Temmer, corporate executive, and newspaper editor in an earlier life, for detailed editing of the book. Any errors that remain are surely mine. Brent had a difficult task in converting the literary equivalent of a southern drawl into readable English.

Carol Thorup, retired executive in the nuclear industry, Secretary and Board member of the Committee for Sandy Springs, Recording Secretary for the Governor's Commission on Sandy Springs (surely the most overqualified secretary in history) for her great diligence in reading, proofing and offering suggestions on the book.

Fred Bentley, Cecil McClendon and Bill Riley
For their contribution of pro bono legal work to the city and for the use of various contracts in this book.

Citizens of Sandy Springs, who volunteered untold days, weeks and months of time to implementing the city. This is their story.

DEDICATION

*To Pat Porter, my beautiful and supportive wife,
who graciously allowed me to give up a year of our
lives to implement the City of Sandy Springs*

PREFACE

It is January 1, 2006, as I begin to write this book. The sounds of "Happy New Year" and "Auld Lang Syne" still hang in the air as I reflect on the events of the year 2005.

In less than twelve months, the seventh largest city in the state of Georgia has been created. The City of Sandy Springs, a community of almost 90,000 people has been incorporated as Georgia's first new city in 50 years. "they said it couldn't be done" is too weak a phrase to capture the amazing progress from nothing, to a functioning municipal government in less than eleven months.

Of equal magnitude, was the organizers' decision to look to private industry as the principal supplier of the new city's services. The resulting contract with the international firm of CH2M HILL incorporates the widest range of services to be found in the United States. As such, Sandy Springs believes that it may become the model for the 21st century municipal government.

This book has a dual purpose:

(1) to serve as an aid to other communities that may be considering incorporation

(2) to offer a guide to existing municipalities that may be interested in contracting with private industry

To aid the reader in focusing on an area of interest, the book is structured to allow those interested in the second topic, i.e. contracting with private industry, to skip ahead to Chapter X, Competitive Contracting.

A history of the approximately twenty-five year struggle to gain approval by the Georgia General Assembly to allow the citizens to vote on their local government, would be very interesting. However, the author has chosen to focus solely on the process of the implementation of the city. References to the legislation are at times vital to understanding the implementation process, and will therefore appear in various chapters.

Possibly, a few words about me are in order to let the reader better understand the viewpoint from which the book is written.

First, it may be rather obvious that I am not a professional writer. My career was in the corporate world with one of the world's largest companies. I held a wide variety of positions including: engineering, planning, finance and marketing. In addition, I have had an extensive history of volunteer work, including having been the national chairman of two major charities in the health field. That experience extended to organizing many state and local not-for-profits. In retirement, I am an artist, with oil painting as my preferred medium.

My involvement with the effort to create the city of Sandy Springs began about seven years ago when I was asked to join the Board of the Committee for Sandy Springs.

Since that time, there have been a number of roles that involved me in every aspect of the start-up of the city:

(1) Chairman of the Charter Commission

(2) Volunteer Interim City Manager

(3) Chairman of the Governor's Commission on Sandy Springs

My contributions to the decision by Sandy Springs to seek the resources of private industry to serve the municipality included:

(1) Researching, introducing, and selling the concept to our leadership

(2) Drafting the massive Requests For Proposals (RFP's)

(3) Leading the Evaluation Team on RFP responses

(4) Leading the Contract Negotiation Team

All of the above roles, but especially the 50 to 60 hour work weeks of the past year, as the volunteer Interim City Manager, have provided me with a rather unique view of the formation of a new city, and in the value of contracting with private industry.

So, this book is not a novel, nor a history. It is intended to be a primer, to share our experiences, and to assist others in forming a city and/or the advantages of harnessing the resources of private industry in municipal government.

CONTENTS

CHAPTER I

*"The greatest test of courage on earth is
to bear defeat without losing heart."*

BACKGROUND

Sandy Springs, Georgia, is a community of almost 90,000 residents, burgeoning to about 125,000 during a workday. The area of the new city is 38 square miles, located immediately north of Atlanta. Sandy Springs is a vibrant component of the larger Metro Atlanta area, and includes both commercial and residential areas.

The commercial area is largely situated along two north-south corridors. One corridor being the "interstate like," limited access GA-400, with high-rise modern structures, which predominately house office complexes; and the other being Roswell Road, which serves as the retail "main street" of the community. This corridor primarily consists of low-rise buildings dating from 1950-1960.

Residential development, until recent years, has been single-family homes of medium to above-average cost for the region. Sandy Springs has some of the metro areas finest homes. The community is considered to be among the more affluent in Georgia.

In the past 20 years, with the introduction of rapid transit and GA-400, there has been a substantial buildup of apartments and condominiums, particularly along the two corridors.

Sandy Springs is a diverse community, with a minority population of approximately 28 percent that is rapidly growing, particularly in the Latino component.

The community has existed for more than 100 years, and for the past thirty of those years, has been seeking self-government. The author will not burden the reader with the politics, both partisan and personal, that thwarted the will of the community for all those years. Suffice it to say that party politics blocked the citizens' right to self- determination for that entire period.

The state elections of November 2004 overturned the party that had been in power for more than one hundred years. With the shift in control of the House to match the 2002 shift in control of the Senate and the governorship, cityhood became a realistic opportunity.

Throughout the long years "in the Wilderness," a dedicated group of citizens had kept the dream of self-government alive.

Organized as the Committee for Sandy Springs (CSS), the group had lobbied the Georgia General Assembly and continued to mold community sentiment in a determined manner. It was from this group that the Charter Commission described later in this chapter was formed. Further, the Committee was the driving force in shaping the bills necessary to form the city. (See Chapter IV).

It was against this backdrop that the community entered the year 2005, with greatly improved hopes of achieving its aspirations to obtain self-rule.

A. CHARTER COMMISSION

Several years before the City of Sandy Springs was incorporated, a Charter Commission was formed to study and codify the powers, structure and organization of the future city. The Commission was created by the Committee for Sandy Springs as an important step in the effort to gain cityhood. The author was asked to organize the Commission and was appointed to be the Chairman.

Members of the Charter Commission were recruited from all the geographic areas of the community to assure as strong a representation of views as possible.

Under Georgia law, there are three acceptable forms of municipal government. In general, these may be characterized as:

(1) Strong Mayor—the mayor is the chief executive and manages the administration

(2) Weak Mayor—the Council directs the administration

(3) City Manager—the City Manager directs the administration

No member of the Commission had ever participated in the effort to create a charter, so the work began at ground zero. Various governmental agencies and other local communities were contacted to obtain sample charters. The Georgia Municipal Association offered a model charter. Representatives of other government and academia were invited to make presentations and answer questions on the positive and negative aspects of the alternative forms.

Very quickly, it was recognized how complex and detailed the task of creating the charter was to be. There were as many views on each major component as there were members of the Commission. Therefore, the Chairman decided to divide the charter into three sections and to divide the Commission into subcommittees to address each section. The sections may be generally described as:

(1) Powers and Limitations

(2) Organization

(3) Legal

Each subcommittee brought forth, in turn, recommended language for their respective sections. There was general debate on each section by the Commission as a whole and every major provision was approved or amended by a majority vote.

The Charter Commission's final draft was presented to the Committee for Sandy Springs, which approved the draft. Subsequent bills filed with the Georgia General assembly were based on this charter. Over the years between the Charter Commission's work and the passing of the bill by the General Assembly, changes crept into the bill, usually of unknown origin, but generally attributed to legislative staff. The Chairman of the Commission would review the proposed Bill each year, and attempt to return it to the original form, sometimes with limited success.

For the most part, the surviving document reflected the work of the Charter Commission, which, in turn, reflected the desires of the community.

A brief outline of the content, and associated reasoning behind the Charter might be helpful to the reader.

First, the final document created a hybrid form of government, combining, in the opinion of the Charter Commission, the best features of the Strong Mayor and City Manager forms.

The intent of this hybrid was to place the policy-initiating function in the hands of a single official, the Mayor, responsible to the voters and elected by a citywide vote.

The second important intent was to have the best available professional city manager to manage the day-to-day operations of the city.

Highlights of the Sandy Springs Charter

    I. Powers of City enumerated – a very broad list

       A. Boundaries set

    II. Structure

       A. Mayor

B. Council – Six members elected by district with a residency requirement

Recommendation:
May be preferable to have a district residency requirement, but elect on an at-large basis.

C. Terms of Office – 4 years, nonstaggered

Recommendation:
Consider staggered term

D. Compensation

Recommendation:
Compensation was set quite low:
Mayor $25,000/year and Council members at $15,000/year

The desire was that these offices be part time, and basically performed by individuals desiring to be public servants as opposed to professional politicians. The salary level was intended to cover the campaign costs of the elected official.

E. Boards, commissions, and authorities nominated by Mayor, confirmed by Council

III. Powers of the Mayor and City Manager

A. Powers and Duties of Mayor enumerated.

The Mayor is the Chief Executive Officer, and as such is:

– The policy originator and public spokesperson

– Responsible for appointing the City Manager subject to confirmation by the Council

– Able to appoint Judge(s)

– Given a strong role in the budget process

B. Powers and Duties of the City Manager enumerated.

The City Manager is the Chief Administrative Officer, and as such is:

- Responsible for the day-to day-operations of the City

- Authorized to hire and fire city employees

- Responsible for preparing the budget

IV. Courts – powers and structure

V. Finance and Fiscal matters

VI. Called for a complete review of the charter by a new Charter Commission in five years

The Charter Bill is provided in its entirety in Appendix (B).

B. PRE-IMPLEMENTATION STRUCTURE

In Sandy Springs, and the other communities that I have advised, a volunteer organizing group has initiated the implementation process. In the case of Sandy Springs, the Committee for Sandy Springs had existed for about 30 years. However, all the effort had been focused on the attempt to gain the approval of the Georgia legislature to hold a referendum and form the city.

As it became apparent that legislative success was at hand, the organizers were ill prepared to begin the implementation phase. The Board of Directors of the Committee for Sandy Springs, which numbered about 25 volunteers, had a number of talented and dedicated people. But with the legislative focus, it had not developed a management team that could take on the implementation activities. Given this structure, the introduction of an Interim City Manager, or some similar position, was vital to providing the required focus and leadership. When there is a short time frame and a multiplicity of decisions, "leadership by committee" simply will not work.

The workload during early 2005, was divided into three components:

(1) The continuing legislative effort

(2) A referendum campaign

(3) Implementation of the city

The first component, the legislative push, was successful and ended in April. Then there was need for focusing on obtaining the governor's signature as soon as possible to meet a very short time line to have the bill reviewed by the Justice Department, and to have the referendum placed on the ballot.

The Board of the Committee for Sandy Springs also was active in seeking the governor's appointment of the Commission on Sandy Springs.

The referendum campaign group began the formal campaign immediately following the passage of the legislation.

When the incorporation of Sandy Springs broke the fifty-year drought of new cities in Georgia, a number of communities were encouraged to begin their own incorporation efforts (at least six of which the author has been advising in different degrees).

In a second community that the author is advising, Dunwoody, Georgia, the start up situation is quite different from that of Sandy Springs. This community has no history of an incorporation effort. This has led to an almost simultaneous attempt to conduct a legislative push, referendum campaign, and implementation effort.

Using the Sandy Springs charter bill, and planning processes as a template, the adjacent community of Dunwoody rapidly organized. The prime mover, a state senator, put out a call for volunteers. From the initial group of about seventy people, a Steering Committee of three was selected. The Steering Committee supervised the formation and provided the charges to the required task forces. These task forces were modeled on the Sandy Springs structure, and initially numbered fourteen. The author was retained as an advisor for every phase of the implementation. As of this date, success of the legislative effort is still undecided.

Recommendation:
The implementation phase should be led by no more than three people. There are too many decisions that must be handled quickly and decisively to be managed by a larger group.

Start-Up Needs

Organizers need several basic tools to begin their implementation efforts. Among the more important are:

(1) A fundraising program

   The community will need funds to support:

   (a) a fiscal viability study

   (b) a referendum campaign

   (c) limited operating expenses for the organizing committee

   (d) consulting fees (optional)

(2) Large mail and email lists

(3) A website

(4) Volunteer leadership

   Qualifications should include the following:

   (a) a willingness to make a major time commitment

   (b) possession of skills that include planning, financial, organizational, and communications

   (c) an ability to make decisions

   (d) an ability to cooperate with others

The foregoing may seem to be a large order, but if one person cannot be identified with these characteristics and experience, possibly two or three can form a leadership team.

C. WESTON

Significant credit for the success of Sandy Springs should be given to the example and helpfulness of the city of Weston, Florida; and to its progressive City Manager, John Flint. Weston is a beautiful planned development set in the wetlands west of Fort Lauderdale.

Early in 2005, the author, now the Interim City Manager (ICM) for Sandy Springs, learned of Weston's status as a "contract city." Having begun as a planned development and grown to a population of about 40,000, by 1996, Weston had chosen to incorporate and to continue working with private-industry providers for most of its services.

The initial review of Weston's published material revealed a well-run city with strong finances. The author presented the case to the Committee for Sandy Springs and sought their approval to make an exploratory visit to Weston.

Mr. Flint was extremely hospitable and informative. His enthusiasm for forming operating partnerships with private industry and the improved efficiency and responsiveness of this method was infectious. Observing the level of competence that the firms brought to the city manager's weekly staff meeting was most impressive. The City staff consisted of the leaders of the firms' respective service-delivery teams. Responses to the City Manager's questions were clear and concise. If, on rare occasion, a staff member did not have an immediate answer, the response was "I will have that to you in two hours, or tomorrow at the latest." The City's contractor representatives served up no bull and engaged in no evasion. It was clear that Weston's people were on top of their jobs.

While the leaders were impressive in their competence and their cooperative spirit, the icing on the cake was the author's opportunity to observe and speak with other lower level employees of the firms at their worksites. When queried on their responsibilities (out of sight of their supervisors) they were clear. There appeared to be no doubt in their minds that satisfying the citizenry was their primary responsibility. As many said in one-way or another "everyone I meet must go away happy." The author thought, "just like our county employees" – NOT!

It was certainly clear that this was an innovative and improved way of performing municipal services.

Later in the year, contacts were made with the City Manager in Centennial, Colorado, John Pazour. Centennial had chosen to do a great deal of private contracting and John was quite helpful in offering advice and pointing out potential pitfalls.

During private conversations with the companies serving Weston, the Interim City Manager questioned whether they thought that their firms might be interested in extending services to Sandy Springs. Upon receiving a positive response, the ICM was emboldened to ask two more questions to which he really did not anticipate an enthusiastic answer. However, proceeding in the spirit of "nothing ventured, nothing gained," the questions were put.

(1) Sandy Springs will receive the vast majority of its revenue in the second half of the year. Do you think that your firm would be willing to defer payment for services for most of the year?

Then the big one:

(2) Sandy Springs has no authority to make contracts until the city is incorporated. Do you think that your firm might be willing to spend the funds necessary to implement the city in advance of having a contract?

The answer to both questions was a very encouraging, and surprising, "yes."

It was upon these informal and completely nonbinding assurances that the ultimate creation of the new city was founded.

As an aside, neither of these two companies chose to enter a bid proposal for the Sandy Springs' contracts.

The next step in the process was to arrange for the Weston team, the city manager, and leaders from the two principal contractors to travel to Sandy Springs and tell their stories to the Committee for Sandy Springs.

The team agreed to come at their own expense and their testimonies had a profound and favorable influence on Sandy Springs' organizers.

The result was that the Interim City Manager was authorized to pursue the option of seeking proposals from private industry for a broad array of municipal services in Sandy Springs. To our knowledge, the result was the largest municipality ever started with such a significant range of private industry contracted services in the nation.

It all began with a visit to Weston.

CHAPTER II

"I've Been on a Calendar, but Never on Time"
Marilyn Monroe

TIMELINE

The timeline for implementing Sandy Springs was extremely short. Attachment (A) at the end of this chapter shows the original time line, or action plan that the author constructed in December 2004. This rudimentary plan was the first attempt to capture the actions necessary to implement the city in the time required. It was obvious that a major problem loomed for the organizers. Too many objectives had to be achieved in the last few weeks of the year because the election was scheduled so late (November) in the period. However, this was the time specified in the authorizing legislation, and we had to deal with it. The recognition of the extraordinary difficulty involved with meeting the schedule was a significant factor in driving the author's search for unconventional approaches for starting the city. A recommendation for establishing a more workable timeline will be offered later in this chapter.

The legislation that the Georgia General Assembly passed and was signed into law in April, 2005, provided for incorporation of Sandy Springs on December 1, of the same year. During that period, the bill had to receive the governor's approval, and a referendum had to be conducted to allow the community to decide on the creation of the new

13

city. This allowed a scant five months after the referendum for the city to be implemented.

On June 6, 2005, the citizens spoke. After almost thirty years of being frustrated by partisan politics, the people of Sandy Springs cast 94 percent of their votes in favor of forming a new city.

There was a great deal of legitimate concern about the timetable. First, the required bills were delayed in the House of Representatives until the last day that would allow them to go to the Senate. Then the Senate, in the last hour of the last day of the 2005 session, passed the bills.

The governor then delayed signing the legislation until April 15, 2005. Although that signing would appear to allow adequate time to enable the referendum ballots to be prepared, in southern states there is an additional problem. Georgia continues to be burdened with the Voting Rights Act of 1965, which requires a review by the Justice Department of any change in voting patterns. The creation of a new city triggers such a review, which may, and often does, consume up to sixty days.

If Justice had taken the full time allowed, and with the County requirement for a thirty-day lead time to prepare the referendum, the Sandy Springs vote could not have been held on time. The domino effect would have been to delay the election of Council and the start of the city by almost a year.

Fortunately, every effort had been made to understand Justice's potential concerns and to construct the Sandy Springs Council districts to eliminate any possible geographic or racial concerns. This effort, along with prenotification to Justice, allowed a faster than normal review.

With the overwhelming approval of the new city by the voters, the next political milestone was the election of the Mayor and Council members on November 8, 2005.

Finally, the community had official leaders, but only three weeks before incorporation! Elected officials still had no authority to act on behalf of the City.

A schedule of significant events follows that may clarify the timeline for Sandy Springs.

Date	Event
January 13, 2005	Task Force 3 organizational meeting
March 20	House passes bills
March 31	Senate passes bills
April 15	Governor signs bills
June 6	Referendum passes
June 23	Governor's Commission appointed
June 29	Governor's Commission meets and issues Requests for Proposals (RFPs)
August 14	Pre-proposal conference
August 31	Proposals submitted
September 14	Governor's Commission selects top proposal and authorizes negotiations
September 24 - October 11	Candidates for elected office training
October18	Governor's Commission recommends contracts
November 8	Elections
December 1	Incorporation; City begins planning, zoning and permitting responsibilities
December 6	Runoff elections
December 20	Contract with private firm signed
January 1, 2006	Full operations assumed by city
February 15, 2006	City Manager begins work

It should be obvious from the foregoing timetable that there was hardly sufficient time to efficiently form the city. The city officials were elected only three weeks before the city was officially incorporated. Even after election, the new mayor and council had no authority to act on behalf of the city until incorporation. The problem could have been complicated further by runoffs that would not occur until six days after incorporation. Fortunately, there were only two runoffs for Council seats, allowing a quorum to be seated on Day One.

A major improvement in a new city's ability to start operations would be to have created a better timeline. An interval is needed, six months minimum, between the time that the elected officials or an appointed body, has the authority to make binding deals and the start of operations.

Authorizing the elected officials to form contracts and make other commitments well in advance of the city's start date, will pay big dividends. If the preferred alternative for providing services is to use private industry, the ability to commit to contracts will result in greatly reduced costs. This will be discussed more fully in the chapters on private industry, but in short, it is a matter of risk. If firms are asked to expend funds in advance of having a signed contract as was necessary in Sandy Springs, two factors drive up costs:

(1) Fewer companies will be willing to submit proposals

(2) The companies that do bid will build a risk premium into their proposals.

Even if the city plans to provide services in the traditional do-it-yourself mode, it will be necessary to hire personnel, acquire assets and systems, and make many other decisions well in advance of the start date. None of that can be done efficiently without authority.

In Sandy Springs, there were only two original hires since we were contracting all the other work. Those hires were the Deputy City Manager and City Clerk. Fortunately, both of these people were willing to give notice to their existing employer thirty days before starting work with Sandy Springs. They did that even though there could be no binding agreement that the jobs would be theirs.

The new city was fortunate to be able to acquire top quality employees under these conditions.

Recommendation:
Establish the incorporation and election of city officials at least six months before beginning the city's services.

ATTACHMENT (A)

INITIAL TIME-LINE

<u>*Action Plan to establish city of SandSprings*</u>
<u>*11-29-04*</u>

Month 2005	J	F	M	A	M	J	J	A	S	O	N	D
Create Action Plan	X						X = done					

I. CONDUCT REFERENDUM
	J	F	M	A	M	J	J	A	S	O	N	D
A. Bill passed	X											
B. Bill signed		X										

	J	F	M	A	M	J	J	A	S	O	N	D
C. Charter												
1. Review bill	xxx											
2. Amend bill	x											

	J	F	M	A	M	J	J	A	S	O	N	D
D. Public Awareness campaign												
1. Establish PA task force	X											
2. Create campaign plan	xxx											
3. Execute plan		xxxx	x	xxxx								

	J	F	M	A	M	J	J	A	S	O	N	D
E. Conduct Referendum												
1. Establish Referendum Committee	X											
2. Determine procedures and date for referendum		xxx										
3. Review referendum language			xxx									
4. REFERENDUM				X								

II. ELECTIONS
	J	F	M	A	M	J	J	A	S	O	N	D
A. Election										X		
1. Recruit candidates						xxxxxxxxx						
2. Provide candidate data for ballot								xxx				

Month 2005	J	F	M	A	M	J	J	A	S	O	N	D
3. Campaigns									xxxxxx	x		
4. Pretrain Candidates					xxxxxxxxxxx							

III. ESTABLISH CITY

	J	F	M	A	M	J	J	A	S	O	N	D
III. ESTABLISH CITY												X
A. Recruit Interim City Manager	X											
1. Interim City Manager Coordinates all task forces to implement City	xxxxxxxxxxxxxxxxxxxxxxxxxxxxx											
B. Finances												
1. Establish Finance Task Force	X											
2. Determine sources of funds		x	xxx									
3. Determine timing of transfer			xxx									
4. Negotiate for fund transfer									xxxxxxxxx			
5. Create prelim budget					xxxxxx							
6. Estimate initial funds needs							xxx					
7. Negotiate Line of Credit									xxxxxx			
C. Personel												
1. Establish Human Resources Task Force	X											
2. Search for City Manager												
a. Prepare job description			xxx									
b. Select Headhunter					xxxx							
c. Advertise							xxxxxx					
d. Prelim interviews								xxxx				
e. Finalist list									xxx			
f. Mayoral interviews											xxxx	
g. Hire City Mgr												X
3. City Staff												X
a. City clerk												X
b. Finance Mgr												X
c. Other												
4. Prepare prelim.budget									xxxxxx			

Month 2005	J	F	M	A	M	J	J	A	S	O	N	D
D. Legal/Courts												
1. Appoint Judge										X	X	
2. Determine Facilities needs for court, detention etc.				xxxxx								
a. Coordinate with Properties Task Force						xxxxx						
3. Retain City Attorney									xxxx	X		
4. Prepare prelim budget								xxxxxxxxx				
E. Services												
1. Establish Service Task Forces	X											
2. Determine services to be provided by City			x	x								
a. Police												
b. Fire												
c. Public Works												
d. Parks												
e. Other												
3. Contact other Gov'ts for data		xxxxxx										
4. Determine source (hire or contract)				xxxx								
a. Hiring process							xxxxxxxxxx				X	
b. if contract: Negotiation process							xxxxxxxxxxxx				X	
5. Prepare prelim. Budgets								xxxx	xxx			
E. Accounting/MIS System												
1. Establish Accounting Task Force		X										
2. Determine Needs		x	xxxxxx									
3. Determine source(buy or contract)												
a. if buy: procural process						xxxxxxxxxxxxxxxxxxx						
b. if contract: negotiation process						xxxxxxxxxxxxxxxxxx						
4. work with county to set up sub accts							xxxxxxxx					
5. Prepare prelim. budget									xxxxx			
6. Council approves											X	

Month 2005	J	F	M A	M J	J	A	S	O N	D

F. Ordinances

  1. Establish Ordinance Task Force   X

    a. Review ordinances   xxxxxx

      - Fulton County, Roswell, Alpharetta, etc.

    b. Prepare draft ordinances   xxxxxxxxxxxx

    c. Council review   xxxx

    d. Approve ordinances   X

G. Administration

  1. Establish Admin. Task Force   X

    a. Coordinate with all Task Forces to   xxxxxxxxxxxxxxxxxxxxxxx
      aggregate needs

    b. establish initial staffing needs

    c.. Create preliminary budget   xxxxxxxxxxxxxxxxx

  2. Council approves budget   X

H. Physical Facilities

  1. Establish Properties Task Force   X

  2. Determine facilities that city will own   xxxxxx

    a. Negotiate turnover of facilities/records   x   xxxxxxxxxxx

    b. Transfer facilities   X

  4. Determine requirements for leased   xxxxxx
      facilities

    a. Negotiate leases   x   xxxxxxxxxxx

    b. Council approve leases   X

  5. Prepare prelim budget   xxxxxxxxx

  6. Determine Temporary Facilities   xxxx
      Needs

    a. identify locations   xxxx

    b. negotiate for space   xxxx

    c. Sandy Springs Board approves   X

Month 2005	J	F	M	A	M	J	J	A	S	O	N	D

I. Community Development

1. Establish Comm. Dev Task Force — X (Jan)

2. Review organization& codes of other Gov'ts — xxxxxxxx (F–M)

   - Fulton county,Roswell, etc. — xxxxxxxx (M–A)

3. Prepare Prelim. zoning codes

4. Recruit Zoning Board — xxxxxxxx (M–J)

   a. Zoning Board named by Council — X (N)

5. Prepare Prelim. building codes

   a. Determine requirements to enforce codes — xxxxxxx (M)

   b. Identify resources — xxxxxxxx (J)

   c. Council approves — X (N)

6. Determine Planning requirements on city

   a. make preliminary plans to meet requirements

7. Prepare prelim. budget — xxxxxxxxx (A–S)

J. Transportation

1. Establish Transportation Task Force — X (Jan)

2. Review other Gov'ts to identify needs — xxxxxxx (M)

3. Identify sources for resources — xxxxxx (M)

4. make "acquire vs contract" recommendation — xxxxxxx (M)

5. Prepare prelim budget — xxxxxxxxx (A–S)

K. Professional Assistance (consultants)

1. Interim city Manager investigates — xxxx (J)

2. Determine desirability & availability — x xxxxxx (J–F)

   a. Vinson Institute

   b. Ga. Municipal Assoc.

   c. other

3. Make recommendation to Board — X (M)

4. Board hires consultants as needed — X (M)

Month 2005	J	F	M A	M J	J	A	S	O	N	D

L. Misc.

1. Name official Spokesperson(s)   **X**

Notes:

(1) Every effort has been made to initiate each function as early as possible.

(2) Many functions are by necessity squeezed into the last six weeks of the year due to the Dec.1, 2005 start date.

C H A P T E R   I I I

VIABILITY
Capable of Success or Continuing Effectiveness

VIABILITY STUDIES

An important step leading to the implementation phase for the city was the production of an economic viability study. Actually, in the case of Sandy Springs, there was a study and then two updates, with the final version being completed at the end of 2004.

These studies are vital for several reasons:

(1) To assure the organizers that the city can succeed

(2) To assure the legislature of the economic viability of the city

(3) To assure the community that the new city would not result in unreasonable taxes

To accomplish these objectives, it was necessary that the study be conducted by a respected and objective third party. Sandy Springs was fortunate to be able to draw upon the resources of the Carl Vinson Institute of Government, a branch of the University of Georgia with extensive experience in government. The Institute has the advantage of a record of working with the Georgia General Assembly on many economic studies. The Institute's excellent reputation was very helpful in satisfying the concerns of all the involved parties.

From the work of the Vinson Institute, and other sources, it was very clear that Sandy Springs was definitely subsidizing, and by a large margin, other portions of Fulton County. Several studies released by the county staff also had identified this subsidy, although the amounts differed significantly.

While the degree of subsidy varied between studies, there was no doubt that Sandy Springs could use the surplus of revenue over expense to easily support a new municipal government.

The knee-jerk reaction, and a fairly logical one, of citizens is that a new level of government will result in greater cost to the taxpayer. The economic viability study showed that our taxpayers already were paying more than enough to support a municipal government; we just had not been receiving ithe services!

The point for those considering forming new city governments is this: Do not fool yourselves. Pay the price, conduct the necessary objective fiscal viability study, and proceed accordingly.

A word about what should be expected from a viability study: The study team can look at the revenue and costs that have been collected and expended in the area of the proposed city. This can be more or less difficult, depending on the existing government's ability to isolate finances to the area. In the case of Sandy Springs, the study was aided by the fact that we were in a Special Services District. This helped to isolate costs. Another option is to compare the costs of similar cities as a benchmark.

Regarding revenue, Ad Valorem taxes and Special Service District taxes could be estimated within reason.. The division of a special sales tax known as Local Option Sales Tax, or LOST, had to be estimated. LOST was shared between the county and the ten existing cities within the county. The proper division of LOST, to include the new city, had to be specified within the Enabling Act.

There were approximately 22 other less significant, but important in the aggregate, revenue sources that had to be estimated.

Do not expect that the viability study will provide a working budget, but it will indicate whether a successful budget is possible. Remember also that the study is identifying costs at the previous level of service. If your community demands improved levels of service, and most will have such a desire, those will come at an extra cost. These are the budget decisions that ultimately should lie at the feet of the elected officials, and not the implementers.

Once a reliable viability study is in hand, the organizers will be able to consider the results. Although there is likely to be a great deal of enthusiasm for moving forward without regard to the finances, that should be done with caution. To the more fervent city-hood enthusiasts, there may be legitimate reasons for creating the city other than financial benefits. These other benefits may include local control, efficiency, and improved services. Without question, those benefits may outweigh financial considerations to the enthusiast. Just be aware that to many citizens, probably the majority, the only question is going to be, "will my taxes go up?" A viability study that shows that a tax increase will not be necessary is an enormous plus for the referendum campaign.

The cost to have a viability study performed by a reputable objective entity in Georgia, has ranged from $30,000 to $50,000. It is worth every penny.

CHAPTER IV

"If you like laws and sausage, you should never watch either one being made."

-Otto Von Bismarck

LEGISLATION

A. DUAL BILLS

In Georgia, municipal governments may be established only by the General Assembly. Since there had not been a new city incorporated in Georgia in fifty years, the laws of the state did not encourage such activity. In fact many statutes and even constitutional provisions served as obstacles.

Sandy Springs was required to draft two Bills to effect incorporation. The first was an Enabling Act to amend state laws to allow the formation of the city. (Georgia House Bill 36; April, 2005), See Appendix A; and the second was the Charter Bill (Georgia House Bill 37, April, 2005), See Appendix B.

1. Charter Bill

The Charter was discussed in more detail in Chapter (I A), Charter Commission, however, there were several provisions that dealt with concerns other than normal charter provisions. The most important among these being the establishment of a referendum for the residents of Sandy Springs to vote on incorporation.

2. Enabling Act

The Enabling Act was an amendment to existing statewide statutes that removed obstacles and allowed the formation of new cities.

First among the statutes that had to be changed was the one dealing with the "three mile limit." Georgia law prohibited the incorporation of a new city within three miles of an existing city.

Since Sandy Springs abutted the city of Atlanta, that provision had to be eliminated entirely.

A second provision concerning the delivery of services was modified to provide a two-year period for new cities to arrange to qualify by providing certain minimum services.

One of the more unusual provisions was the creation of a five-person commission to be appointed by the governor to assist in the preparation of the new government. (See Chapter VII, Governor's Commission)

A critical new provision provided the formula by which Local Option Sales Taxes would be allocated to a new city.

There were more than a dozen additional changes covered by the Enabling Act, to allow Sandy Springs and potentially other communities, to break the fifty-year drought on new cities in Georgia.

B. LEGISLATION DEFICIENCIES

This discussion of the two Sandy Springs bills will offer suggestions to other communities on changes that would improve the cities' implementation processes. No criticism of the bills drafters is intended. They were working under the combined pressures of politics and of time in trying to gain approval of the legislation.

We, the organizers, created the largest problem by insisting that the city must be started as soon as possible. This led to the situation in which it was necessary to conduct the entire implementation effort with volunteers who had neither authority nor funds.

The single most important recommendation that the author can make with regard to an authorizing bill is to adopt a more favorable timeline.

Specifically, there should be a minimum of six months between the incorporation of the city, with nearly concurrent election of city officials, and the time when city services are to begin. In all probability, revenues also will be delayed for the same period. (If limited funds are needed during that period, banks will be very amenable to lines of credit). The critical point is that during this period, the elected officials must have the authority to enter into binding contracts, and/or employment agreements.

This recommendation is important. Consider the plight of Sandy Springs. During the entire implementation period, the volunteers had no authority to make a single binding agreement, right up to midnight on November 30. One minute later, 12:01 a.m. December 1, the city had to be operating. Could it be done? Obviously, yes – we did it. However, there is clearly a better way. The lesson is, give yourselves some time and authority.

If you are considering contracting with private industry for key services and functions, the ability to negotiate and approve contracts will be a tremendous asset.

Day One Processes

A second area of concern in the Sandy Springs' bills was the failure to spell out any method for the initial establishment of ordinances and codes. When a new city government begins operation, it has an immediate need to have laws in place. Without legislative action, it is extremely difficult to enact laws on Day One.

The absence of statutes would leave a city in a very vulnerable position. Legal opinion was that the new city of Sandy Springs could not rely upon the existing county ordinances and code. It was necessary to adopt and/or modify those statutes officially. Further, it was necessary to follow the charter provisions on notice and hearings. Failure to scrupulously follow these procedures would probably result in a court challenge to the city's legal authority to enforce the ordinances and codes. Zoning and licensing decisions, and enforcement, were particularly vulnerable to challenge by developers, landowners and businesses. If the statutes could be shown to have been approved without proper process, then all subsequent decisions and actions of the city would be illegal and unenforceable.

The Charter legislation had sufficient detail concerning the approval process for ordinances and codes once the city was in full operation. Such approvals require public notices; in some cases multiple hearings, and must allow for public comment. When Day One of the new city arrives, there is no opportunity to have provided notice, because there has been no authority to issue notices. The multiple hearing processes also may preclude passage of vital statutes and resolutions on Day One.

Recommendation:
A section of the authorizing legislation should include specific language that spells out the procedure for adoption of ordinances and codes on Day One.

That language must provide specific exemption from normal public notice requirements, and a waiver of multiple hearings.

State law likely will hinder the establishment of new cities. After all, laws often are designed to restrict rather than to create. One would hope that other states' laws were not as constricting as Georgia's. Because we had not authorized the creation of a new city in fifty years, there had been a long period when the legislature could ignore the issue.

Just as an example of the benign neglect, let me cite (in layman's language) the following:

Many new cities, such as Sandy Springs, with "back end loaded revenue" (we will receive most of our property tax revenue in October) will need to borrow funds early in the year to tide them over.

The Georgia constitution says that a city only can issue Tax Anticipation Notes (TANs), which is the preferred method for cities to float their expenses, in an amount not to exceed three fourths of their previous year's revenue. Now, while this is a prudent measure to apply fiscal restraint to existing cities, it does not require the mind of a mathematician to determine the amount of borrowing available to a new city—ZERO.

Another example: Sandy Springs opted to conduct competitive bidding for private industry to provide the major portion of the city's services. Naturally, any such contract would be enhanced by having a multiyear term. Under Georgia law, a city cannot make a binding multiyear contract. Sandy Springs was able to offer a six-year term, but was careful to make bidders aware that each year the contract must be reauthorized by the City Council

Still another: The various forms of Open Meeting/Open Records acts that many states have enacted are valuable. In Georgia, these laws are applied correctly to the functions of state and local government. However, these laws can be abused by the press, if it tries incorrectly to apply them to volunteer groups such as the Sandy Springs Task Forces. Volunteer groups with no public funding and no authority, are clearly not included in the laws' definition as affected parties. Actually, this is not a legislative deficiency, but an example of the abuse of the law that is possible if you are not diligent in your understanding of the existing statutes.

Let me hasten to clarify that Sandy Springs always had, and followed, a policy that meetings were open to the public. However the highly restrictive, and costly, provisions regarding advertising, agendas, and minutes that apply to government agencies under Georgia's Open Meeting/Open Record laws would have significantly inhibited citizens' rights to serve in the formation of the new city voluntarily.

A number of other examples exist of inhibiting laws that Sandy Springs had to overcome, or work around to get the job done. The point here is that the organizers of any new city should make the effort to identify all the "restrictive" laws early in the process.. It is so much simpler to find alternatives before you run into the wall of "thou shalt not" than after.

And still another: The enabling legislation should specify a method whereby major assets such as properties will be divided between the new city and the governmental area from which the city area is currently served. Examples of such properties are parks, fire and polices stations.

The absence of such legislation can lead to great divisiveness and ultimately to the courts. In the case of Sandy Springs, where it has been demonstrated that the citizens of the community had for many years been paying a larger share of the taxes per capita, the new city argued that it had already paid for the properties within the city's new boundaries. Conversely, the county asserted that it could not allow the city to have the property at less than market value. This controversy is more fully described in Chapter VIII, A.

Recommendation:
The method for an equitable separation of assets should be specified in the enabling legislation.

CHAPTER V

"Nevertheless, the people are the masters of our country, and this fact will never change..."
-Chen Shui-bian

REFERENDUM

In Georgia, after passage of the charter by the General Assembly, a referendum of the people in the area of the proposed city is required. For Sandy Springs, that referendum was held in June 2005. With the bill being signed by the governor in April, there was little time to prepare the citizenry. The Committee for Sandy Springs mounted a strong campaign to get out the vote and inform the voters on the merits of the city.

The campaign began with a final poll to determine the top service issues that concerned the voters. By a large margin, the number-one issue was zoning. Number two was traffic by a narrow margin over public safety. With these issues in mind, and the ever- present concern with taxes, the campaign was formulated.

Seven brochures were published dealing with the major issues. One was in Spanish to reach the growing Latino community. Precincts were evaluated to determine voting patterns. The result was that five large precincts with high voter turnouts were targeted for extra attention, such as door-to-door contacts. The large email list was utilized to provide very inexpensive contacts, along with providing data on the web site. Every opportunity to speak to homeowners' associations and civic clubs was taken.

Probably the greatest free assistance came from the county commissioners who opposed the city. It seemed that every blast from that group resulted in a large increase in the vote for the city. Never underestimate the power of your opponents to help you!

The result of the campaign was clear on election night. A large and vocal group of supporters gathered at the historic site of the springs for which the community is named, to await the referendum results. The first precinct that reported was one that had been a concern, and when it came in at more than ninety percent in favor of the city, the crowd went wild. As results poured in, it became clear that the referendum was a landslide for the city. In the end, in an off-year balloting, more than one third of the voters had cast ballots. Ninety-four percent of the voters had voted "yes." This result exceeded the wildest expectations of any of the organizers, and provided a mandate to create the city!

While the subject of this book is limited to the implementation of the city and is not intended to cover the political aspects of gaining cityhood, there are some obvious areas of overlap between the subjects.

One such area involves decisions on how much information to release, and when. The volunteer task forces were hard at work gathering data and forming recommendations. There is a natural tendency among those who are trying to win any type of political battle to want to release as much favorable information, and hold back as much unfavorable, as possible. There is also a strong desire to refute every argument by the opposition, and to do so immediately. Let me offer several reasons why you may want to refrain from following those impulses.

With regard to the preliminary data that the task forces were gathering and evaluating, there was much risk in going public with unfinished work that might subsequently prove to be wrong or at least subject to question. In Sandy Springs the initial opposition was all "knee-jerk" in nature, That is, it was founded on poor assumptions, without facts to support the position. An example of that type opposition was the oft-stated "fact" that taxes would have to be increased. That was erroneous.

Another area of attack was that there was no budget, therefore, the organizers do not know whether the city is viable or not. That too was erroneous. The Accounting Task Force had begun creating an increasingly reliable series of budgets from early in the process. However, any data that was released would immediately have been subjected to misinterpretation and distortion. The choice was made to rely upon the original viability study by a reputable third party (see Chapter III, Viability Studies) and to release no budget data before its time. It proved to be a winning strategy, plus the task forces could do their work without constantly defending budget assumptions.

In short, the opposition had little to offer. After stating their initial unsupported claims, unless we provided them unreliable data, they could do no more than continue to repeat the same opinions, over and over. The public grew tired of their refrain, and we maintained credibility by not rushing in with partial data.

The author is no political strategist, but is firmly convinced that it is ultimately far more important that the public be able to rely on the information provided, as opposed to providing early answers. Premature release of information can be very damaging to the referendum campaign.

CHAPTER VI

"Nothing will ever be attempted, if all possible
objections must be first overcome"
-Samuel Johnson

IMPLEMENTATION

A. INTERIM CITY MANAGER

In December 2004, the author realized the need for a single person to take responsibility for the implementation of the city. Due to the need for rapid action and a focused approach, management by committee was not a viable option.

Over the many years leading up to that point, the organizing group (Committee for Sandy Springs) had been focused on the very difficult political process of getting a charter bill through the Georgia legislature. Other than a cursory plan drafted by the author, no work had been attempted toward the actual implementation of the city.

It was clear that the organizers' immediate attention would continue to be on the legislative process, and then, if successful in securing passage, would shift to the referendum campaign.

Therefore, after much serious consideration of the requirements for the position, and the time commitment that serving would entail, the author decided to volunteer his services.

Among the capabilities and experience that were considered as important to the position were the following:

- Engineering/technical

- Financial

- Planning

- Organizational

- Personnel

A history of organizing new entities and proven leadership skills were also assets that the author brought to the table.

The reader might note that experience in government at any level was missing. While such experience may have been of value in the latter stages of implementation, it might have been a hindrance as we sought to find new and "out of the box" solutions for setting up the new city.

In January 2005, the Committee for Sandy Springs voted to accept the author's offer of services and approved the use of "Interim City Manager" as a working title. At that time, although it was not a requirement, the author volunteered that he would not run for any office, nor accept a paid staff position with the city. It was felt that such a commitment would eliminate any future perception that the Interim City Manager had something to gain from the many actions and decisions that would be necessary. The role was accepted as a year of public service.

As an aside, the author since retirement from the corporate world, had become an active painter, and therefore had business cards that read "Artist." In the earliest days as Interim City Manager, when these cards were presented to leaders in others in government, there was an almost visible recoiling. It became necessary to have new cards printed with Interim City Manager as the title. This clearly opened doors more effectively.

It also was amusing that the media, particularly the major newspaper in the area, seemed to be particularly concerned about the title. Their immediate question was "How can you have such a title as a volunteer?"

The response of "Who else is there?" seemed to add to their confusion. The point is that whether there is legal authority, or not, some individual must step forward and assume leadership.

There is a chapter on media relations that is recommended for anyone considering a city startup. In some cases it is definitely more "do what I say" than it is "do what I did" advice.

For anyone considering accepting the "Interim City Manager" or equivalent position, to lead the formation of a new city, you may want to be aware of the commitment required.

(1) **This is a full-time assignment.** The time commitment grew rapidly to a level of 50 to 60 hours per week, and sometimes more.

(2) **The Interim City Manager must be prepared to attend a number of night meetings.** Most of the volunteer task forces prefer evening meetings.

(3) **You must be flexible.** You will be dealing with volunteers. You must seek and accept the community's input. At the same time, you must establish a clear and concise direction for their work and keep them on track.

(4) **You must be a tireless promoter.** There is a constant requirement to sell the concept to the volunteers and to the public in general, and to keep them informed of the progress.

(5) **You must manage media communications effectively.** There is a need to deal with the media, who will tend to seek to report only negative or inflammatory issues. I hope that the media that you deal with will be more positive and professional than that which we faced.

(6) **You must be vigilant about legal issues.** Chapter IV B, Legislation Deficiencies outlines some of the Georgia laws that might have derailed our process. Few laws are designed to aid in creation; many are crafted to restrict activities.

Whether it is an Interim City Manager or some other title, there is a critical need for an individual leader throughout the implementation stage.

B. THE CHALLENGE

Imagine, you are asked to implement a new city, in less than eleven months with:

(1) no authority to make contracts, or any form of binding agreement

(2) no funds

(3) no staff

That was exactly the challenge that we faced in January 2005, as we anticipated the passage of two bills that would be the first steps toward the incorporation of Sandy Springs.

To compound the problem further, the bills that would authorize a referendum on the formation of the city had not yet been passed by the Georgia General Assembly, and both still were undergoing amendments.

Just to make it even more interesting, the referendum to approve the city could not take place until early June, leaving only six months to make the city happen, and still would provide no authority, funds nor staff!

These were the daunting circumstances under which we began to work. Neverethe less, we saw the goal drawing nearer and were excited.

Task Forces

It was clear that the entire job had to be carried out by volunteers. Fortunately, the community of Sandy Springs had abundant talent and management experience. The challenge was to attract this talent, and then to harness it, and to keep it committed for the full year.

Step one – the creation of a simple plan that identified all the critical services and functions that the city would need and timelines for the provision of the services. The section on timelines later in this chapter illustrates the timeline and plan.

Step two – We issued a call for volunteers to serve on a set of task forces that addressed virtually all of the identified services and functions. Initially, twelve task forces were formed. Later two additional task forces were added to address public information and emergency 911 (E911) service.

A listing of the task forces follows with a brief description of the area of responsibility for each. In addition to the specific tasks that follow, every task force was to create preliminary budgets for the area of service and functions that they addressed. A brief description of the charge to each task force follows with more details in Chapter VI, C.

Task Force	Description
Administration	Organizational structure, head count, ethics and insurance policies
Accounting	Accounting system, cost budget and auditing
Finance	Identification of revenue sources, bank selection
Human Resources	City Manager search, employee salary and benefit plans
Information Technology	Identify IT needs and sources
Legal	Draft ordinances and create municipal court system
Police	Identify needs and structure Police Force
Fire	Identify needs and structure Fire Department
Public Works and Transportation*	Identify needs and design operations
Parks and Recreation	Identify existing parks and programs and plan for continuation
Community Development	Establish methodology and organizational needs for Planning, Zoning, and Permitting
Properties	Identify all properties owned by the county within the boundaries of the new city
Public Information	Keep public informed on progress of the task forces
E911	Identify needs and sources for E911 service

Note: these functions were combined due to the specific experience of members. They could be separate task forces.

At the peak of activity, there were more than 120 volunteers involved in these active task forces.

The commitment and talent that were shown by these citizens groups were exemplary. For months the task forces met and explored every aspect of their assignments. To report in detail the output of their work would take a separate book. Suffice it to say these volunteers designed a city from the ground up. The implementation of the city of Sandy Springs was as fine an example of democracy in action as can be found in today's society.

C. THE CHARGE

It is important that each task force receive a clear and unambiguous charge. One that:

(1) excites interest

(2) provides a strong sense of direction, while leaving latitude for the task force members to exhibit their creative abilities.

The most difficult aspect to drafting a charge, and managing the process, is to keep the task force focused on "Day One," the start day for the new city. The volunteers will want to begin with long-range planning. The charge must be to do only those things necessary to prepare the city to be ready to run on the chosen start date.

The charge to one Sandy Springs task force follows:

TASK FORCE WORK PLAN

Finance Task Force

Chair:

    I.   Form task force

      A.   Review tax provisions in bill

    II. Determine sources of revenue

      A.   Negotiate process for transferring revenue from county

    B.   Negotiate process for transferring Local Option Sales Tax

    C.   Establish process for collecting new revenue (fines, licenses, franchises etc.)

  III. Determine timing of revenue

  IV. Identify capital needs

   V. Recommend sources for meeting capital requirements

  VI. Identify short-term credit needs

 VII. Issue RFP for bank

VIII. Negotiate line of credit to meet short-term needs

VIII. Prepare preliminary revenue budget

  IX. Prepare preliminary cost budget for Finance Department

   X. Complete data gathering phase by the date of referendum

---

The timeline for the progress of the Sandy Springs Task Forces was divided loosely into three phases:

(1) Data gathering and identification of alternatives

(2) Narrowing alternatives

(3) Negotiation

In the case of Sandy Springs, the three periods coincided with the intervals between:

(1) Filing the Bill in the legislature, and the referendum

(2) The referendum, and release of the RFP's

(3) RFP issuance, and start-up of the City.

Although we had no idea that the city would ultimately be served by private industry, when we established the time periods, this schedule turned out to be a good fit for our needs.

D. TASK FORCE RESPONSIBILITIES

ACCOUNTING

The Accounting Task Force's primary responsibilities were twofold:

(1) to make recommendations on the type, form and cost of accounting systems that the city would require

(2) to aggregate a cost budget and cash flow analysis for the city

The task force moved quickly to understand the accounting procedures and standards for municipalities in Georgia. Sources of aid in this effort were other municipalities and the Georgia Municipal Association. All of this work was a necessary first step to prepare for the city and also to be able to formulate the budget.

A stroke of good fortune got the effort off to a great start. A senior vice president of accounting in one of the major national banks had just retired and moved to the Sandy Springs area. She agreed to chair the task force and did a terrific job.

After completing the data gathering and recommendations on providing the accounting system, the task force turned to the major task of generating budget estimates for costs and later to the cash flow analysis. The revenue component was being developed simultaneously by the Finance Task Force.

As each of the other task forces developed the service needs for its area of responsibility, they also developed headcount and other costs to form a preliminary departmental budget. The Accounting Task Force priced out the budgets using gross-ups derived from comparable cities. Finally, the task force analyzed and refined the data, and aggregated the components into a preliminary city budget. This budget, which covered the first two years of operations, is discussed in more detail in the next section of this chapter: budgets.

ADMINISTRATION

When the Administration Task Force was formed, it was intended that this group would be the consolidator of the budget. As events progressed it became obvious that the budget task was more closely related to the accounting area and the experience that emerged on that team. The Administration Task Force then focused on gathering data on head-counts from other municipalities to serve as a comparison to the projections of the service task forces.

In addition, administration also accepted the assignment of studying and making recommendations on the city's insurance needs and the matter of an ethics code.

As the actual incorporation neared, the task force did a good job of identifying sources for insurance to cover the city's needs. Municipal coverage is a fairly specialized area and ultimately the city settled on coverage through the Georgia Municipal Association's pooled insurance. This decision was after a thorough investigation of private-company offerings. It is difficult for companies to evaluate the risk of a city emerging in as large and as rapid a manner as Sandy Springs. The risk was made even more unique by the broad scope of services from private industry.

COMMUNITY DEVELOPMENT

Community Development is a catchall name for the city's planning, zoning, and permitting functions. This was probably the area of greatest interest to the residents of the new city. As such it was not at all difficult to fill the task force membership to a workable level quickly. The difficult task was to maintain a good balance of interests and opinions. Two very capable chairmen came forward; one with a legal and community planning background, and the other with a long history of zoning experience. Under their leadership the desired balance was forthcoming. Basically there appeared to be two opposing interests, the homeowners and the developers. As the work of the task force proceeded, it became clear that there were actually more shared than opposing interests. Homeowners were interested in maintaining their property values with a good quality of life. Developers had many economic reasons for seeking the same result. The challenge was to adopt codes and procedures that served developers' and homeowners' objectives effectively.

One of the initial questions that the task force faced was how ordinances and codes would be placed in effect. Many in the community, and initially on the task force, were solidly against adopting all, or any, of Fulton County's codes. After an in-depth analysis, the task force determined that the county's codes were not that bad. The problem was in the enforcement and variances that had been allowed. With that understanding and the imperative of adopting legally acceptable codes on Day One, the task force did recommend the adoption of the county codes. However, work began immediately on drawing up modifications to recommend to the new city council for early consideration.

In addition to the codes, significant attention was given to processes. On the one hand, residents desired more opportunity to be involved in zoning and building permit issues. The developers were interested in shortening and streamlining the processes. The task force worked hard at doing both. Means were developed for incorporating more public notice and input earlier in the processes, while giving the developer/builders more clear direction early enough to allow proper planning.

The task force also had an impact through the staffing recommendations on increased enforcement activity. The requirements as identified by the task force were met on Day One as the new enforcement officers were sworn in. This staff represented a significant increase in the number that had been available under the county.

E911

The E911 Task Force was one of the last task forces formed. Originally assigned as a function of the Information Technology (IT) Task force, the technical and political complexity of this emergency response system; and the need for inter-task force participation by the Police and Fire Task Forces, and cooperation with other jurisdictions, led to the establishment of a stand-alone group. E911 is a very costly service to establish. There are significant economy-of-scale opportunities, which led to the task force exploring partnerships with established entities. E911 service must be flawless. One mistake can cost a life.

The initial recommendation was to seek a contract with the county to provide E911 for a period of time. This resulted in an eleventh-hour agreement with Fulton County to continue service for six months. For a service as complex as E911, this was a very short time. The task force identified a number of options, including:

(1) A long-term contract with the county

(2) Joining an Authority being considered jointly by the city of Atlanta and the county

(3) Joining another municipality's service

(4) Creating a Sandy Springs Service

(5) Creating a Public Safety Authority for about four potential new cities and three existing cities north of Atlanta.

None of these options were easy to implement. There were economic and timing problems associated with all the options. At the time of this writing, no final decision has been made. The city is seeking an 18-month extension of the contract, with the county to provide the time to identify and implement one of the other options. A decision by the county is expected soon. It would appear that the extension would be in all parties' best interests, but politics sometimes do not follow the course of reason. The county has indicated it is not willing to provide the service beyond the potential 18 months.

Assuming a favorable decision on the extension, Sandy Springs is leading an evaluation of the Public Safety Authority concept. The author has had meetings with other communities to introduce the the idea. Establishing the Authority would require no new legislation, because recent legislative action has created the mechanism for setting up various types of authorities in Georgia. The envisioned Public Safety Authority could include a wide variety of services beyond E911. These include:

- Fire
- Police
- Training
- Jails and Detention Centers
- Courts
- Special Ops
- Vehicle Maintenance
- EMS
- HazMat
- Traffic management centers
- Non-Emergency call centers

The concept envisions a "cafeteria" approach wherein participating cities could select services to meet their individual needs. The major advantages of the Authority would include economies of scale and the ability to fund capital projects jointly. A great deal of work remains to finalize any decision on the Public Safety Authority.

The most difficult factor in establishing an E911 system is not obtaining the equipment and staff to answer and respond to emergency calls. The problem is in setting up the dispatch transmissions. Radio frequencies are controlled by the FCC and are severely limited. Towers and other equipment are costly. This is an area that a potential city must address early and often.

FINANCE

The Finance Task Force was charged with several missions:

(1) Provide an estimate of revenues for the city

(2) Aggregate capital needs from the other task forces and recommend a vendor or vendors

The important task of identifying the amount, source and timing of the city's future revenue is more fully described later in the chapter. See (F2), Revenue Sources.

To address the city's need for banking services, the task force issued a Request for Information to a number of national and local banks. There was substantial interest in the city's account by all the banks. There was a preference by the community to use a local bank, but there were requirements for services that ruled out the smallest banks. One of the major needs was for a $10-million line of credit to float the city through the early months of operations. All of the banks indicated a willingness to meet that need.

The task force did an excellent job identifying the expected revenue stream for the city, which was a great help in getting the city off to a solid start.

FIRE

The Fire Task Force was charged with the task of determining how Sandy Springs could provide its own fire service and what resources would be required to do so. In that regard, the group did provide some guidance on resources that would be required.

It was clear that establishing a fully equipped fire department was extremely difficult in the short 5 months between the referendum and the incorporation date. Because the continuity of fire service is so essential, the focus of the task force moved significantly toward the consideration of alternatives for delivering the service. The task force became committed to the idea of the need for a long-term contract with the county. As the months progressed, the Negotiating Team of the Governor's Commission sought to buy some time by contracting with the county. That effort was successful, but only at the last moment. Even then the contract was for 6 months, leaving the pressure on to make a more long-term arrangement.

By the time the city was started, little progress toward a long-term solution had been made. The Fire Task Force, which actually had a number of firemen in the group, had described a number of problems that could arise if the city chose to create its own force. Included among those was the problem of limited advancement opportunities in a small force. This could inhibit the ability to attract and maintain top-quality employees. There also are significant capital requirements involved with the housing and equipping of a new fire department.

In the first couple of months since the city was incorporated, officials have sought an extension of the service contract with the county. An extension of the contract will provide the opportunity to establish our own fire department, or to explore the Public Safety Authority concept (see E911)

HUMAN RESOURCES

The two principal tasks of the Human Resources Task Force were to lead the search for a City Manager and make recommendations on salary and benefit packages for the new city. The search for the City Manager is outlined more fully later in this chapter (section G).

The subject of salaries and benefits is in many ways more difficult for a new city then an established municipality. To be able to attract employees, the new entity must be competitive with the other employers in the area. It is easier to gauge the salary levels that may be required than to try to match the myriad of benefit plans that job candidates may have been experiencing. On the other hand, having the "clean sheet of paper" in front of it allowed the task force to draw up some recommendations that will have a long-term effect on the city.

Because private industry would be delivering the vast majority of Sandy Springs' services, the number of city employees was limited. At Day One, there were only two full-time employees: the Deputy City Manager (serving as Acting City Manager) and the City Clerk. Part-time positions for a City Attorney and City Solicitor were filled. In the first month, the positions of Clerk of the Court and Police Chief also were filled, making a total of four full time jobs in the city. All other functions were performed under contract except for the later addition of the City Manager.

The intention is to end the contract with the county for the provision of a police force in seven months. At that time, Sandy Springs will have its own startup force in place. This force of around sixty will be supplemented to approach eighty by the end of the year. Since the city is seeking to extend the six-month contracts for fire and E911 by an additional 18 months, the police needs will dominate the city's initial salary and benefit decisions.

The basic approach by the task force was to (1) recognize that "one size does not fit all." Customized packages were necessary for key employees, including the Chief and several of the top-echelon police force. For the remainder of employees, a package was required that would balance the need to attract people but not create a monster in the form of future benefit commitments.

The committee was well aware that it was not necessary to offer better packages than other employers to attract people to Sandy Springs. The community is considered a very desirable work location that sells itself without excessive pay and benefit incentives. For example, within the first thirty days, there were more than 500 applicants for the police force.

The most important recommendation of the task force was that the city should opt for a defined contribution rather than a defined benefit plan. This is significant in the long-run finances of the city.

Health care programs that were competitive, but with electives and caps that the employees could choose, also were recommended. Because the police were to be the only early forces under the plans, there were several benefit options applicable to their specific needs. To achieve the optimum recommendation, the Human Resources Task force worked closely with the Police and Fire Task Forces.

INFORMATION TECHNOLOGY

Information technology (IT) is obviously a highly technical subject that requires people with experience in the field. Several volunteers emerged with skills in that area. The team overcame some challenges related to differences in philosophy and approach, and produced a useful analysis of the city's technology needs. The committee reviewed several potential vendors of systems and software, and identified a leading contender for a turnkey solution.

Because of the city's desire for no more than two major contractors, the IT vendors were not in the running unless they could partner with other firms to provide a broader scope of services. The leading IT firm, as identified by the task force, was able to find a good partner and ultimately was a participant in the winning proposal. It is far easier for the city to have the primary contractor coordinate all the IT needs under its umbrella, than for the city to try to manage separate vendors. All of the arguments about who is responsible for a function are eliminated under one master contract.

Sandy Springs was very interested in being a leading edge city with regard to technology. To a major extent, we seek to have a paperless environment. The coordination and compatibility of all the various systems needed to provide such up-to-date services and functions are best provided under one firm. The recommendations of the IT Task Force were definite factors in defining the future capabilities that the city desired.

LEGAL

The Legal Task force studied the city's needs and recommended a course of action for the municipal courts.

In addition, the task force reviewed relevant ordinances from other municipalities, the county, and model ordinances. This major undertaking yielded a set of recommended initial ordinances to be offered to the new city Council. The Legal Task Force also worked to identify jail facilities for the City.

The intention was to start up the municipal courts in the first month of operations for two reasons: (1) the City would need to deal with code violations cited from Day One, and (2) the police would generate citations that required action and that would result in much-needed revenue to defray the costs of the courts. The municipal court was established in about 45 days. Part of the delay resulted from the absence of proper courtroom space. The solution was to share the temporary Council chambers, which required some elevation of security and other facilities for the courts. Two judges, each serving part-time, were sworn in and the process is working well.

The jail needs were worked out through a contract with a neighboring city. The willingness of Roswell, Georgia to share their facility with Sandy Springs was deeply appreciated and there was little haggling over terms.

The recommended ordinances were a major undertaking. Pro bono work by a couple of legal firms enabled the creation of a set of preliminary ordinances which were distributed to all candidates for public office during the candidate training sessions discussed later in this chapter. Multiple editions were necessary to capture the desires of the future officials, and most important, to assure that the proper steps were taken to address any legal challenge of the new ordinances. To this end, as many of the existing county ordinances as possible were incorporated into the city's initial set. Any potential city should give detailed and early attention to the production of its ordinances. A review of the agenda for the first Council meeting in Sandy Springs, which is included later in this chapter under Elected Officials, will provide an idea of the detail and complexity of the ordinances.

PARKS AND RECREATION

The Task Force on Parks and Recreation was populated with a number of people with a great deal of enthusiasm for the task.

Many had served in volunteer community groups that had supported parks and other community programs for years. At first, such prior involvement can be a bit of a problem, because committee members desire to focus on long-range plans for growth in the parks. We found we needed to continue reminding the members that the focus of the task forces is to have the city ready to function on Day One.

The group settled in and was very diligent in capturing the data on the existing parks. Working with the Properties Task Force, the Parks and Recreation Task Force catalogued physical park spaces, completing that task early. Thereafter, the task force discovered a more complex task when it conducted an assessment and inventory of programs run within the parks.

The task force also conducted an inventory of the many nonprofit organizations formed over the years to carry out certain civic activities normally sponsored by a city. The working group desired to continue all of this activity, but first the nonprofit groups' functions and financial needs had to be understood. The task force did a thorough job inventorying the activities in all these areas.

The City's initial goal was to see that no existing parks and recreation programs would be discontinued or diminished.

Sandy Springs had already been significantly "under parked" compared to the rest of the county, and could not afford to cut back in this area. With the work of the task force and the recommendations passed on to the city at incorporation, the transition of programs went smoothly.

The unresolved issue on Day One was the ownership of the parks. Negotiations with the county to transfer the properties had been unsuccessful. In fact, the county commissioners refused to deal with the Governor's Commission on the matter. A footnote to the issue is that by Georgia law, the county is not permitted to operate a park in a city of more than 50,000 population. At the last moment, a one-year contract was arranged for the city to lease the parks for $60,000. As it appeared that the county would continue to desire to sell the parks for "market value," without recognition of the Sandy Springs' taxpayers' contribution to the purchase of the properties, there did not seem to be a chance to resolve the issues without court action.

At this writing, a bill has been introduced and passed the Georgia Senate that proscribes: (1) the necessity of the transfer of properties (2) a recognition of the tax contribution of city residents to the purchase and (3) a formula for the sale of the properties.

If this should be made law, it will clarify greatly the entire issue of asset transfers for Sandy Springs and future cities as well as precluding the need for court resolution.

POLICE

With public safety ranking very high (third) in the citizens' priority list, there was substantial interest in the plans for police service. Many assumed that the city would have to continue relying on the county for service for many years. Within thirty days of the formation of the task force, there was an initial plan for starting our own force. The plan originated with the Chief of Police in another organization, and contained all the elements necessary to operate the city's police force. The plan was detailed and comprehensive enough that the Interim City Manager was confident that the job could be done. The only obstacle to having the police force ready on Day One was the lack of authority and funds to hire and equip the required force

The Police Task Force continued to revise and refine the plans during the transition year. The county agreed to a six-month contract for police services. That was all that was needed to be ready to have a Sandy Springs police force on the job on July 1, 2006.

The hiring of the Chief is described later in the chapter under "personnel." With the Chief hired in December 2005, the process of bringing his top management team on board began. Within sixty days, a team of eight had been assembled with 500 applicants for other positions. The City Council has approved contracts to purchase 62 fully equipped vehicles, radios, vests, and other needed equipment. Sandy Springs will have a fully functioning police force on July 1, 2006.

The new force will begin with more officers than had been supplied by the county. The force will be capable of doubling by the end of 2006. Budget decisions by the Council will control the rate of growth.

PROPERTIES

The Properties Task Force was charged with researching and accumulating data on all real properties that the county owned within the bounds of the new city of Sandy Springs. The properties of principal interest were parks, fire, and police stations. It was necessary to examine all properties to confirm that the above listed types were captured, as well as undeveloped properties that might offer future use for these purposes.

In total, about 100 properties were included in the study. Many of these turned out to be of little interest. Parcels included rights-of-way and very small isolated lots.

The task force's charge called for a great deal more data than the physical location and description of the parcels. The additional data included:

(1) Cost of the property

(2) Cost of additions and improvements

(3) Dates of acquisitions

(4) Current market values

(5) Source of funding for the acquisitions

The last category, the source of funding, became important in negotiations with the county. Sandy Springs' position in the negotiations was that for properties for which the source could be determined to have been from the taxes paid by the community, then the property had been paid for and should be transferred at no additional cost.

The county's initial position was that the new city should pay full market value without consideration of the previous tax contribution. With regard to determining the source of funds, a further problem was the county's records, which were sometimes incomplete and inaccurate.

In spite of the obstacles, the task force did an excellent job in accumulating the data. Their findings were presented to the Negotiating Team appointed by the Governor's Commission on Sandy Springs, for the purpose of negotiating with the county.

Whereas the other task forces were dealing with service areas that eventually would become functions/departments of the city, and therefore influence future operations, the Properties Task Force's work was completed.

PUBLIC INFORMATION

The role of the Public Information Task Force will be outlined in more detail later in this chapter.

PUBLIC WORKS AND TRANSPORTATION

Originally charged as two separate Task forces, the groups were merged immediately due to the close relationship of the functions, and the overlapping experience levels of the members of the teams.

This team faced a lot of hard work in defining the scope of activities under in its area, and gathering data on the county's operations and the level of ongoing projects that the city would inherit. Because public works/transportation projects often stretch over several years there was the potential for much greater financial impact on the new city from incomplete projects than in any other functional area. Coordination with federal, state, and county programs was required.

Under the general heading of public works, the largest function to be considered was storm water plans and code enforcement. The task force made recommendation in this area including deriving a preliminary budget for the functions.

The definition of transportation did not include long-term capital improvements for the city's roads nor issues such as mass transit. The task force's charge was:

(1) To determine the ongoing programs and estimate associated potential costs

(2) To identify short term solutions to traffic problems

(3) To determine force and budget requirements to perform routine road maintenance in the city

This issue of traffic control was of high priority, since traffic conditions had been identified as the citizens' number two issue, second only to zoning. Road maintenance is, of course, always a highly visible concern. No one likes potholes.

It was known that the county had been devoting very little attention to traffic problems in Sandy Springs. The task force estimate (from a good source–a county traffic engineer was on the task force) was that the county devoted only three-fourths of one person's time to implementing traffic control studies. As a result, there was a total lack of synchronization of the 160 plus traffic signals in the city. Later work by the contracting firm confirmed that of the signal control boxes, 70 percent had either missing or malfunctioning equipment.

The public began expressing approval in the first ninety days for the improvements in this area. Potholes were being fixed, and by two-man crews versus the old "one working – seven watching" methods. New signs were up, stormwater drains were being cleaned, and new drains were installed where needed. Water runoff codes were being enforced. Traffic-signal boxes were being evaluated and repaired, and streets were being cleaned.

It appears that the task force did a good job of sizing up needs and priorities for the new city.

TASK FORCE SUMMARY

Without the work of the talented and dedicated volunteers on the above Task Forces, the city of Sandy Springs could not have been formed in the time that was allotted by legislation. Most of the individuals involved have not received and will never receive public acclaim for their contribution. It is to be hoped that all will have derived an enormous amount of personal satisfaction for a job well done!

E. ALTERNATIVES

All the Task Forces were charged to consider three alternative methods for performing the required services and functions.

These alternatives were:

(1) Create the organization and staff to perform the services

(2) Contract with the current government (county) to perform the services

(3) Contract with the other local governments (city or county) to perform the services

Several months into the process, a fourth alternative was added:

(4) Contract with private industry to perform services

Throughout the year, every effort was made to keep all alternatives open as long as possible. The importance of this strategy was evident when several services were negotiated at the last minute, and to the City's advantage.

Prematurely committing to one source or another could have prevented selection of the most beneficial solution.

For Sandy Springs, keeping our options open became a necessity and a tremendous advantage as we became involved in considering the use of private industry.

By the time of the referendum, the goal of gathering all necessary data and identification of the alternatives had been fulfilled by most of the task forces. In addition, a great deal of progress had been made by each task force in creating a "bottoms up" budget for their respective areas of responsibility. The charge in developing these budgets was to:

(1) Budget for the barebones resources that would be required to start the government, while

(2) providing service levels no worse than currently being provided by the County

This budget work was invaluable as the task forces shifted focus from identifying alternatives to beginning to narrow the alternatives to the most promising paths. Since by this point, the alternative of contracting with private industry was starting to appear to be a realistic option, this budget work could become a very valuable benchmark for evaluating the financial merit of any proposed contracts. More detail on budgeting is provided in Chapter VI, Budget.

Suffice it to say that while financials were very important in the consideration of alternatives, the dollars were never of greater than equal weight than considerations of service and responsiveness to the community.

Without going into detail about the methods and/or negotiations involved, it may be helpful to the reader to have a synopsis of the resulting utilization in Sandy Springs of the four alternatives outlined above.

ALTERNATIVE	SERVICE/FUNCTION
I – "do it ourselves"	Courts, City Clerk, Clerk of Court Office of City Attorney Future – Police, Fire, E911
II – Current Government (county)	Police, Fire, E911 (all under 6-month contract), Sewer
III – Other Governments	Jails, enhanced Library service, Water
IV – Private Industry	Accounting, Finance, Information Technology, Administration, Human Resources, Administrative support of: Courts, Police and Fire. Parks and Recreation, Community Development (Planning, Zoning & Permitting), Public Works, Transportation, Solid Waste (one-year nonexclusive contract, evolving into franchises

F. BUDGET

1. EXPENSES

Proper finances are of the utmost importance to the successful beginning of a new city. The creation of a series of budgets allowed Sandy Springs to become increasingly more assured about its ability to function as a city. I say budgets –plural, as there were a number of iterations. The budget was refined as more data became available over the early months.

For example, initially there was financial data, gathered from comparable communities in the area, and from the existing county government. Metrics were developed from that data that enabled the creation of a "comparative" budget. This was the first locally developed indicator of the new city's ability to meet its financial needs and provide a satisfactory level of service. We characterized this as a "top down" budget since it was based on outside sources.

As the Sandy Springs task forces began to deliver on their charge to determine the level of service required within their respective areas of responsibility, they also provided budget estimates. The Accounting Task Force aggregated these estimates to form another draft budget. This budget was a living document that experienced a number of additional iterations (about four) before it could be designated as a final budget recommendation. The final draft was presented to city officials and the newly formed staff for their use in developing the actual budget after the city was incorporated.

Note that the budget the city ultimately adopted was very different from the work of the task forces. The reason for this divergence was the introduction of "competitive contracting" into the equation. The massive contracts with private industry had a major effect on both the form and bottom line of the budget.

The Sandy Springs contracts were based on fixed costs for the first two years, which represented more than half of the total budget. The next largest segment of the budget also consisted of contract expenses with the existing county and other municipalities. Less than ten percent of the cost budget was for other non-contract expenses.

With the dramatic restructuring of the budget dictated by private industry contracts, it may not be obvious why all of the preliminary budget work was necessary. Believe me, it was vital.

First, a community might not know in the early stages whether it will choose to work with private firms. Building preliminary budgets for a traditional do-it-yourself government will yield important data for that decision. The choices on how services are to be provided are not all-or-nothing. A community may choose among alternative ways for delivering individual services. The preliminary budgets facilitate the financial basis for these decisions.

Second, the preliminary budgets were vital to evaluating the responses to the RFPs from private firms. Absent the task forces' budgets, there would have been no benchmark for evaluating the benefits of the private firms' proposals. Naturally, because the RFP process was competitive, there was a certain amount of control on costs, but only in the comparison of one company versus another. With the task force budgets, Sandy Springs was able to make judgments on the relative merits of contracts with private industry versus traditional government-provided services, or versus contracts with other governments.

A sample of the budget prepared by the Sandy Springs task forces follows at the end of this chapter (Attachment A). As you may see, it consists of large matrices for both revenue and expenses. Revenue for Sandy Springs flowed from **21** sources. Seventeen of the tax categories already were collected by the county or state. There are four new categories that the city will generate. Each source involved a separate method for collection and timing of the receipts. Therefore, a monthly spreadsheet is required. An example is the Local Option Sales Tax (LOST), which will not begin to flow to the city until April 2006, four months after the city was incorporated. Because this source provides approximately $1.5 million per month, it was important to get the timing right.

The cost budget overview (Attachment A, page 2) displays 40 expense line items by month. There were 17 individual budgets by department/function that were aggregated to create this budget overview.

In addition to the budget overview, there were individual department/function budgets that contained additional details.

2. REVENUE SOURCES

An extremely important factor in establishing a city is a reliable estimate of revenues. To obtain such an estimate, it is necessary first to identify the many potential sources of the funds. Then, to determine:

(1) The anticipated amount

(2) The timing of the revenue flow

(3) The method by which revenues would be obtained

The last issue can lead to either striking contracts with the current billing and/or collection source, or having to establish the city's own processes. Either of these methods may require protracted planning and negotiation.

Warning: The author is aware of one start-up city in which a consultant missed the revenue projection for the first year by $10 million, or about 50 percent of the actual revenue. This necessitated a drastic cut in the expense budget for that year. The detailed and laborious work of the Finance Task Force is paying off in a more reliable revenue flow for Sandy Springs. The task force identified 17 separate existing sources, and four new sources of funds.

It was important to capture data for two years, because there were certain revenues that would not flow for all, or part, of the first year. The best estimate was for a total of approximately $63 million in Year One (2006) and $75 million in Year Two (2007), with normal growth thereafter.

3. CASH FLOW

The final budgeting output was the cash-flow analysis. This document was vital to the determination of the month-to-month fiscal viability of the new city.

From the beginning, the organizers were aware of a potential cash flow problem. While on a calendar year basis, there appeared to be adequate revenue to support the expense budget, this revenue was primarily back-end loaded; that is, it would accrue late in the year. Establishing the timing for the receipt of the revenues was essential to projecting cash flows. Failure to recognize cash flows properly on the revenue and expense sides can lead to disaster. For example, in the case of Sandy Springs, the new city would be operating for more than three-fourths of the year before property taxes were due. Local option sales taxes would also be delayed by at least three months under the authorizing legislation. In short, 55 percent of the city's revenue would be received in the final quarter of the year. Many other taxes and fees are delayed, or staggered during the year. With a monthly cash flow analysis it was clear that there was a shortfall of cash in the early months of each year and particularly in the inaugural year. This dictated the timing and amount of a loan or line of credit that would be needed.

Many cities may find this sort of "back-end loading" in the calendar year to be a reality. For an existing city, this may not present a problem. If adequate reserves are in place, the early year shortfall can be funded. For a new city there is, of course, no reserve from which to draw. A sample of the task force's preliminary cash flow projection follows this section (Attachment B).

The solution is to borrow money at the beginning of the year to cover costs until the revenue picks up late in the year. Banks in the Sandy Springs community were very anxious to have the new city's business, and were forthcoming with credit. A Tax Anticipation Note (TAN) was issued in the amount of $10 million on January 1, 2006.

An alternative consideration was the establishment of a line of credit for the same amount. Careful budgeting had to be accomplished to be certain that the revenue for the start-up year would allow repayment by December 31, 2006. Georgia law prohibits a municipality from carrying over operating debt from one year to the next.

If your state does not have laws such as those on the books in Georgia, back-end revenue loading may not be such a problem.

Recommendation:
Have a detailed knowledge of laws governing municipal borrowing and repayment terms

Budgets were created for two years. The startup year was an anomaly, with less revenue than would be the norm in future years, and with more costs due to the 2005 start-up costs being added to normal operations of 2006. The budget for 2007 reflected levels that were more representative of the ongoing finances.

From a public information viewpoint, the 2007 budget was more useful as it illustrated the continuing viability of the new city, while the 2006 numbers were vital to managing through the startup year.

In Thousands $

EXISTING REVENUE SOURCES	Jan	Feb	Mar	Apr
Real Property Tax				
Motor Vehicles	108	108	108	108
Bus. Occupational Tax - Alcohol				
Bus. Occupational Tax - Other	4808	1227	1227	4907
Insurance Premium				
Alcoholic Beverage Tax	163	163	163	163
Rents Royalties	79	79	79	79
Intergovernmental Revenues				
Intangible Taxes	70	70	70	70
Real Estate Transfer Tax	21	21	21	21
Hotel Motel Tax	55	55	55	55
Development Review Fees	27	27	27	27
Planning & Zoning Fees	6	6	6	6
Fire Dept. Revenue	0.25	0.25	0.25	0.25
Parks & Recreation Rev.	6	6	6	22
Other	15	15	15	15
Total Existing Sources	5359	1777	1777	5473

NEW REVENUE SOURCES				
Court Fines	178	178	178	178
Utility Franchise Fees	341	341	341	341
Intergovernmental	27	27	27	27
Local Option Sales Tax				1490
Total New Revenue Sources	19880	546	546	546
Total Revenue	5906	2323	2323	7509

In Thousands $

May	Jun	Jul	Aug	Sep	Oct	Nov	Dec	Total
				2438	14630	4879		24383
108	108	108	108	108	108	108	108	1296
								0
98								12286
								0
163	163	163	163	163	163	163	163	1951
79	79	79	79	79	79	79	79	952
								0
70	70	70	70	70	70	70	70	842
21	21	21	21	21	21	21	21	248
55	55	55	55	55	55	55	55	680
27	27	27	27	27	27	27	27	325
6	6	6	6	6	6	6	6	69
0.25	0.25	0.25	0.25	0.25	0.25	0.25	0.25	3
24	22	6	6	6	6	6	6	125
15	15	15	15	15	15	15	15	185
868	567	561	561	2989	15180	5427	2989	43306
178	178	178	178	178	178	178	178	2139
341	341	341	341	341	341	341	341	4096
27	27	27	27	27	27	27	27	320
1490	1490	1490	1490	1490	1490	1490	1490	13414
2036	2036	2036	2036	2036	2036	2036	2036	19980
2702	2603	2509	2587	5025	17216	7483	5024	63286

Attachment A
In Thousands $

EXPENDITURES	Jan	Feb	Mar	Apr
Salary/Benefits	1534	1554	1582	1610
Seasonal	13	13	13	13
ProfessionalDevelopment	21	21	21	21
StipendAccounts	1	1	1	1
ProfessionalFees	186	186	186	186
EmployeeRecruitment	1	1	1	1
CouncilMemberFees	1	1	1	1
EquipmentR&M	10	10	10	10
VehicleR&M	42	42	42	42
GroundsR&M	21	21	21	21
BuildingRental	12	12	12	12
FacilityR&M	16	16	16	16
RentalEquipment	3	3	3	3
Communications	32	32	32	32
Advertising	4	4	4	4
Printing	12	12	12	12
Travel	8	8	8	8
MaintenanceContracts	99	99	99	99
GeneralSupplies	59	59	59	59
Uniforms	44	44	44	44
Utilities	76	76	76	76
Meals	3	3	3	3
LeaseParks				
Promotions	2	2	2	2
CapitalProjects	180	180	180	180
Machinery&Equipment	61	61	61	61
EmployeeRecognition	3	3	3	3
EmployeeWellness	2	2	2	2
ManagementContract	183	183	183	183
Contingency	183	183	183	183
ContingencyforContract	300	300	300	300
TransferstoCIPFund	276	276	276	276
TransferstoGrantFund				
TransferstoE911				
VehicleInsurance	17	17	17	17
Property&EquipmentInsurance	3	3	3	3
Gen.LiabilityInsurance	11	11	11	11
LawEnforcementLiab.Ins.	4	4	4	4
PublicofficialLiabilityInsurance	2	2	2	2

Total

In Thousands $

May	Jun	Jul	Aug	Sep	Oct	Nov	Dec	Total
1638	1666	2076	2097	2117	2138	2158	2184	22335
13	13	19	19	19	19	19	19	188
21	21	32	32	32	32	32	32	320
1	1	2	2	2	2	2	2	20
186	186	279	279	279	279	279	279	279
1	1	1	1	1	1	1	1	9
1	1	2	2	2	2	2	2	20
10	10	16	16	16	16	16	16	157
42	42	63	63	63	63	63	63	623
21	21	31	31	31	31	31	31	310
12	12	18	18	18	18	18	18	175
16	16	24	24	24	24	24	24	243
3	3	5	5	5	5	5	5	51
32	32	47	47	47	47	47	47	488
4	4	7	7	7	7	7	7	66
12	12	18	18	18	18	18	18	176
8	8	12	12	12	12	12	12	129
99	99	149	149	149	149	149	149	1489
59	59	89	89	89	89	89	89	884
44	44	69	69	69	69	69	69	697
76	76	113	113	113	113	113	113	1134
3	3	4	4	4	4	4	4	38
								0
2	2	4	4	4	4	4	4	39
180	180	241	241	241	241	241	241	2407
61	61	1261	1261	1261	1261	1261	1261	3813
3	3	5	5	5	5	5	5	51
2	2	3	3	3	3	3	3	29
183	183	275	275	275	275	275	275	2700
183	183	275	275	275	275	275	275	2700
300	300	450	450	450	450	450	450	4500
276	276	414	414	414	414	414	414	4143
17	17	26	26	26	26	26	26	255
3	3	5	5	5	5	5	5	50
11	11	17	17	17	17	17	17	162
4	4	5	5	5	5	5	5	55
2	2	3	3	3	3	3	3	31

53438

Attachment (B)

Sandy Springs Projected Cash Flows Rounded (000)

	Total	Jan	Feb	Mar	April	May	June	July	Aug	Sept	Oct	Nov	Dec
Existing Rev.	43,306	5,359	1,777	1,777	5,473	666	567	551	551	2,989	15,180	5,427	2,989
New Rev.	19,960	546	546	546	2,036	2,036	2,036	2,036	2,036	2,036	2,036	2,036	2,036
Total Rev.	**63,266**	5,905	2,323	2,323	7,509	2,702	2,603	2,587	2,587	5,025	17,216	7,463	5,025
Salary & Ben.	22,335	1,534	1,554	1,582	1,610	1,638	1,666	2,076	2,097	2,117	2,138	2,158	2,164
Other Exp.	31,101	1,873	1,873	1,873	1,873	3,073	3,073	2,911	2,911	2,911	2,911	2,911	2,906
Total Exp.	**53,436**	3,407	3,427	3,455	3,483	4,712	4,740	4,987	5,008	5,028	5,049	5,069	5,069
Rev.-Exp.	9,830	2,498	(1,105)	(1,133)	4,026	(2,009)	(2,137)	(2,401)	(2,421)	(4)	12,167	2,394	(45)
Cumulative	0	2,498	1,393	260	4,286	2,277	140	(2,261)	(4,682)	(4,686)	7,481	9,875	9,830
Borrowing							12000						-12000
NetCash		2,498	1,393	260	4,286	2,277	12,140	9,739	7,318	7,314	19,481	21,875	9,830

G. PERSONNEL

Earlier in this chapter, the four alternatives that Sandy Springs considered for providing the myriad services were discussed. It should be clear that each choice creates a different set of staffing needs. Briefly recounted, the alternatives are:

1. City Provided

   In this traditional form of government, all required personnel must be hired, trained and equipped, in advance of the start up of the service. The task force estimates were that a force of more than 700 employees would be required in Sandy Springs. (Population 90,000). With the extremely short time frame for establishing the municipality, this option was ruled out.

2. County (existing Government) Contracts

   While numbers for this alternative were never fully developed, there would have been a requirement to establish a core operation for the new city, with key positions in Administrative, Accounting, Information Technology, Legal, Finance, Human Resources, as well as personnel to monitor the contracts with the County in all of the service area such as Planning, Zoning, Permitting, Parks, Recreation, Courts, Public Works, Transportation, Police, Fire, and E911.

   There is a significant overlapping of personnel needs under this alternative, since the County also will be continuing to perform core operations functions. A reasonable estimate for city personnel under this alternative would have been about one hundred people.

3. Contracts with Other Governments

   Basically the personnel needs would be similar to those under Alternative Two, above.

4. Contracts with Private Industry

   With the massive contracts with private industry for almost all services other than public safety, and initially contracting with other governments for the public safety functions, Sandy Springs required only **four** administrative employees.

Those were:

City Manager, Deputy City Manager, City Clerk and

Clerk of Court.

As the Legal Department and Courts were established, a City Attorney and Solicitor were hired, and two judges were appointed to part time positions.

With the decision to establish a Police force at the end of a six-month contract with the County for police service, a Police Chief and several top level staff members were hired to:

(a) monitor the contract

(b) begin the process of hiring the new force.

At the time of the writing of this book, the decision on extending the contracts for Fire and E911 services had not yet been determined, but if the contracts are not to be extended, there will be a requirement to hire the leaders for those two services in the near future.

The reader must surely see that the difficulty in acquiring adequate trained personnel to start a new city is not to be underestimated. The use of contracts, particularly with private industry was the major factor in making the startup of the city feasible. The resources and competence of the selected firm, CH2M HILL, in providing a professional staff cannot be overemphasized.

SEARCH PROCESSES

1. Internal Search Teams

Sandy Springs, in choosing Alternative IV, Private Industry, greatly simplified the hiring needs

However, because the organizers of Sandy Springs had no authority to hire personnel, the search for personnel to fill key positions still was handicapped. The obstacles were overcome in several ways.

First, the Governor's Commission was used to conduct searches that could be accomplished without the use of a professional search firm. In this category were placed the positions of Deputy City Manager, City Clerk and Clerk of Court.

The Commission formed search teams about sixty days in advance of Day One of the city. The search teams prepared job descriptions and posted job-opening announcements on the website of the Georgia Municipal Association (GMA). It was anticipated that paid job advertisements might be required but the overwhelming response to the GMA ads made that step unnecessary. Within the first 24 hours there were a number of responses, including one from Alaska! It appears that municipal employees, at least those in Georgia, are frequent scanners of the GMA site.

If the jobs had not been typical municipal positions, then an outside source might have been more needed.

The search teams evaluated all the resumes as submitted, conducted phone interviews and narrowed the applicants to a group of finalists for each position. The finalists were given individual in-person interviews and a selection was made. Still, no job offer could be extended. The actual hiring only could be done by the elected officials after the city was officially incorporated. However, tentative terms were discussed, with hiring made contingent upon the approval by the Council on Day One.

In the cases of the Deputy City Manager and the City Clerk, both were confident enough in the process to give notice to their present employer, thirty days in advance of having a formal offer of employment.

The natural source for these municipal positions is other existing and nearby cities. To be able to attract top personnel from the other municipalities, we had to be willing to offer reasonable salary increases. In general, those salary terms were in the area of ten percent above the candidates' current pay. In addition, we pledged to meet the benefit packages currently available to those employees. This did not entail exact duplication of every segment of their benefits, which would have been difficult in some cases. The object was to assure that the overall package would be of equivalent value to the respective employees.

I would like to mention that the leadership, both elected and staff, of the cities from which Sandy Springs drew personnel was more than gracious in allowing us the opportunity to approach and hire the individuals. It seems to be recognized that in this area of municipal employment, there are not a great number of opportunities for internal advancement within cities of fewer than 100,000. Therefore, individuals commonly must seek positions with other governments to fulfill career objectives. Still we appreciate our sister cities.

The final position that was filled at the direction of the GCSS was the Chief of Police. The search team appointed by the GCSS utilized a Georgia based search firm that specialized in the area of public safety. The firm was instructed to focus on individuals with chief's experience in metropolitan police work, preferably in the Atlanta metro area. The position was advertised in the major metro paper, the Georgia Municipal Association web site, and with the Georgia Police Association. More than fifty applications were received. The firm narrowed those to six, which were further narrowed to three by the Search Team for final interviews. The selected candidate was recommended to the city and subsequently hired by the Acting City Manager. It is preferable that the City Manager be in place and make such important hiring decisions, but the very difficult time constraints that were faced in Sandy Springs precluded that process.

2. Executive Search Firms

The Human Resources Task Force (HRTF) was given the charge of managing the search for the City Manager. That position was viewed as the single most important selection to be made for the city. Therefore, the HRTF chose to mount a nationwide search to obtain the best available candidate. The initial intent was to have the candidate selected and committed by the first day of the city's operation. To that end, the HRTF's first step was to initiate a search for a professional executive search firm that had experience with locating key municipal employees.

The firm had to be willing to take the risk of conducting the city manager search at its own expense, with no promise of payment—an unusual requirement. Of course, the expectation was that the elected officials would vote to make payment, but there could be no guarantee. Everyone told us that executive search firms would not accept that condition, however, as often is the case, everyone was wrong. Several firms did indicate a willingness to proceed on that basis. The search was narrowed to three firms and after reviewing the proposals and in-person interviews, The Mercer Group was selected to conduct the search for the City Manager.

Unfortunately Georgia has a "gratuities" law, which our legal advisors' interpreted as making it illegal for the search firm to be paid at a later date by the City council. This arcane obstacle sent the HRTF back to the drawing board. Finally, an anonymous donor agreed to provide the funds to pay the search firm's fees and the process began.

The HRTF provided to the firm general specifications for the type of candidate that would be considered, along with salary and benefit ranges. In collaboration between the firm and the HRTF, a brochure was created to describe the job and to sell the city to candidates. The advertising of the job was nationwide, using the International City Managers Association network and other media.

More than 130 applicants were received, from coast to coast, and the firm began the process of weeding out the less attractive candidates. The firm did an analysis of the candidates and a preliminary group of 16 candidates' resumes was presented to the HRTF for screening. The firm had conducted telephone interviews with this group, and also provided data from the calls and other background information.

The HRTF narrowed the potential candidates to six, and conducted telephone interviews with the reduced group. After the interviews the candidate group was further reduced to the three finalists. These candidates were presented to the Mayor and City Council for final interviews and selection.

This extensive process dictated that the city would have to begin operations without a City Manager. In fact the City Manager did not actually report until February 15, 2006, two and a half months after Day One.

The Deputy City Manager, who was selected under the internal search process described earlier, served admirably during the interim. He should be a prime candidate for a City Manager position in another city, particularly a start up situation, although Sandy Springs would hate to lose him.

In summary, although the obstacles were formidable, the end result was worth the efforts to make the selection processes legal and effective.

H. PUBLIC INFORMATION

It was important that the people of Sandy Springs receive timely, accurate and comprehensible information. To properly achieve that goal is not as easy as it might sound.

Let us focus on the timeliness and type of information that was required. Early in the year, before the referendum, it would have been counterproductive to have released preliminary, and therefore possibly misleading data. In the financial area, the decision was made to release only the Fiscal Viability Study produced by the Vinson Institute of the University of Georgia.

This data had the advantage of being from an objective and reputable source. It was still criticized by opponents of the city, but could not be discounted. The opponents were quite vocal in demanding a "budget". While the task forces had generated preliminary cost and revenue data, we were determined not to give the community anything that could later be shown to have been erroneous or poorly derived. The same approach was followed in all the service areas. We talked about the progress of the work, invited anyone to participate, but did not release preliminary decisions. The author believes that this was a good policy. Opponents of the city were waiting for any data or position that they could attack. If we had prematurely stated a position and then had to back away, it would have been a great boon to the opposition.

The risk was that the public would not feel informed and would vote against the city. To counter that concern, we tried to focus on the openness of the process and the opportunity for all citizens to be involved. The high level of citizen participation certainly worked in our favor.

After the referendum, the necessity for providing information receded a bit. The community's decision to create a city had been made. Now the interest turned to the question of how the job would be done. It was during this time that the Governor's Commission and the issuance of the RFPs to private industry began finally to awaken the press's interest. From this point on, the focus shifted from trying to get solid information out to the public, to trying to make sure that the press was publishing correct information. There was much more to report as the task forces began to formulate recommendations, and the Governor's Commission swung into action.

Recommendation:
Do not be too eager to release preliminary information that can be misused or later shown to be inaccurate.

1. MEDIA

> *"Before I refuse to take your questions, I have an opening statement."*
> *Ronald Reagan*

The dealings with the press will be discussed more fully, but first, let us focus on the distribution of information. In today's world there are many channels for providing information, some more readily available than others. The natural choice would be to utilize the media. For Sandy Springs that was a problem.

a. Radio and Television

There are a number of local radio and television stations in the metropolitan Atlanta area. Electronic media outlets throughout the Atlanta area seemed to ignore the story until the month before the city's incorporation. Even then the short sound-bite coverage did nothing to inform the public on issues. In 2005, a new low-wattage station, "Radio Sandy Springs" was created by a private investor to serve the area of the new city. The new station broadcast the Governor's Commission meetings live as a public service. The creators of this local station desired to cover the developments and issues surrounding the startup. However, the station's audience reach was limited by lack of power and by scant public awareness.

b. Newspapers

For most of thirty years, Sandy Springs had struggled to gain the notice of the local press. In large part, the community's efforts to gain cityhood were ignored. The only major daily newspaper in the area, the Atlanta Journal Constitution (AJC), on the rare occasions when it published anything on the subject, opposed the incorporation of the new city. In the past couple of years, that position was modified, but still the community's efforts received little coverage.

As the year of implementation began in January of 2005, the paucity of coverage continued. Only after the Sandy Springs' bills passed the legislature and were signed into law did the interest begin to pick up. Still, the media had not awakened to the fact that the first new city in Georgia in fifty years actually could begin in only a few months. The organizers had hoped for favorable reports featuring the citizen's right to self-determination before the referendum. That never materialized. Instead there was criticism to the effect that the effort was being run by a "small group of insiders" and other poorly researched views.

With the amazing 94-percent approval vote in the referendum, the press finally appeared to awaken a bit, and coverage picked up. The AJC still was not aware of the unusual nature of the city that was being implemented, while the two weekly community papers had begun to recognize the impact of the plans.

It was only with the formation of the Governor's Commission on Sandy Springs, and the issuance of the two massive RFPs to private industry, at the first meeting in late June, that the AJC began to realize the potential of the story. Not only was cityhood right around the corner, but also the extensive use of private industry was a major departure from the norm in municipal government. In addition, there was going to be a major impact on the remainder of the county as both services and revenues were reduced.

It was ironic that once the referendum was over, we were no longer interested in media exposure. There was much work to be done and spending time responding to media mistakes was not high on our agenda. As the AJC coverage picked up, it also became more negative. The author is still unsure as to whether the negativity was the result of a true bias, or just a lack of professionalism. Whatever the cause, the coverage focused on the most improbable aspects of the Task Forces' activities. For example, the Community Development Task force was formed to deal with the single most important function of the new city, according to the polls. One of the meetings of the Task Force involved in-depth discussions of potential zoning and permitting codes and processes for the new city. The AJC covered the meeting, and chose to report on the lack of chairs and the table that the task force gathered around. This was a total trivialization of an important meeting, and a single example, among many, of the truly poor coverage of an amazing volunteer effort to create a city. This wonderful exercise in democracy at work was consistently characterized as the work of a small group of insiders. It became apparent that the AJC was far more interested in selling papers by trying to drum up controversy than it was in accurate reporting.

Even more damaging than the negative coverage, was the AJC's insistence that all of the volunteer task forces were subject to the state Open Meeting/Open Records laws. Any reading of the statute makes it perfectly clear that the law applies to governments, and cannot possibly be construed to apply to volunteer groups with no authority to do anything. In spite of the clear and unambiguous language, the AJC chose to insist that Sandy Springs' volunteer groups were subject to the Open Meetings/Open Records laws. The paper issued numerous information requests citing the Open Records law as its basis.

As a matter of fact, by policy and practice, all of the Sandy Springs meetings were open to the public. However, the requirements under the

Open Meetings laws, which were designed for governmental bodies and agencies, would have been extremely onerous to the volunteer groups. These groups were meeting, sometimes in homes, and at short notice. With no funds, the cost of placing legal advertisements would have been prohibitive and of benefit to no one except- guess who- the newspapers. Meetings were posted on the community website, and there was never a complaint from the community about not being able to attend.

The old saying is "never get into an argument with anyone who buys ink by the barrel," but it is important that the community should not let the press run all over them. We stood on principle and it did not hurt in the long run. To have done otherwise would have hampered the effort to create the city to a great degree.

Recommendation:
Be intimately familiar with your state's laws on meetings and records, and stick to your guns.

The two weekly papers that served portions of the area in the proposed new city proved to be more factual than the major paper. Both were slow to begin significant coverage, but still well ahead of the AJC. Once started, the local weeklies did a much better job of conveying factual and needed information to the public. However, our ability to get out information in a timely way through these two channels was inhibited by both their lack of frequency and that collectively they probably reach less than half the residences. Neither delivers to apartments, which have become a high percentage of residences in Sandy Springs.

2. PUBLIC INFORMATION TASK FORCE

Absent the ability to rely upon the channels of mass media to inform the citizen's the author formed another Task Force, the fourteenth, on Public Information.

This task force was a bit late in forming, but did the best it could to play catch up. Some of the activities included:

Hosting an information tent at the Sandy Springs Festival, a longstanding and well-attended event in the community. Writing and placing news releases. Hosting community meetings to distribute information and answer questions. Updating the Sandy Springs web site.

The formation of the Public Information Task Force could have been handled more effectively if we had recognized the need for such a task force a few months earlier. We tried too long to rely upon the media and should have begun an effort to do the job ourselves. Fortunately, this was not a critical problem, and in the end, the public was generally satisfied with the available information.

I. CITY HALL

Once the referendum was a success, and the public was convinced that the millage rate was not going up, the most frequently asked question of the Interim City Manager was "Where will City Hall be?" While the acquisition of a city hall was to be important later in the year, it was not at the top of the priority list for the first half of the implementation year. To the public, however, it seemed to be really big. Possibly, if they had realized just how complex the startup of a new city was proving to be, the fixation on the location of a city hall would have been diminished.

For readers who may be considering the creation of a new city, the following narrative outlines Sandy Springs' quest for a city hall/operating space.

It was fortunate that a board member of the Committee for Sandy Springs was in commercial real estate, and agreed to head up the search for suitable quarters. The Interim City Manager's original estimate of space requirements was 30,000 square feet. This estimate was based on projection of force requirements for the city's elected officials, staff, and contractor staff.

As the search began, there appeared to be an almost ideal location. A major grocery store had abandoned a building in the heart of the Sandy Springs business district. The vacant building offered about 30,000 square feet of open space. Naturally, the build-out costs would have been substantial, but not unreasonable. The site provided ample parking with an attractive exterior that could have been made to look like a city hall at little cost.

The ownership situation was a bit complex. The grocery store had sublet the property through a previous occupant who in turn had a lease with the owner. However, the prospects for reaching an agreement seemed good, because the current holder of the lease did not want to reopen a store at that location, and we surmised, did not want a competitor to have the space.

A diligent effort to negotiate a lease was mounted. After several months, it became clear that getting a decision through the corporate structure of the large grocery chain was not going to happen in our required time, which now was growing short.

The decision was made to drop that location and seek an alternative. At that point, a local developer offered a new location. This property was not as desirable due to location and size, but seemed to be acceptable. There was a whirlwind negotiation and the developer should be given credit for making every effort to accommodate the city's needs. However at the last minute, the city became aware that the property might not be available for more than a year due to future development plans. This, coupled with the location and space factors mentioned previously, led to an eleventh-hour decision to pull back.

There now was less than three months until the city had to open for business, and few options seemed to remain. Many properties were simply not available to the city, because we had no authority to form a binding contract. The few property owners who might have been willing to take a chance with us were not willing to accept the substantial cost of building out space with no lease.

In the earliest version of the RFPs for the city's services, there had been a provision that the contractor had to provide for the city hall/operating spaces. That provision had been removed as the organizers focused on obtaining the former grocery property.

Now, with time fleeting, the Interim City Manager approached the firm that had emerged as the recommended vendor from the RFP process, with the request that the firm become the lessee of space for the city.

In the spirit of partnership, which would come to permeate the entire relationship, the company agreed to be the leaseholder if the city could identify suitable property. The arrangement provided for the cost of the lease to flow through to the city.

With that agreement, the search took on a wholly new look. Whereas we had been limited by the city's inability to make contracts, which scared most potential landlords away or inhibited their willingness to build out the property; now we were viewed as being backed by "deep pockets." With this advantage, a much wider array of properties became available. The problem became one of making a quick, but considered choice between a number of sites.

A site was chosen with the initial five-year lease for 30,000 square feet and first right of refusal on an additional 20,000 square feet.

The company (CH2M HILL) took on the contract negotiations. Now the immediate problem was that even with the company's support, too much time had elapsed to complete the design and build out of the site before Day One of the new city.

The new city required temporary operating space. Once again, CH2M HILL came through. There was empty space in the building that houses CH2M HILL's operations in Georgia. The company took a short-term lease and built out the space for the Sandy Springs temporary operations. It was amazing to watch the rapid growth in the space as cubicles, computers communications and staff popped up like mushrooms.

Initially, there was opposition to the "temporary city hall," because it not located in Sandy Springs. The truth is that it was only about a block outside the city limits. As soon as we ceased referring to the location as "temporary city hall" in favor of "temporary operating space," all opposition faded away. Semantics do matter!

For the temporary quarters for council meetings, zoning hearings and municipal court sessions, CH2M HILL set up multi-use temporary quarters in the unleased portion of the new city hall building. This was to be utilized until the leased space build-out was completed. Their temporary setup has proved so successful that the council does not want to move.

All is well that ends well.

J. CANDIDATE TRAINING

One of the unique programs that was introduced in Sandy Springs was for "candidate training." The newly elected city officials would face not only the task of running a city of substantial size, but also, the daunting necessity of starting the city. Everything from new ordinances, zoning and building codes, hiring, contracts etc, would have to be passed immediately.

As a matter of fact, the first Council meeting was set to begin at 12:01 A.M. on December 1, 2005: one minute after midnight on Day One. The agenda for that meeting is offered in the following Section (K), to illustrate the magnitude and complexity of the initial tasks before the City Council.

The typical new municipal office holder can expect to take a seat in an ongoing operation, surrounded by incumbents who are available to provide a degree of continuity. Not so with Sandy Springs, where every aspect of government and every government official was to be new.

We could not wait until after elections to conduct training. There was not sufficient time, because the city would be incorporated only three weeks later.

The solution was to invite all candidates, both mayoral and council, to attend training sessions during their campaign period. It was recognized that the time commitment was large in the midst of a busy campaign, however, we did point out that a failure to attend would be viewed by the community as a possible lack of commitment.

All of the 20 candidates made the commitment and participated actively in the discussions. There were four sessions, labeled as "Interactive Information Exchanges" rather than "training." (The largest newspaper in the area had been trying to make an issue that Sandy Springs was a creature of a small group of insiders, so we wanted to avoid the errone- ous impression that candidates were being brainwashed.)

The program was built upon the work of thirteen Task Forces (the E911 Task Force having been activated by that time). Each Task Force Chair provided the candidates with an overview of the work of the task force and the resulting recommendations. From the following schedule, the reader can observe the far ranging scope of the training.

The program consisted of four sessions. The first was an all-day, weekend session, and the others were three night sessions of three hours each.

The candidates generally were very appreciative of the learning opportunity, and the vital nature of the information presented. One candidate, probably with a bit of hyperbole, offered that: "I learned more than I did at college." One would hope not, but certainly more was learned about the requirements for starting and managing the city, than could have been learned elsewhere.

The proof of the value of the training was in the smooth conduct of the first Council meetings and the tremendous amount of work that was accomplished in the first month of city operations.

The letter announcing the training and urging candidate participation follows:

CANDIDATE INTERACTIVE INFORMATION SESSIONS ON IMPORTANT ISSUES

SCHEDULE

Sessions will be conducted for all candidates for elected office in Sandy Springs on the following dates/times.

The location will be provided at a later date when estimates on the numbers of candidates have become more firm. Final qualifying to run for office is on September 16.

Candidates were provided dates at the July 21 meeting. Please note the updated schedule.

All candidates are strongly urged to attend all sessions. Vital information, and discussion, will be provided that will enable the candidates to be informed on the needs and issues that will be before them the moment that they take office.

Sept. 24, Saturday,   9:00 A.M. – 5:00 P.M., one hour lunch break

Sept. 29, Wednesday,   6:30 P.M. – 9:30 P.M.

Oct. 5, Wednesday,   6:30 – 9:30 P.M.

Oct.11, Tuesday,   6:30 P.M. – 9:30 P.M.

For further information, contact Oliver Porter

770 393 8898 or oliverporter1@comcast.net

The training program is outlined in the following material that was directed to both the Candidates and Task Force Chairs:

INTERACTIVE INFORMATION SESSIONS with CANDIDATES

Since the beginning, it has been our plan to introduce a unique program to aid in the implementation of the City. The program involves the provision of information and training to the candidates for elected office. Remember, that all the great effort by the Task Forces will have no effect until adopted by the elected officials. I hope that you can play a vital role in this effort.

The suggested schedule and other instructions follow. Please contact me, if you have questions.

SCHEDULE   Total hours =16

Date	Time	Minutes	Subject	Presenter
Saturday Sept 24	9:00 A.M. - 5:00 P.M.			
	9:00 - 9:30	30	Introductions	Porter
	9:30 - 11:00	90	Charter	Porter
	11:00 - 12:00	60	Ordinances	Riley/Belafonte
	12:00 - 1:00	60	LUNCH	
	1:00 - 2:00	60	Ordinances	Riley/Belafonte
	2:00 - 4:00	120	Contracts	Porter/CH2M HILL
	4:00 - 4:30	30	Courts	Riley
	4:30 - 5:00	30	Franchises	Porter
Thursday Sept. 29	6:30 - 9:30 P.M.			
	6:30 - 7:00	30	Revenue	Dejulio
	7:00 - 8:30	90	Accounting	Jackson & Budget
	8:30 - 9:00	30	Police	Riley/Anderson
	9:00 - 9:30	30	Fire	Sterling
Wednesday Oct. 5	6:30 - 9:30 P.M.			
	6:30 - 8:30	120	Planning, Zoning, Permitting	Hale/Young
	8:30 - 9:00	30	Human Resources	Kearse/Lewis
	9:00 - 9:30	30	E911	Roskind
Tuesday Oct. 11	6:30 - 9:30 P.M.			
	6:30 - 7:00	30	Information Technology	Palmer
	7:30 - 8:00	30	Public Works	Cleveland/Hill
	8:00 - 8:30	30	Transportation	Cleveland/Hill
	8:30 - 9:00	30	Parks/Recr.	Bain/Wilson
	9:00 - 9:30	30	Administration	Veit

INSTRUCTIONS

1. <u>Allow at least half of your time for questions.</u>

2. Please review the schedule for your assigned segment and confirm your availability by <u>Tuesday, Sept. 13</u>. If you want to ask someone else to deliver, or share, the time, please let me know.

3. Please review allotted time. If you need more, or less, let me know, but try to fit the schedule if you can.

4. We currently expect to need at least 20 copies of all material. Please plan any handout material that you will need. I have arranged for free copying. For the first session, we will need your material by <u>Sept. 19</u>, to be able to use this free service. For subsequent sessions, materials need to be in <u>one week</u> prior to the session.

CONTENT

1. <u>The focus should be on Task Force recommendations. Of most importance are actions that the elected officials must take immediately upon taking office.</u>

2. A short summary of the TF charge and status of on-going activities could precede the recommendations.

MATERIALS

Following are materials that are known to be needed at this time and will be made available.

Charter
Enabling Act   Franchise agreements
Ordinances   Budgets
  – proposed amendments   Police report
Zoning Ordinances   Fire report
  – proposed amendments   E911 report
Contracts   Purchasing manual
  – Administrative   Benefits summary
  – Technical   Ethics code

Please review and prepare to offer the above materials that are under your TF's responsibility, and any others not listed, that should be offered.

We are so proud of the volunteer effort that you and all the other volunteers have made. It is now time to begin the handoff process to those who will be elected to do the citizens' work. I know that all of you are busy, but please give this your immediate attention. It is an important step in the birth of Sandy Springs – the City.

Oliver Porter

K. ELECTED OFFICIALS

This book will not deal with the political elements such as the campaigns and the roles of the officials' post election. It should go without saying that the opinions of these officials were important, and that the future of the city rests upon their well-qualified shoulders. However, prior to the incorporation of the city, their role as a Council was not yet in play. As individuals, several of the elected officials were prominent contributors through their work on the various Task Forces. The new mayor had been the driving force behind the movement to incorporation since the very beginning. Her knowledge and determination to make the city a reality was beyond value. She had been informed, and was in accord, with the implementation efforts at every step as we progressed toward city-hood. Everyone was comfortable that her leadership as mayor would be a very positive factor in the city's success. Many of the new Council had also been involved in the implementation efforts. Of the mayor and six council members, five had been on the board of the Committee for Sandy Springs; four had been members of Task Forces, with one serving as a chair; all had been active participants in the Candidate Training Program, described in the previous section, which outlined the efforts that were made to prepare the future elected officials to be ready to govern.

Some years ago, when the Charter Commission was engaged in the difficult decisions on the form and structure of government to be proposed, we often discussed the fact that no structure would work well, if the people that would be elected to office were poor choices. So, as we approached the start of the new city, every effort was made not only to have an informed Council, but also to insure that there was buy-in to the service structure that was being implemented, i.e., the "competitive contracting" concept.

The fact that the Council did adopt the contract with the private firm, without amendment, when it was presented, gave evidence of their buy-in. Time will tell whether the initial spirit of partnership will survive through the full terms of this council, into succeeding administrations. The first years of service will greatly impact the future. If the citizens continue to be pleased with this innovative form of municipal government, one would hope that future administrations would be able to support the private industry partnership.

Due to the incredibly tight time line for Sandy Springs, there was a concern about the elections, which were to occur on November 8, 2005. With two mayoral, and 18 council candidates, there was a strong possibility of the necessity for run-offs. The date for runoffs was December 6. If more than three runoffs were necessary there would not be a quorum to allow the transaction of business on Day One, December 1, 2005. The problems that would have ensued due to the lack of the ability to pass ordinances and codes immediately are outlined more fully in Chapter (IV B), Legislative Deficiencies, but in short, it could have been a disaster. As the elections approached, we watched the council races very closely and became fairly confident that sufficient seats would be filled to provide a quorum in the first election. Under the charter, this would allow the seating of the elected officials and give them the authority to conduct vital business. The expectations were fulfilled as the mayor and four council members were elected on the first ballot.

The plan for the first Council meeting was to present only the issues that were vital to initiating the city to this group. Other important issues such as a budget could be deferred until the full Council was in place.

Due in large part to the efforts of our partnering firm and legal counsel, the first midnight session of the Sandy Springs Council went off like clockwork and the city was born – big and healthy Every effort was made to assure the legality of the proceedings and of all measures adopted, to avoid any future challenges.

The mayor and council-elects, along with the four candidates still in runoffs were convened twice in the three weeks between the initial election and the runoff.

At these sessions the future officials were briefed on the issues that would be placed before them at the initial meeting. The members were issued laptop computers that would be loaded with the agendas, including resolutions and ordinances to be considered. Agreement was reached on the frequency and schedule for Council meetings. All of these preliminary meetings were advertised and open to the public.

Included at the end of this segment is the agenda for the 12:01 A.M.. meeting on December 1, and the continuation session at 7:00 P.M., that made up the first official session of the Sandy Springs municipal government. The agenda serves to indicate the complexity and the precision required to start a city. No stone had been left unturned in assuring the smooth startup for Sandy Springs.

◇◇

CITY OF SANDY SPRINGS, GA

Eva Galambos, Mayor

CITY COUNCIL

Dave Greenspan/Oz Hill – District 1 (Runoff)
Dianne Fries – District 2
Rusty Paul – District 3
Ashley Jenkins/Joey Mayson – District 4 (Runoff)
Tibby DeJulio – District 5
Karen Meinzen McEnerny – District 6

District 6 Thursday, December 1, 2005   Special Call Meeting
of

12:01 A.M.

Council Meeting

Agenda

1) WAIVER OF NOTICE APPROVED BY MAYOR AND CITY COUNCIL

2) CALL TO ORDER

3) INVOCATION

4) ADMINISTER OATH OF OFFICE TO THE ELECTED OFFICIALS

5) PLEDGE OF ALLEGIANCE

6) ROLL CALL

7) **APPROVAL OF MEETING AGENDA** *(of items for consideration at this Special Meeting)*

8) REPORT OF ELECTION RESULTS

9) **ADOPTION OF ROBERT'S RULES OF ORDER TO GOVERN COUNCIL MEETING RULES OF PROCEDURE**

10) ORGANIZATIONAL ITEMS:

a) Resolution: Appointment of Deputy City Manager and designate as Acting City Manager

A RESOLUTION APPOINTING AARON BOVOS AS THE DEPUTY CITY MANAGER FOR THE CITY OF SANDY SPRINGS, GA AND DESIGNATING THE DEPUTY CITY MANAGER AS THE ACTING CITY MANAGER EFFECTIVE DECEMBER 1, 2005 AND CONTINUING UNTIL A CITY MANAGER HAS TAKEN OFFICE.

b) Resolution: Appointment of City Attorney and naming of City Solicitor

A RESOLUTION APPOINTING WENDELL K. WILLARD AS CITY ATTORNEY FOR THE CITY OF SANDY SPRINGS, GA, PURSUANT TO ARTICLE III, SECTION 3.08 OF THE CITY CHARTER EFFECTIVE DECEMBER 1, 2005 AND NAMING WILLIAM F. RILEY AS CITY SOLICITOR.

c) Resolution: Appointment of the law firm of Bentley, Bentley & Bentley as Assistant City Attorneys

A RESOLUTION APPOINTING THE LAW FIRM OF BENTLEY, BENTLEY & BENTLEY AS ASSISTANT CITY ATTORNEYS FOR THE CITY OF SANDY SPRINGS, GA, PURSUANT TO ARTICLE III, SECTION 3.08 OF THE CITY CHARTER EFFECTIVE DECEMBER 1, 2005.

d) Resolution: Appointment of City Clerk

A RESOLUTION APPOINTING JEANETTE MARCHIAFAVA AS CITY CLERK FOR THE CITY OF SANDY SPRINGS, GA PURSUANT TO ARTICLE III, SECTION 3.09 OF THE CITY CHARTER EFFECTIVE DECEMBER 1, 2005.

i) Administer Oath of Office to City Clerk and

    ii) Administer Oath of Office to Assistant City Clerk

  e) Swearing in of City of Sandy Springs, GA Code Enforcement Officers

11) RESOLUTION: To Approve the City Seal for the City of Sandy Springs, GA

12) NEW BUSINESS:

  a) Ordinance: Providing for The Continuation of Ordinance and Law during the transition period legislatively established for the City of Sandy Springs, GA

**AN ORDINANCE TO PROVIDE FOR
THE CONTINUATION OF ORDINANCE AND LAW
DURING THE TRANSITION PERIOD LEGISLATIVELY
ESTABLISHED FOR THE CITY OF SANDY SPRINGS, GA
AND THE ADOPTION OF ORDINANCES BY
THE CITY OF SANDY SPRINGS, GA.**

  b) Resolution: To Accept and Award Placement of City Insurance

**A RESOLUTION ACCEPTING THE BID OF THE
GEORGIA INTERLOCAL RISK MANAGEMENT AGENCY
(GIRMA)
FOR THE PLACEMENT OF INSURANCE FOR THE CITY OF
SANDY SPRINGS, GA
AND AUTHORIZING THE MAYOR AND CITY CLERK,
OR THEIR DESIGNEES, TO EXECUTE ANY AND ALL
DOCUMENTS NECESSARY
FOR THE IMPLEMENTATION THEREOF.**

  c) Resolution: To impose a Temporary Moratorium of one (1) month on the issuance of Licenses, Permits, and activities which are subject to Zoning until December 31, 2005 for the City of Sandy Springs, GA.

**A RESOLUTION TO IMPOSE A TEMPORARY
MORATORIUM OF ONE (1) MONTH TO FINALIZE**

THE ZONING APPLICATION, APPLICATION FOR SIGN PERMITS, USE PERMITS, BUILDING PERMITS, LAND DISTURBANCE PERMITS, WHICH ARE SUBJECT TO ZONING, OR OTHER APPLICATIONS ADDRESSING THE USES AND DEVELOPMENT OF PROPERTY WITHIN THE TERRITORIAL BOUNDARY OF THE CITY TO ALLOW FOR THE CONSIDERATION AND ADOPTION OF ZONING ORDINANCES, AS DEFINED AND REQUIRED BY THE GEORGIA ZONING PROCEDURES LAW; PROVIDED, HOWEVER, THIS MORATORIUM SHALL NOT APPLY TO ANY PERMITS NOT SUBJECT TO ZONING REQUIREMENTS.

d) Resolution: Designation of Fulton County Daily Report as Newspaper for Official Publications and Notices (Legal Organ).

e) Resolution: To have published a notice in the city's legal organ informing the public of a public hearing by the City Council to receive comments and consider adoption of ordinances establishing procedures and zones, or districts, within the territorial boundaries for the City of Sandy Springs, GA.

A RESOLUTION TO HAVE PUBLISHED A NOTICE IN THE CITY'S LEGAL ORGAN IN THE FORM AS ATTACHED HERETO AS APPENDIX 1, INFORMING THE PUBLIC OF A PUBLIC HEARING BY THE CITY COUNCIL TO RECEIVE COMMENTS AND CONSIDER ADOPTION OF ORDINANCES ESTABLISHING PROCEDURES AND ZONES, OR DISTRICTS, WITHIN THE TERRITORIAL BOUNDARIES OF THE CITY REGULATING THE USE AND DEVELOPMENT STANDARDS OF PROPERTY WITHIN SUCH ZONES, OR DISTRICTS, INCLUDING ADOPTION OF A ZONING AND COMPREHENSIVE ZONING PLAN AND MAPS ILLUSTRATING LOCATION OF PROPERTY WITHIN THE CITY BY ZONING CLASSIFICATIONS, CURRENTLY AND THE FUTURE FOR THE CITY OF SANDY SPRINGS, GA.

f) Ordinance: To adopt and approve an Ordinance relating to Business Occupation, Tax & Regulation for the City of Sandy Springs, GA.

g) Resolution: To impose a Moratorium for the issuance of Business Licenses to any businesses within the territorial limits of the City of Sandy Springs, GA.

A RESOLUTION TO IMPOSE A MORATORIUM FOR THE ISSUANCE OF BUSINESS LICENSES TO ANY BUSINESSES WITHIN THE TERRITORIAL LIMITS OF SANDY SPRINGS, GA, PREVIOUSLY LICENSED BY FULTON COUNTY, GA, TO CONDUCT A REGULATED BUSINESS PURSUANT TO CHAPTER 11: BUSINESS OCCUPATION TAX, LICENSES AND REGULATIONS, ARTICLE 6: ADULT ENTERTAINMENT; ARTICLE 7: MASSAGE THERAPISTS; AND ARTICLE 8: ESCORT SERVICES, OR ANY NEW APPLICANTS WHICH WOULD HAVE BEEN REGULATED PURSUANT TO ANY OF SAID SECTIONS OF THE FULTON COUNTY ORDINANCES.

h) Ordinance: To adopt and approve an Ordinance relating to Alcoholic Beverage Licenses for the City of Sandy Springs, GA.

i) Ordinance: To adopt and approve an Ordinance relating to Building Codes for the City of Sandy Springs, GA.

13) OTHER BUSINESS:

14) RECESS MEETING

◇◇

CITY OF SANDY SPRINGS, GA

Tuesday, December 13, 2005 – Special Called Council Meeting Agenda 7:00 P.M.

15) CALL TO ORDER – (Continuation of Special Called Meeting held on December 1, 2005)

16) ADMINISTER OATH TO THE NEWLY ELECTED OFFICIALS (runoff election) – Supreme Court Justice Harris Hines

17) ROLL CALL

18) WAIVER OF NOTICE FOR SPECIAL MEETING APPROVED BY CITY COUNCIL MEMBERS DISTRICTS 1 & 4

19) INVOCATION – Reverend Don Southworth, Northwest Unitarian Universalist Congregation

20) PLEDGE OF ALLEGIANCE

21) QUESTIONS BY DISTRICTS 1 & 4 TO ACTION PREVIOUSLY TAKEN BY THE CITY COUNCIL

22) APPROVAL OF MEETING AGENDA *(add or remove items from agenda)*

23) CONSENT AGENDA *(none at this time)*

24) REPORT AND ACCEPTANCE OF FULTON COUNTY ELECTION RESULTS FOR THE DECEMBER 6, 2005 RUNOFF

25) ORGANIZATIONAL ITEMS:

   a)   Election of Mayor Pro-Tem

   b)   Adoption of Rules of Procedure for the City Council Meetings and Public Hearings

26) REPORTS AND PRESENTATIONS:

   a)   Mayor and Council Reports

   b)   Staff Reports

      i)   Fiscal Year 2006 Budget Calendar *(Presented by Aaron Bovos, Acting City Manager)*

      ii)   Presentation of 15-Month Council Agenda Calendar *(Presented by Aaron Bovos, Acting City Manager)*

iii) Presentation and Reporting of City Activities and Staff Functions. *(Presented by Aaron Bovos, Acting City Manager)*

iv) Update on Current Revenues and Expenditures through December 12, 2005. *(Presented by Don Howell, Operations Manager)*

c) Other

27) **UNFINISHED BUSINESS:** *(none at this time)*

28) **NEW BUSINESS:**

Intergovernmental Agreements:

1) Consideration and Approval of Intergovernmental Agreement for Animal Control Services with Fulton County. *(Presented by Aaron Bovos, Acting City Manager)*

2) Consideration and Approval of Intergovernmental Agreement for Police Services with Fulton County. *(Presented by Aaron Bovos, Acting City Manager)*

3) Consideration and Approval of Intergovernmental Agreement for Fire Services with Fulton County. *(Presented by Aaron Bovos, Acting City Manager)*

4) Consideration and Approval of Intergovernmental Agreement for E-911 Services with Fulton County. *(Presented by Aaron Bovos, Acting City Manager)*

5) Consideration and Approval of Intergovernmental Agreement for Sewer Services with Fulton County. *(Presented by Aaron Bovos, Acting City Manager)*

Ordinances and Resolutions:

6) Approval of an Ordinance Amending Chapter 2, Administration, Article 1, General Provisions, Section 1, Meeting Times, Subsection (a) of the Code of Ordinances of the City of Sandy Springs. *(Presented by Wendell Willard, City Attorney)*

AN ORDINANCE AMENDING CHAPTER 2,

ADMINISTRATION, ARTICLE 1, GENERAL PROVISIONS, SECTION 1, MEETING TIMES, SUBSECTION (A) OF THE CODE OF ORDINANCES OF THE CITY OF SANDY SPRINGS, GA

7) An Ordinance to adopt the following Articles of Chapter 14, Land Development and Environmental Protection in accordance with State Model Codes as amended:

Article 3: Floodplain Management/Flood Damage Prevention

Article 4: Illicit Discharge and Illegal Connection

Article 5: Post-Development Stormwater Management for New Development and Redevelopment

Article 6: Stream Buffer Protection

Article 7: Soil Erosion and Sedimentation Control

Article 8: Tree Preservation

(Presented by Nancy Leathers, Community Development Director)

AN ORDINANCE TO ADOPT ARTICLES 3, 4, 5, 6, 7, & 8 OF CHAPTER 14, LAND DEVELOPMENT AND ENVIRONMENTAL PROTECTION IN ACCORDANCE WITH STATE MODEL CODES AS AMENDED.

8) Approval of an Ordinance Adopting the International Property Maintenance Code, 2003 Edition as amended. *(Presented by Nancy Leathers, Community Development Director)*

AN ORDINANCE TO ADOPT THE INTERNATIONAL PROPERTY MAINTENANCE CODE, 2003 EDITION AS AMENDED.

9) Approval of a Resolution Naming an Appointee to Post 4 of the Sandy Springs Design Review Board. *(Presented by Nancy Leathers, Community Development Director)*

A RESOLUTION NAMING AN APPOINTEE TO POST 4 OF

**THE SANDY SPRINGS DESIGN REVIEW BOARD, WHO
SHALL SERVE A TWO (2) YEAR TERM TO COMMENCE
DECEMBER 1, 2005, PURSUANT TO SECTION 12B .3 OF
THE ZONING ORDINANCE OF THE CITY OF SANDY
SPRINGS, GA.**

10) Approval of a Resolution Accepting the Motions and Actions Taken by the Governor's Commission of Sandy Springs and Directing the City Clerk to Provide a Certified Copy to Fulton County. *(Presented by Oliver Porter, Consultant)*

**A RESOLUTION OF THE CITY OF SANDY SPRINGS
ACCEPTING THE MOTIONS AND ACTIONS TAKEN BY
THE GOVERNOR'S COMMISSION OF SANDY SPRINGS;
AND DIRECTING THE CITY CLERK TO PROVIDE A
CERTIFIED COPY TO FULTON COUNTY, GEORGIA**

11) Approval of an Ordinance Adopting of the Fiscal Year *(Presented by Aaron Bovos, Acting City Manager)*

**AN ORDINANCE TO SET AND ADOPT THE FISCAL YEAR
FOR THE CITY OF SANDY SPRINGS, GEORGIA AS JULY 1
THROUGH JUNE 30, AND FOR OTHER PURPOSES.**

12) Approval of an Ordinance to Require a nonexclusive Solid Waste Contract to Operate in the City of Sandy Springs. *(Presented by Aaron Bovos, Acting City Manager)*

**AN ORDINANCE ESTABLISHING SOLID WASTE
COLLECTION SERVICES WITHIN THE CITY OF SANDY
SPRINGS; PROVIDING FOR THE SCOPE AND NATURE
OF THE OPERATION; PROVIDING FOR THE DISPOSAL
OF GARBAGE, SOLID WASTE AND REFUSE; PROVIDING
PROCEDURES FOR THE HANDLING OF COMPLAINTS;
PROVIDING FOR A CONTRACT FEE; PROVIDING FOR
THE ESTABLISHMENT AND ADJUSTMENT OF CHARGES;
REQUIRING INDEMNITY INSURANCE; PROVIDING FOR
REVOCATION AND AMENDMENT; PROVIDING FOR
PAYMENT OF TAXES BY CONTRACTEES; PROHIBITING
ASSIGNMENT AND SUBLETTING OF THE CONTRACT**

WITHOUT CONSENT: PROVIDING FOR FORFEITURE; AND MAKING OTHER PROVISIONS.

12) Approval of a Resolution authorizing the City Manager and City Attorney to negotiate and formalize a Cooperative Agreement between the City of Sandy Springs and the City of Smyrna for library/book services. *(Presented by Aaron Bovos, Acting City Manager)*

A RESOLUTION AUTHORIZING THE CITY MANAGER AND CITY ATTORNEY TO NEGOTIATE AND FINALIZE A COOPERATIVE AGREEMENT BETWEEN THE CITY OF SANDY SPRINGS, GEORGIA AND THE CITY OF SMYRNA FOR LIBRARY AND BOOK SERVICES

14) Approval of a Resolution Outlining the Terms for the Use of Fulton County Parks and Recreation facilities located within the City of Sandy Springs. *(Presented by Aaron Bovos, Acting City Manager)*

A RESOLUTION TO OUTLINING THE TERMS FOR THE USE OF FULTON COUNTY PARKS AND RECREATION FACILITYS LOCATED WITHIN THE CITY OF SANDY SPRINGS BY THE CITY OF SANDY SPRINGS, GA

29) PUBLIC COMMENTS

30) ADJOURN

CHAPTER VII

"It is difficult to steer a parked car, so get moving"

-Helen Mears

GOVERNOR'S COMMISSION on SANDY SPRINGS

As discussed elsewhere, there was no one with authority to conduct business for the new city during the entire implementation period. In an attempt to overcome this obstacle, an entity was created to aid in the facilitation of services for the new city. To that end, the following language appeared in the Enabling Act.

"As of the date a chartering Act is approved by the Governor or becomes law without such approval, the governor is authorized to appoint five persons to serve as interim representatives of the newly incorporated municipality until the election of the municipality's first governing authority. The interim representatives shall cease to serve as of the time the members of the first governing authorities take office. The function of the interim representatives shall be to facilitate the provision of municipal services and facilities, the collection of taxes and fees, the negotiation of intergovernmental agreements in preparation of the establishment of the new municipality. **The interim representatives shall not have the ability to enter into any binding agreements, to expend public funds, or to incur any liability on behalf of the new municipality.**"

The obvious problem with this section of the Bill was that the Governor's Commission on Sandy Springs (GCSS) had no actual authority to do anything except facilitate. As emphasized in the bold print, the Commission could not make contracts, hire employees, expend funds, nor did it have any staff at its disposal.

However, as the saying goes it was "the only game in town", so we attempted to make maximum use of the limited authority.

The GCSS met within the first week that it was appointed, and as its first act elected the author to be the Chairman.

Next, of great importance at the first meeting, the GCSS voted to issue two massive RFPs to private industry that covered virtually every service/function required by the new city.

A listing of other resolutions and actions by the GCSS follows, but the willingness of this commission to take the vital and extremely unusual step of issuing those RFPs at the earliest possible moment, proved to be essential to the success of the new city.

(See Chapter (X) for information on the RFPs)

Governor's Commission on Sandy Springs
<u>Summary of Activity</u>

June 24, 2005

Commission appointed

June 29, 2005

(1) Issued two massive RFPs to solicit proposals from private industry to serve Sandy Springs

(2) Established a five-member Negotiating Team to meet with Fulton County

(3) Passed a resolution that assets purchased with Special Service District Funds should be the property of Sandy Springs

July 6, 2005

(1) Passed resolution stating that the County had the obligation to continue performing services in December 2005, having collected a full year's taxes.

(2) Approved mandatory proposal conference for RFPs

(3) Named Negotiating Team

July 25, 2005

(1) Amended the RFPs to extend the submission date and reduce bond provision.

(2) Accepted briefings from Citizen Task forces

August 10, 2005

(1) Further amendments to RFPs and extension of filing date to August 31, 2005

(2) Appointed RFP Evaluation Team

(3) Received first report from Negotiating Team, August 24, 2005

(4) Continued monitoring of negotiations with the county

September 14, 2005

(1) Received the recommendation of the RFP Evaluation Team that the firm of CH2M HILL was the top ranked firm for both proposals.

(2) Authorized the initiation of contract negotiations with CH2M HILL.

(3) Authorized search teams for fire and police chiefs.

October 18, 2005

(1) Continued monitoring of negotiations with the county

(2) Notified the county that the City would assume responsibility for planning, zoning, new building permits; and Municipal Courts on December 1, 2005

(3) Authorized a search for the Deputy City manager, the City Clerk, and the Clerk of Court.

(4) Approved in principal, subject to legal review, a recommendation to the future city officials to accept the contract with CH2M HILL

November 2, 2005

(1) Continued monitoring negotiations with the county

(2) Gave notice to the Fulton County Tax Commissioner with regard to procedures for processing and collecting 2006 fees and licenses, on behalf of the City

November 16, 2005

(1) All business completed, the commission dissolved and authorized the remaining Employee Search Teams to report directly to the city officials upon incorporation.

Of course, there were a number of procedural actions and resolutions taken by the GCSS, but the outline above includes the significant steps taken that had major impact on the future of the new city.

One function of the GCSS was to serve as the focal point for community input and information. The meetings drew a great deal of public interest and were well attended by the citizens. At each meeting the GCSS called for public comment, and initially there were many statements, both pro and con, about issues before the GCSS. As time and events passed, the public's concerns appeared to dwindle and the level of trust in the Commission apparently grew. This conclusion is drawn from the reduced level of public statements during the last few months of the Commission's five month existence.

The GCSS made every effort to facilitate as much as the authority granted to it would allow, and at times, probably stretched that authority. Still, it is clear that there should be a better vehicle for starting a city. The GCSS was an instrument created to fill the void in authority set up by the legislation.

The author has recommended in an earlier chapter that the city be officially incorporated, with officials elected well before operations are begun. If this is not possible, then a governor's commission, or similar body, should be established, in advance, with powers to execute agreements on behalf of the new city.

Two mutually exclusive recommendations follow:

(1) **If possible, a new city should have city officials elected with authority to make contracts with other entities and individuals at least six months before the city begins operating.**

(2) **If legislation to carry out the first recommendation is not deemed feasible, then a commission should be established, and given the power to execute the necessary contracts on behalf of the city.**

CHAPTER VIII

*"To secure ourselves in this use, each contracts,
or will ultimately contract, with his fellows not
to encroach upon those portions of the earth
which they are actually using, in return for their
agreement not to encroach upon that portion of the
earth which he is actually using."*

-Benjamin Tucker

CONTRACTS

A. RELATIONSHIP WITH CURRENT GOVERNMENT

The community of Sandy Springs did not enjoy a good relationship with the Fulton County Commissioners responsible for serving the unincorporated area. In short, it was the poor treatment at the hands of the commissioners, and a general lack of responsiveness by the county that led to the desire to form a city. The Commission is composed of seven commissioners and a huge staff. The people of Sandy Springs grew very dissatisfied with the attitude of the Commission and the gross inefficiencies of the bloated staff.

On the positive side, the situation with the county made the task of convincing a majority of citizens to vote for a new city quite easy. The inefficiency made the task of funding the new city easier, because expenses could be cut significantly simply by operating more effectively.

Most issues that were presented to the Commission were decided by a four-to-three vote, with Sandy Springs on the short end. In fact, the commonly used term for the county's method of operation was "government by four." This division within the Commission offered little hope of shifting, or growing more conciliatory, in the future, due to the demographics of the county.

So as Sandy Springs began the work of implementing the city, the relationship with the politically motivated Commission was strained, to say the least. On the other hand, the cooperation of the county staff was rather good. Our impression was that County staff members recognized the reality of the situation and wanted to do the right thing. However, they always had to operate with one eye on the Commission to avoid losing their jobs.

Early in the year, the Interim City Manager (ICM) recognized the delicacy of the county staff's position and attempted to alleviate as much strain as possible. The Task Force members were instructed not to contact the county staff for information or data until a proper link had been established. To set up the required links, the ICM first contacted the County Manager to determine how he wanted to handle requests. It was agreed that the single point of contact was to be with the Deputy County Manager (DCM). The ICM then made that contact, and an agreement was reached that the first request for data from each task force would flow through the ICM to the DCM. The DCM then would obtain the information for the city, or would designate someone for the task force to contact directly. This may seem cumbersome, but following this procedure led to a fairly smooth flow of information. In every case, the DCM chose to name a point of contact, and from that point on, the task forces had direct contact with an approved source of data. In only one case was there a need to resort to an Open Records request. Because such requests are both time consuming and irritating to all parties, avoidance of that process was a big plus.

The foregoing does not intend to imply that all requests resulted in obtaining all of the desired data. In many cases, the county records simply were not complete, nor accurate enough to be very helpful. I suspect that may be true in many long-standing government operations. Fortunately the creation of a city, as complex as it is, does not require the same degree of accuracy as a moon shot. If it did, we would have ended up drifting in space.

Expect a huge task with records transfers. Depending on the level of mechanization of the existing government, the amount of paper records to be transferred can be awesome. For Sandy Springs, acquiring zoning and permit records alone required the transfer of more than 600 large boxes of material.

Even when there is a high degree of mechanization, the transfer is not necessarily easy. At minimum, systems must be compatible enough to effect the transfer. Sandy Springs found that after assuring compatibility between such large systems as GIS, there remained a problem with the accuracy of the database being transferred. It is possible that the purification of data will be ongoing for years.

1. CONTRACTING

After reviewing alternatives, Sandy Springs chose to approach Fulton County for a contract to deliver public-safety services. Services included Police, Fire, and E911. Given the very short time available for starting the city, the hiring, training, and acquisition of the physical assets for the city to be able to provide public safety services dictated the need for contracts. Sandy Springs viewed the contracts as a stopgap measure until it could begin performing services itself. Actually, the new city could have been ready to provide police coverage on Day One, but the county refused to contract for any of the services unless we agreed to all. Further, the county demanded that the terms for all services be co-terminus. After much negotiation, an agreement was reached for a six-month contract for the three services. The county commissioners delayed their approval until December 29, two days before the deadline for the new city to start providing the service. The sad part about this delay is that it was obviously in the county's best financial interest and certainly that of the affected employees, to engage in the contract. The statutes provided that the county should receive the full cost of providing services but should not be allowed a profit.

It would have been extremely difficult for Sandy Springs to have begun providing fire and E911 services even if the decision to do so had been made early in the year. Any new city with a lead-time of less than two years must make as early a decision as possible on the method of providing these services. If a relationship with the existing provider is reasonably good, the preferred choice is likely to be to continue under a contract with that provider.

Sandy Springs' current plan is to initiate a police force on July 1, 2006, at the conclusion of the initial six month contract. A Chief of Police and key staff had been hired as of January, and more than 500 job applications are in hand. Fully equipped police cars have been ordered. The plan is to move from the county staffing level of about 40 beat policemen, to around 80 by year-end. At that force level, Sandy Springs will still be under staffed as compared to surrounding communities and national averages for a city of this size.

Fire and E911 remain problems as of this writing. Negotiations continue with the county to extend these services with individual contracts that are not co-terminus. If this can be accomplished, the city will have time to create its own services. The county must not be allowed to delay the decision until the last moment again. A deadline for decision of March 31, 2006 has been set. If no contract is finalized by then, the city will initiate emergency measures to provide the service.

The preferred method for performing the Fire and E911 services in the long run may be the formation of a Public Safety Authority. Such an authority, under Georgia law allows multiple local governments to join in providing defined services. Sandy Springs may seek to be the catalyst for an authority that could include as many as seven cities.

The important point for those who may be considering the formation of a new city is that public safety is a paramount issue that must be addressed early and well. One would hope that the relationship with the existing government would be cordial enough to allow an early contract agreement.

While it should have been obvious to all concerned that the residents of Sandy Springs were not, by virtue of the formation of a city, seceding from the county, many seemed to assume that to be the case. Possibly the major metropolitan newspaper contributed to the confusion. In fact, the residents of Sandy Springs will still be major contributors to the county's revenue stream, and the county still owes Sandy Springs residents a wide variety of services such as public health, libraries, courts, and a regional trauma center. Our citizens actually will pay more tax to the county than to the city and it is incumbent upon the county to continue the required services.

2. STAFF PERSONNNEL

An obvious source of personnel for the new city is the staff of the existing government. However, there are pros and cons to hiring these people. On the positive side, they have experience on the job. However, the city very likely will want to do things differently. After all, dissatisfaction with the way things have been was among the strongest reasons for desiring a city. So, a massive transfer of the existing staff may not be popular with many people. That was the case in Sandy Springs. As a result, only a select handful of the thousands of county staff employees were hired to serve the new city.

The police and fire forces were viewed differently from staff positions. Familiarity with the community was an important factor in those areas and therefore the existing force was given special consideration. However, even here, the majority of the jobs may be filled from other organizations once the six-month contract with the county expires. The recently hired police chief and the second tier of management were primarily from outside sources.

3. ASSET DIVISION

The division of assets represents one of the most difficult issues that Sandy Springs has faced in its dealings with the county. Asset-division issues arose primarily with regard to parks and fire stations. However, points of contention may crop up in any area where the existing government owns sizable assets located in, and needed by, the new city.

Sandy Springs had only four parks with recreational programs run by the county, and another half-dozen with passive programs or with programs provided by nonprofit groups.

There were three fire stations located in the community and a fourth that served a portion of the community from outside the boundaries.

In all of these locations, the new city felt that it had paid all or part of the cost of acquiring and maintaining the facility through property taxes over the years.

The county commissioners, as might be expected took a different view, demanding at various times that either full cost or market price be paid for the properties. Attempted negotiations through the Governor's Commission were rebuffed by the county, which first refused to deal with anyone other than Sandy Springs' elected officials, then after they were elected, refused to negotiate with them.

As January 1, 2006, approached, the parks presented a dilemma. By Georgia law, the county is prohibited from operating parks in cities of over five thousand population. To avoid a shutdown of the parks, Sandy Springs offered to lease the parks for $60,000 for one year. In addition, the city agreed to maintain the parks and fund the programs. The county accepted the offer December 29, 2005.

With a year to negotiate, we hope that we can reach a reasonable settlement on the transfer of the assets.

A very recent development that may offer hope for an equitable solution to the asset transfer problem is a bill filed by the neighboring community of Dunwoody. The bill is one of a package of bills seeking a referendum on cityhood for their area.

Now that Sandy Springs has broken the logjam, the author has been advising several potential cities about how to avoid key pitfalls. One such area is the aforementioned asset-transfer issue. To avoid future disputes, the author has been counseling that this issue should be addressed in legislation. As a result, a statewide bill has been introduced that calls for the transfer of assets such as parks, fire and police stations, upon the incorporation of a new city. The financial settlement for the transfer is to be based upon two factors:

(1) The ratio of taxes paid by the new city, to that of the total county

(2) The ratio of the class of assets (example: parks) being transferred, to the total assets in that class in the county

If the taxes-paid ratio equals, or exceeds, the asset ratio, then the new city is considered to have paid for the properties. Nothing is owed.

Conversely, if the taxes paid ratio is less than the asset ratio, then the city must pay the county to make up the identified shortfall.

As a general proposition, the method of division for any assets, liabilities, revenues, and expenses should be specified in the authorizing legislation. Failure to do so will spawn a high probability of litigation.

Recommendation:
A SETTLEMENT METHOD FOR THE TRANSFER OF ASSETS SHOULD BE INCLUDED IN THE AUTHORIZING LEGISLATION.

THE METHOD SHOULD RECOGNIZE RESIDENTS' PAST CONTRIBUTION TO THE OWNERSHIP OF THE PROPERTIES

4. IMPACT ON COUNTY

There is no question that the act of creating a city from a former unincorporated area of a county will impact that county. In the case of Sandy Springs there was great concern expressed by the opposing factions that there would be a negative impact on the remainder of the county. That concern was realistic. Any time a segment of an entity that has been subsidizing the others is removed from the mix; there will be an impact on the remaining area. Sandy Springs had been subsidizing the remainder of the county for decades. The author estimates that Sandy Springs may have produced a subsidy of one billion dollars over the past twenty-five years!

There will definitely be a requirement for belt tightening for the remainder of the county as the substantial subsidy is removed. Further, it is likely that the county's problems will get worse as at least four other communities are now following Sandy Springs in seeking self-determination. There should be no tears for a county that has enjoyed the largess of these communities' taxes for so many years. Its inefficiencies and inequalities are coming home to roost.

B. RELATIONSHIPS WITH OTHER GOVERNMENTS

Sandy Springs was fortunate to have several municipalities nearby that were very willing to assist in forming the new city. In Fulton County, both Roswell and Alpharetta had been in existence for more than 100 years. Roswell is adjacent to Sandy Springs, and its population and area are nearly identical. Alpharetta is on the opposite side of Roswell and was about forty percent as large, but less dense, in population.

As the year of implementation began, one of the first steps was to make contacts in the two existing cities. Everyone from the mayors down promised, and delivered, cooperation.

Following the old adage that "no good deed goes unpunished", we later drew some of the best employees from both cities to work with our private contractor. To our credit, we did recognize the possibility that such a "raid" might occur, and in the first meeting with the Mayor of Roswell, we offered to pledge to not take their employees. His generous response was: "Take any that you can. That is the only way that folks in municipal government have much opportunity to advance." We did tell him that we would exercise care not to start an escalation in the typical salary ranges for the area.

The key person that we recruited was the Finance Director from Alpharetta. He was extremely helpful in providing information on accounting, finance, and budgeting requirements for the new city. We came to admire his skills so much that we eventually offered him the position of Deputy City Manager, with the understanding that he would serve as Acting City Manager until the City Manager was in place.

Both these cities cooperated in sharing data, sample contracts and processes that were of great value to the Sandy Springs Task Forces. We attempted, as we had with the county, to establish a channel for requests through the City Managers, to avoid the confusion resulting from separate data requests from too many people.

Contracts with other municipalities had been one of the four alternative methods for providing services that we had considered from the beginning. As it turned out, this option was not widely used. In most cases the other municipalities being somewhat smaller than Sandy Springs, did not have the capacity to offer the services without major expense increases or capital expenditures.

There were two services that could be provided jointly with others. Roswell had the capacity to provide jail space. A contract was drawn that allows Sandy Springs to transport prisoners to the Roswell facility. This is especially advantageous because that is the closest jail facility to Sandy Springs and should cut transport time by at least 75 percent, versus taking detainees to the county facility. Roswell will benefit financially from the contract. We certainly did not haggle over the price!

The City of Smyrna also has been helpful to Sandy Springs. Smyrna is a city several tiers away to the west. There was a need to provide "enhanced" library service. The county will continue to operate the one existing library in Sandy Springs. The libraries throughout the county are financed through the General Fund, and will continue as a county function. It was clear that there was a need for enhanced library services to reach people in Sandy Springs that could not, or would not, use the single library. Included in that category are the elderly, less affluent members of the community and the more transient apartment dwellers.

In cooperation with Smyrna, a number of remote lending library sites were established and serviced to meet their needs

There was a strong second need to provide the enhanced service. Under Georgia law, a city must provide at least three of six specific services to be eligible to receive a share of the Local Option Sales Tax (LOST). Sandy Springs' portion of the LOST amounts to about $20 million a year, so it was imperative that the city qualify to receive its share as soon as possible. From the outset, there were problems in being able to provide a number of the services. However, the law stipulates that:

(1) Contracting for a service is equivalent to direct provision of the service

(2) Qualification may be by "enhancing" an existing service

The opportunity to provide enhanced library service was very attractive because several service contracts with the county—for fire, police and sewer, and with the city of Atlanta for water services—did not materialize until the last possible moments, the library contract with Smyrna was huge in meeting the qualifications for LOST.

Recommendation:
Fully understand every aspect of your state's laws and processes with regard to tax revenues.

If Sandy Springs had not started early to understand and to prepare to meet qualification requirements for LOST, the city would have been in financial jeopardy from Day One.

CHAPTER IX

"One of the things that you have trouble with politicians… is when you get mad at them and you can't touch them; you can't punch them; you can't yell at them."

-Frank Luntz

RESPONSIVENESS

The Official Seal of the City of Sandy Springs bears three words. At the sides are the words "Honesty" and "Efficiency," but the seal rests on the word "Responsiveness."

Citizens might desire to form a city for any of numerous reasons. Some of the more common may include concerns for taxes, service levels, and zoning issues. The people of Sandy Springs had all of these issues, plus traffic and public safety concerns. However, responsiveness was the preeminent issue for this community.

Certainly, it was clear that our community was tired of subsidizing other portions of the county for as long as we could remember. We estimate that in the past 25 years, at least a billion dollars has flowed out of Sandy Springs to be spent elsewhere. We could almost hear the whooshing sound of funds being sucked out of the area.

Just as certain was the imbalance of services. Sandy Springs was grossly under force in the vital public safety functions of police and fire. The favored (by the county) areas had eleven times the park space per capita. Few resources were assigned to traffic design and management. The litany of deficiencies covered every area of service.

Yet, with all that, the most disturbing, even galling, issue to the community was the total lack of responsiveness by the political representatives at the county commission. Pay more, receive less, and keep your mouth shut, seemed to be the motto of the majority.

The feeling of isolation by the northern suburbs in Fulton County is exacerbated by both geography and the large population of the county. The county is about sixty miles long north to south, split in the middle by Atlanta. It is a decided chore for the residents of Sandy Springs to travel to the county offices in downtown Atlanta, find a place to park, and attempt to conduct any business with the commission or the staff.

With five districts, each commissioner represents an average of about 180,000 people. Given those numbers, it is impossible for the average citizen to feel any sense of contact or shared goals with a representative on the commission. These conditions contribute to the lack of responsiveness even before the politics of race enter the picture.

When dealing below the political level, the situation is a little different. The obvious animosity of many of the commissioners for the northern suburbs is not so evident at the staff level. At the upper staff levels there is a willingness to serve and to cooperate. The problem that Sandy Springs has with the county staff is one of inefficiency caused by the programs and staffing policies of the political leaders. That the county staff is bloated is undeniable. The workers often refer to it as the "Fulton County jobs program." The county had the highest cost per capita of any county in the metropolitan Atlanta area, and probably in the state. While common sense would seem to dictate that more people would provide more resources available to be responsive to the public's needs, it seems to have had the opposite effect. There is a general malaise in which no one is responsible or responsive.

Considering these conditions, it is little wonder that the basic human desire to have someone listen to our needs and respond in a truly concerned manner was not being met. The expectation that the new city will satisfy that need is palpable.

This high level of expectation is a challenge that the Sandy Springs leaders and the company serving the city have begun to meet. So far, the community has indicated that their expectations are being met extremely well.

CH2M HILL recognized the community's desire for a more responsive government from the earliest days of their involvement.

One of the strengths of their RFP response was in the plans to establish programs that produced timely responses to inquiries and encouraged citizen involvement. Most prominent among the plans was the establishment of a non-emergency call center. The commitment associated with the call center was that all calls would receive a response within two days.

Calls that were "emergency" (not E911) such as "a lot is being cleared of trees" would receive a response in two hours or less. Plans were included to be visible in the city immediately. For example, we would have code enforcement people on the streets from Day One. The codes for signs, noise, storm water, and other common violations., were to be addressed immediately. Traffic signals and potholes were to be surveyed and corrections begun.

Parks and recreation programs were to go forward unabated. The community was to be invited in for planning sessions and to express concerns. New street signs were to begin going up. Happily all of these plans were carried out within ninety days, and most within thirty days. In short, Sandy Springs citizens were hungry for someone to respond to their needs. Initial feedback indicates that these needs are being met.

CHAPTER X

"Competition is the keen edge of business, always
shaving away at costs"
-Henry Ford

COMPETITIVE CONTRACTING

A. PRIVATE INDUSTRY

The decision to form the city of Sandy Springs on the foundation of services provided by private industry was driven by two principal considerations:

(1) Over time, private industry would provide more efficient, effective and responsive services.

(2) In the short run, private industry was the only vehicle that could provide a fully operational city in the time required

The decision to consider the use of private industry to provide the majority of services to Sandy Springs was a breakthrough for Sandy Springs. Upon assuming the role of volunteer Interim City Manager, the author began to seek an additional method for meeting the city's needs beyond the initial three alternatives:

(1) Self-provision

(2) Fulton County contracts

(3) Contracts with other governments

Given the extremely short time period to have the city's services in effect, it was clear that out-of-the box solutions were in order.

The reader may refer back to Chapter (I) for a discussion of the identification of Weston, Florida, as a potential source of information on contracting with private industry.

Once the committee for Sandy Springs had agreed to consider the alternative of employing private industry, the ICM's problem became how to proceed. There were no precedents available for creating a city when there was no authority to form contracts.

PREQUALIFICATION

The ICM determined that the first step would be to prepare a Prequalification Letter to send to as many large companies as could be identified as having the experience to potentially offer the required services. Through various sources, a mailing list of national and international firms was compiled.

There were two principal questions that were addressed to these firms.

First, a list was provided of the twelve major areas of service that the city might desire to have under contract. The firms were asked to indicate for each service a reference to any municipality where the firm had provided the service. An opportunity to reference an alternative, but similar location, such as a military installation also was provided.

The second important question was whether the firm would consider making major implementation expenditures before a contract, or even a handshake, could be concluded.

Given the risk implied in the second question, we were pleasantly surprised that about half of the firms replied. Many were somewhat hazy in describing their experience in providing specific services, but all indicated confidence that they could do the job if chosen. Only a few actually would commit to accepting the risk of making expenditures without a signed contract, or even the promise of a contract. A larger number either danced around the issue, or ignored the question all together.

In total, the responses were positive enough to encourage a belief that it was possible to proceed with the concept. Additionally, there was an interesting pattern to the responses with regard to service capability. A matrix was created that listed firms on the X axis and services on the Y axis. The pattern that emerged provided distinct groupings of firms. There were four that covered the eight services that were identified loosely as administrative, and four that were providers of the group of four services identified as technical. Only one company claimed significant capability in both groupings.

B. REQUESTS FOR PROPOSALS

This pattern of service capability, led to the decision to separate the services needs into two RFPs. The first document to be titled:

PROVISION OF ADMINISTRATIVE, FINANCIAL, COMMUNITY SERVICES, EMERGENCY 911, PHYSICAL PLANT, MOTOR VEHICLE, STAFFING, PURCHASING, PROCUREMENT AND CONTRACTING SERVICES

and the second, titled:

PUBLIC WORKS, TRANSPORTATION, STREETS, RIGHT-OF-WAY, FACILITIES, PARKS AND RECREATION, CAPITAL IMPROVEMENTS, PLANNING AND ZONING, INSPECTIONS, CODE ENFORCEMENT, PERMITTING, PURCHASING, PROCUREMENT, AND CONTRACTING SERVICES

These were referred to subsequently as RFP #1 Administrative and RFP #2 Technical. The RFPs are included in Appendix (C) and (D). With each RFP is a suggested Agreement (contract). These tentative Agreements were very helpful in providing a starting point for contract negotiations.

To aid in the creation of the RFPs, the author drew heavily on the Weston documents, and as many other sources as were available, to shape the format and the content.

One of the most difficult challenges in producing any RFP is in specifying the performance criteria. In this rare and complex case in which a new city was being brought to life, the difficulty in providing specific measurements was off the scale. We had no history to rely upon for the city and very little experience from others. Even Weston offered scant data that could be used to form performance metrics.

Given the perceived inability to form measurements of service, the author chose a very different approach. The RFPs placed the burden upon the companies to define the level of services that they could provide. That is, Sandy Springs described the service that was desired, and then asked the company to assist in the creation of performance criteria. After all, the companies had indicated in response to the Prequalification Letter that they had experience with these types of services. This approach caused a lot of head shaking among the responding firms, but ultimately worked. The companies that really did not have substantive experience in serving municipalities tended to fall out of the bidding. There was just too much uncertainty (risk) for them. Companies that knew what they were doing were able to draw up proposals that were quite responsive to our service needs.

Not only were the companies asked to help shape the measurement criteria, but they also were asked to propose an implementation plan with very narrow time limits. It is certain that no firm had been asked to start up a brand new city with such a broad need for services in such a short period of time. The RFPs were approved for issuance by the Governor's Commission on June 29, 2005, and the city was to be born on December 1, 2005.

That was an interval of five months, but recognize that the proposals were not due until August 31, and the successful bidder not selected until September 14, at which point contract negotiations could begin. Five months quickly dwindled to two and a half months for implementation.

Sandy Springs recognized the difficulty of the task that the companies were being asked to undertake, but we were confident that American industry could do it, and were not about to bend in our determination to start the new city on time.

C. RISK

This might be a good point to pause and reflect on why a company might decide to take on such a risky proposition. To recap, the terms were:

"no one has the authority to sign a contract until after the city is incorporated"

"no one is committing to you that even if selected as the top bidder that you will get a contract"

"we can not set firm performance measures"

"if recommended as the top bidder, you have to start the implementation process immediately"

None of these terms were likely to warm the heart of a CEO.

The actual risk to the company was much less than it was perceived to be originally. After all, when the new city Council held the first meeting, to have failed to approve a contract would have left them governing a city virtually without services. There was a greater risk that the Council might decide to significantly modify the recommended contract either with regard to performance levels or costs. Fortunately for all concerned, that did not happen, and the partnership began smoothly.

Referring back to the Prequalification Letter, in addition to questioning the companies about their willingness and ability to serve, we also did a bit of a selling job. It was pointed out that Sandy Springs was going to be the premier showcase for the role of private industry in municipal government in the entire country. Therefore, the firm that got our business would have the spotlight, and a "leg up" on penetrating an enormous market. In Georgia alone, there are 581 cities, few of which have opened their doors to private industry. About 25 percent have some limited contracts in the public works, or transportation area, but not much else. The opportunity to crack a multibillion-dollar market was a terrific incentive to respond to Sandy Springs.

In addition, the challenge we offered was to be a partner in starting a city with a "clean sheet of paper"; the rare chance to do it right. We stated that we hoped to create "a model for the 21st century municipal government." We meant it then, and we believe it to be true now

To our knowledge, there is no municipal government in the country with so broad a scope of services delivered by private industry.

D. COMPETITION

As a start-up city, with little ability to gauge proper costs for its services, Sandy Springs had to substitute competition for knowledge. Multiple levels of competition were established.

First, there was the competition between sources of services.

> Self-provision
>> versus
> County contracts
>> versus
> Other government contracts
>> versus
> Private industry contracts

Second, there was the competition between companies, set up by the RFP process.

This multi-level competition served to assure the new city that it was not paying excessive costs.

COMPETITIVE CONTRACTING

The reader may have noticed that the term "privatization" has not appeared in this book until this point. The reason is that it is an inappropriate description, and for many, a pejorative word; inappropriate, because in a new city there is nothing to "privatize". The negative connotation generally comes because of a loss of jobs by existing employees. In a startup, city there is no such loss. The fact is that the city of Sandy Springs is a net importer of jobs.

If not privatization, then what? The preferred term is "**competitive contracting**." Consider the foregoing choices. Everything was about competition and finding the most efficient and cost effective source. Thus, competitive contracting best describes the model that was followed.

E. OTHER POTENTIAL MARKETS

1. NEW CITIES

As mentioned previously in this book, there are a number of other communities in Georgia that currently have filed, or are in the process of filing, legislation to incorporate. There are five such communities that the author is advising informally, or has been retained to assist.

All of these communities are looking very closely at the Sandy Springs model. Particularly, they are considering the use of private industry as their service vehicle. The success of the Sandy Springs implementation, even after only a short period of operation, is encouraging and attractive to these other potential cities.

One potential city is immediately adjacent to Sandy Springs, and there are some obvious synergies that could be available through sharing the same contractor. However, it is premature to consider this issue. If a cooperative intergovernmental agreement (IGA) can not be arranged, the new cities will have to engage in competitive bidding for their services, as did Sandy Springs.

2. EXISTING CITIES

The advantages that may accrue to existing cities from the introduction of private industry are just as important as for new cities. After observing the effective and professional start-up of services for Sandy Springs, we have no doubt that the same level of expertise could be bought to bear in transferring existing services to the competitive contracting model.

In an existing city, any one of the twelve areas of service/functions that Sandy Springs identified could be opened to private industry without missing a beat.

The obvious concern would be for the existing employees. However, the only reason for their jobs being in jeopardy would be that their current performance was not competitive with alternate sources for the service. The city government owes the citizens the most efficient and responsive services that can be provided, and sometimes must make hard choices. The most productive employees would be very likely to find employment with the replacing service provider. Their experience and productivity would be of great value. Those who had been a drag on service would have to go.

Why should cities not periodically test the waters to find better ways to provide service? Too many have been locked into traditional methods for too long, simply due to inertia. It is the problem of too much baggage; old systems, old methods, old employees that either are not willing, or cannot change.

The bloat found in almost every government, from the federal to the municipal level, is a plague on the nation. There are many reasons for the excesses of governments, but one of the foremost is the reluctance to try new methods. Political leaders come and go, but staffs roll on. No one at any level seems to want to rock the boat.

Traditional city governments are often burdened with employees who have no incentive to innovate, even if they had the ability. Certainly there is no incentive to perform at anything more than the minimal levels necessary to hold on to their jobs.

The political apparatus, and civil service mentality of employees is not the only, or even the most critical, problem with traditional municipalities. Cities often are burdened with inflexible structures. There is no ability to shift forces, or to bring in short term and expert resources as can private industry contractors.

Cities have shown a reluctance to contract for services outside a few functional areas such as public works and transportation projects. Normally those contracts are for capital improvements or maintenance of roads and facilities. The idea that private industry can bring value to such areas as administration, accounting, human resources, finances, community development, information technology and the support of public safety functions has been largely ignored.

Sandy Springs certainly believes that the "competitive contracting" model that we have established will be a good example of private industry's ability to bring value to almost every area of municipal government.

3. ADVANTAGES

Included among the values of competitive contracting are:

a. A more cost-effective means of delivering services. The private sector can deliver services at less cost and better quality. CH2M HILL, will deliver services up to 25 percent cheaper than the city estimated it could provide the same services. The new city has not created a government with the typical inefficiencies of a bureaucracy that include bloated employee costs, retirement programs, health and welfare programs.

b. The private sector is highly motivated to perform. The city has a contract that governs the quality and service level to be provided. The contract provides the city with the right to terminate all, or part, of the contract if there is dissatisfaction with any part of the service. The private sector is motivated to perform for a reasonable profit and there can be incentives to achieve certain performance levels within the contract. Penalties can also be used to as a means of further assuring performance. The city's interests are also protected through the contract terms on liabilities, insurance and bonds.

c. There is more flexibility with the private sector which has the ability to provide varying levels of service and resources as the city grows and needs change. Cities typically hire full time employees and incur all the associated costs (retirement, benefits, etc.) of doing so.

There is the inherent inflexibility of having either too many, or too few employees in a given area, Firms like CH2M HILL can provide incremental resources—only as needed—from its large resource base in Georgia, and the nation. The force, and therefore the cost, can be tailored to provide services as needed.

d. CH2M HILL provided the technical expertise and significant financial resources necessary to cope with the broad scope of services needed by Sandy Springs. The city was not forced to hire, train, and develop qualified personnel. The management systems, processes and tools to manage the city were already in existence and had only to be tailored to the city's needs.

e. Freedom from political influence once a contract is in place. While Sandy Springs has complete oversight of services to the city, it leaves the management of those services to the company within the terms of the contract. The only concern is to avoid political pressures during the process of the competitive contracting.

Recommendation:
Existing municipalities should begin to explore competitive contracting with private industry for a wider array of services/functions.

Cities should be open to opportunities to apply competitive contracting on a service-by-service basis. For example, when a community approaches the need to upgrade information technology; rather than seek bids for new hardware and/or software, why not ask for proposals to provide a "turnkey service" that also provides operating and maintenance in the package? The big payoff comes when all, or most, of the services have been migrated by competitive contracting. Synergies and the flexibility to move resources, both in and out of the city, and between internal functions, will lead to significant cost savings and improved performance.

Many of the firms that can offer services to municipalities have performed in emergency situations all over the world. Stepping in to react to natural disasters and even war zone situations has been a part of their history. They bring a sense of urgency and a desire to excel that in all but the most rare of governments does not seem to prevail.

F. RFP PREPARATION

Preparing the RFPs was a major undertaking. In most cases the process might, in all probability, be the work of a team of people. For Sandy Springs, the author prepared both documents, which were then finalized by a fine legal firm on a pro bono basis. The legal assistance was excellent and much needed. There was a need for constant contact and agreement to be sure that all legal requirements were being met. The law firm that did so much for Sandy Springs is recognized in this book's "Acknowledgments" section.

The RFP process placed the scope of service, performance criteria, timing, evaluation procedures, and processing instructions in the realm of the author. Legal advice was then appliquéd dealing primarily with issues of liability, insurance and performance bonds.

As a note of caution, in this area, Sandy Springs was possibly overcautious in initially specifying bonds that were too difficult and/or expensive for firms to be able to comply. Because the scope of services being sought was out of the ordinary, the bonding agencies were reluctant to meet the requested levels. This, coupled with the perceived risk of implementing services without a contract, led to several firms deciding not to respond.

It is probable that future cities will point to the success of Sandy Springs and eliminate both problems. One might anticipate that the perceived risk will diminish as more cities and companies enter into successful competitive contracting agreements.

Sandy Springs' RFPs and the associated agreements appear in Appendices C, and D. The final contracts with the firm of CH2M HILL are provided in Appendices E and F.

A comparison between the original agreements and the final contracts may be useful to the reader in understanding the dynamics of the contract negotiations.

Contract negotiations required about three weeks. While the Sandy Spring's Contract Negotiation Team felt that the sessions were very intense and drawn out, the firm's team assured us that for a contract of that size, agreement was reached much faster than normal. A factor that helped was that on both sides of the table, there was excitement at the prospect of starting the new city. There was the recognition that this unique opportunity to partner in drawing on the "clean sheet of paper" would not come again.

1. THE RFP PROCESS

It is generally accepted in Georgia that governmental contracts must be offered under a public bidding process. While there are certainly merits to negotiated bids in some cases, open bidding is considered the surest way to protect the public's interest.

The dilemma that Sandy Springs faced was that there was no one with authority to issue an RFP. Originally, the author planned to issue the documents as products of the Committee for Sandy Springs. Legal counsel advised against taking that road, since the committee had no authority to conclude the contract, and could be held liable for the costs of the companies in responding to the RFP.

2. ROLE OF GOVERNOR'S COMMMISSION

The only other body that could conceivably sponsor the RFP's was the Governor's Commission for Sandy Springs (GCSS). The problems with that approach were twofold:

- The legislation only gave the GCSS the authority to negotiate for the city, but not to commit to any contracts.

- Time was growing short and the GCSS had not yet been appointed. In fact, no one was sure when, or if, the Governor might act.

Given that there appeared to be no other alternative, we proceeded with the preparation of the RFPs on the assumption that the GCSS would issue them as soon as possible.

The Governor chose to wait until after the successful referendum (94 percent in favor) to appoint the five-person Commission, doing so on June 24, 2005. The Governor's office asked the author to coordinate the first meeting, which we arranged as quickly as possible for June 29.

Before continuing with the sequence of events, a word about the makeup of the GCSS is in order. The organizers had assumed that individuals from the community who had been involved in the attempt to gain cityhood would be on the Commission. The Governor had other ideas and chose to name a five-person Commission that included four Commissioners who had not been very active in the implementation effort. Two were not residents of Sandy Springs. Let me hasten to say that it was an excellent group of high-quality individuals who worked very well together to assist in the formation of the city. However their learning curve was extremely steep. Had they not been of such high quality and willing to take personal risk on behalf of the community, the whole process could have bogged down beyond repair.

Nothing could better illustrate the Commissioners' willingness to cooperate than the decision at the very first meeting to sponsor the two massive RFPs. They agreed to do so without having the opportunity to make a detailed analysis of the documents. Our law firm and I gave a briefing at which we communicated two facts:

- Nothing was being presented that could not be amended at a later date

- There was great urgency to proceed.

With these assurances, the GCSS took responsibility for the RFPs and approved the issuance.

We next advertised the RFPs, and transmitted information to interested parties. A local printing firm, hopeful of securing the city's future business agreed to print 100 free copies of the four large documents, and these were rushed to mail to the companies that had responded to the Prequalification Letter. Both print media and Internet advertisement produced additional requests for the RFPs.

Sandy Springs was able to post the RFPs to a website, which was a great help in distributing the material to prospective responders. Very few hard copies were needed after the original distribution.

3. PRE-PROPOSAL CONFERENCE

Hosting a mandatory Pre-proposal Conference was the subsequent step in the process. On August 14, 41 companies appeared with a plethora of questions. The author conducted the conference with the assistance of the pro bono legal team. The RFPs were covered in detail, with questions posed and answered at each stage. The procedure for asking additional questions was established. All questions were to be submitted in writing (normally e-mail) to the author by a certain date. The responses to all questions would be distributed to all firms present at the conference. A consensus was reached to extend the date for questions and for the formal submission of proposals by three weeks. It was necessary later in the process to add an additional two weeks because of the complexity and volume of questions that were forthcoming.

It would be fair to characterize the conference as one of uneasiness among many of the prospective responders due primarily to the unusual nature and scope of the RFPs.

Given all of the above, the conference was still fun. No one knew what to expect from this want-to-be city and its unique approach to obtaining services. There was a great deal of concern about our inability to specify metrics for the services. The barrier to entry that the bond levels presented also began to surface. Ultimately, this concern forced a modification to the RFPs.

As the conference concluded, the level of interest expressed was encouraging, but we were concerned about our ability to satisfactorily answer all of the questions that would be forthcoming. If we had really known the volume of the queries, our concern might have turned to panic.

There is no point in providing details on the questions that dealt with specifics on Sandy Springs. An example might be "How many lane-miles of roads will be in the city," or, "What will be the number and length of communication cable runs in the city hall?" The latter question was particularly challenging, as at that point we did not know where city hall would be.

The surprise was that while about half of the questions concerned the scope of services, the other half could be characterized as legal and/or liability issues. An example of such an issue follows:

Question: Will the City/Commission discuss amending the Agreement to specifically provide for the contractor to receive additional compensation if there is a change of applicable law that results in an increase in contractor's cost of performing the Services?

Answer: Yes, the Commission will consider such an amendment.

By the end of the five week process, we had 45 typed pages of questions and answers.

4. MATING PROCESS

Another activity was taking place during the Question and Answer period. At the pre-proposal conference it was obvious that there were a number of smaller firms that were interested in only a portion of the contracts. It also was clear that few, if any of the larger firms could meet all of Sandy Springs' needs without forming partnerships with other companies. From the beginning, companies were encouraged to collaborate, or sub-contract, with others to produce a proposal. It was the desire of Sandy Springs to have only one principal for each RFP, but there could be any number of subcontractors.

To aid in the "mating" process, the author committed to all the companies present, that "advertisements," or similar descriptions of their service capability, that any firm cared to submit, would be forwarded to all of the other firms. There was a lot of this activity as the larger firms worked to build a team response, and the smaller companies sought to fill a niche.

In the end, this matching of companies proved to be a huge benefit to Sandy Springs. It is possible that without this effort, there would have been no satisfactory proposals, especially in response to the RFP for Administration (RFP #1).

5. SUBMISSIONS

For anyone who is not familiar with the RFP process, let me say that the submission of the proposals is a very serious matter to the companies involved. Proper procedures must be set up to receive the proposals, and all parties must adhere to a a clear and inflexible date and time deadline.

For RFPs of such a broad scope and potential value as Sandy Springs represented, companies will devote a great deal of effort, time and expense to the preparation of their proposals. The cost to a company is significant and its reputation potentially is placed at stake. The individuals who may have placed their necks on the line to convince top management of the value of going after the business, want to win the business. The reputation of the company itself also is involved. No major firm wants to be a seen as a loser in a high stakes game.

It is a fact that the company that emerged as the choice in the Sandy Springs RFP competition is viewed by a number of other potential cities as the leading contender for their future business.

With money and reputations at stake, the submission of proposals and the subsequent evaluation process are very serious business.

6. EVALUATION PROCESS

The Governor's Commission on Sandy Springs (GCSS) after agreeing to be the sponsor of the RFPs, then moved on to the selection process. Within the RFPs there was a description of the evaluation criteria by which the various proposals would be judged. The GCSS chose to appoint an Evaluation Team to carry out the critical function of applying the criteria to all of the proposals. It should be remembered that neither the Evaluation Team, nor the GCSS, had the authority to make a binding selection. The job of the Evaluation Team was to objectively apply the criteria and then to present the ranking of the various proposals to the GCSS. The GCSS could then either accept, or override, the ranking, for the purpose of making a recommendation to the future city officials.

The reader may want to refer to the Method of Evaluation section in Appendix C, section 12.2, and D, section 15.2, for more details on the evaluation criteria.

In general, the RFPs stated that the proposals would be ranked under a points system with points being awarded in four categories, as follows:

For RFP #1

(1) Qualifications and Experience

One Hundred (100) potential points based on the offeror's qualifications, experience, and financial position.

(2) Previous experience with providing the specific services

One Hundred (100) potential points based on the offeror's previous experience in providing similar services and duties, divided as follows:

Service/Function	Point Scale
Administration	0 to 10
Accounting	0 to 20
Courts	0 to 5
Finance	0 to 10
Human Resources	0 to 10
IT	0 to 25
Police	0 to 10
Fire	0 to 10
Total	0 to 100

(3) Startup and implementation plans

One Hundred (100) potential points based on the quality, detail and sufficiency of the offeror's startup and implementation plan to have all of the required duties and services operational on the date of Contract Award by the City.

(4) Financial (costs)

One Hundred (100) points to the lowest bid of the submitting offeror. Points for offerors submitting higher bids will be awarded in the following manner:

A ratio of the low bid dollars to the higher bid dollars will be calculated and multiplied by 100.

Low Bid ___ x 100 Points = Bid points
Higher Bid

Composite Score

The sum of the points for (1) Qualifications and Experience, (2) Previous Experience with Similar Services and Duties, (3) Start-up and Implementation Plan, and (4) Financial, will comprise the Composite Score. The maximum Composite Score is 400 Points.

For RFP #2

The scoring was the same for Numbers 1, 3, and 4. For Number 2, the following was substituted:

Service/Function	Point Scale
Public Works	0 to 15
Transportation	0 to 20
Streets, Rights-of-Way and Facilities	0 to 10
Parks and Recreation	0 to 10
Capital Improvement Plans	0 to 10
Planning and Zoning	0 to 20
Inspections, Code Enforcement and Permitting	0 to 15
Total	0 to 100

These evaluation criteria, which were unique to Sandy Springs, seemed to be clear and acceptable to all potential bidders. At least there were no questions with regard to the criteria.

7. EVALUATION TEAM

An Evaluation Team of six well-qualified people was named by the GCSS. Five members were residents of the community with experience in RFP procedure and in evaluation of bids. The sixth member was the County Manager of an adjacent county. The diligence with which the members of the Evaluation Team approached the difficult assignment was highly commendable.

As soon as the responses to the RFPs were officially received, the distribution of the material began. Copies of all submissions were provided to the Evaluation Team and the GCSS. In addition, the proposals were broken up to provide the relevant sections to the Sandy Springs Task Forces. The Task forces were asked for their opinions of the competing proposals and to furnish questions that should be posed to clarify issues.

The Evaluation Team continued to meet at a frequent interval to refine the methodology for the evaluation and to prepare for forthcoming oral presentations by the companies. The Team had the opportunity to consider the four areas of the evaluation criteria in detail. The specifications for each segment and the weighting to be applied to each were made clear. Consensus was reached on additional quantifications within several of the segments, and a format for providing each Team member's evaluation.

The companies were scheduled to make oral presentations. The Evaluation Team prepared questions derived from the submissions, and also questions designed to determine the company's commitment to the new city.

G. ORAL PRESENTATIONS

Each of the proposing firms was given an opportunity to appear for an oral presentation. The Evaluation Team specified that the presentations be brief, and that the only visuals would be those that might be useful in responding to the Team's questions. With the resources that the companies can bring to such meetings, full-scale presentations could have gone on for days. The intent of the Team was to:

(1) Get to know the companies' principal players

(2) Obtain clarifications of the written proposals

Each presentation by the firms was limited to introductions (the largest company team had 14 members) with outlines of each person's role in the proposal, and/or providing future services to Sandy Springs. Key positions that had been filled tentatively since the written proposals were identified. All of the companies would have liked more opportunity to sell their proposals.

The reasons for not allowing the companies to make full-scale presentations were several. First, the Evaluation Team was working under time pressures. Second, oral presentations are not binding. It was important that the evaluation be performed on the basis of the written proposals, which would stand the test of future public scrutiny if necessary. The clarifications to the proposals were documented. Third, the sheer volume of material that could have been presented orally would have swamped the Team.

After the brief company presentations, the Evaluation Team began the question period, rotating predetermined questions between the members. Obviously, as answers were elicited, there was often a need for extensive development through follow-up questions. The companies were very forthcoming throughout the process. The company leaders were encouraged to allow the subject matter experts to provide answers when appropriate, and due to the broad scope of the proposals, that was often the case.

There were a relatively few cases in which the company was forced to offer to provide data, or explanations, at a later date.

Minutes were kept and were provided to all parties at a later date to confirm agreement.

H. EVALUATION PROCESS

Upon the completion of the oral presentations and the provision of follow-up material by the companies, the Evaluation Team began the very difficult task of attempting to rank the proposals. Since there was only one proposal for RFP #1, Administration, the team dealt with that proposal first, with the only decision being to rank the proposal as either Acceptable or Unacceptable. There was unanimity among the team to rank the proposal by the firm of CH2M HILL as Acceptable.

For RFP#2, Technical, there were three competing proposals, including one by CH2M HILL . There were detailed discussions of the proposals within the Evaluation Team. All of the proposals were very well prepared and in varying ways addressed the needs of the new city. Each proposal had certain areas of strength and others that were weaker. The predetermined evaluation criteria were adhered to, and were of significant help in working systematically through the very lengthy (about a foot thick stack), and complex proposals.

During the team discussions, there was no attempt to begin the ranking process. The desire was to be sure that all Team members understood the proposals, and to share views on the relative strengths and weaknesses.

Upon completion of the vigorous Team discussions, each member was asked to independently rank the competing submissions in accordance with our agreed upon methodology.

The consistency of the independent rankings came as a pleasant surprise. There were numerical differences between rankings within every category. Some members tended to rank higher then others, but the relative placements were the same from all team members. This unanimity gave the Team confidence in both the process and the relative merits of the proposals.

The Team agreed that it was ready to present the rankings at the next meeting of the GCSS along with a recommendation to begin contract negotiations with the top ranked firm for both RFPs.

There was some concern due to the fact that the proposal of CH2M HILL had emerged as the top ranked submission for RFP #2 as well as being the selection for RFP # 1. The public might view the recommendation for contracting with one firm for both contracts as putting "all of our eggs in one basket." The team felt that the clear benefits offered by the CH2M HILL proposals were significant enough to over-ride any such concerns. In addition, it should be remembered that the decision to split the RFPs had not been influenced by any particular community need. The split had been driven by the experience levels that the firms had indicated in their responses to the Prequalification Letter. Most firms had indicated experience in only one of the two general areas of service. CH2M HILL had been the only firm that had evidenced experience in both categories.

The Evaluation Team's rankings and recommendations were submitted to the GCSS on September 14, 2005. The GCSS approved the recommendation and authorized the opening of contract negotiations.

I. CONTRACT NEGOTIATIONS

As discussed previously, the Sandy Springs RFPs were not the typical municipal bid request. The scope, complexity, and to some degree, lack of specificity, guaranteed a difficult contract negotiation. On the positive side was the attitude of the parties on both sides of the negotiation table. Everyone recognized the uniqueness of the situation, and the opportunity to do something special. The spirit of partnering was in evidence from the first moment of negotiation, right through the most difficult issues, to the very end. As an integral part of the RFPs, there were attached Agreements. These Agreements were intended to serve as the basis for the ultimate contracts. The RFP contained language to the effect that the Agreements would be considered to be the contracts unless the companies offered changes within their proposals.

The company brought forward a number of issues. Every one of these was addressed with open minds at the table. There was a great deal of give and take as the parties sought common ground on some very difficult points.

The most difficult areas were:

(1) The further refinement of the definition of the scope of service

(2) Performance standards

(3) The degree to which functional costs would be reported

The two negotiating teams worked hand-in hand to reach agreements in all the areas. The scope of service questions were not easy to deal with, since there was no model to follow. Understanding was reached that this was to be a "service" contract. In layman's terms, that meant that the city was requiring that the level of services that were to be provided should in no case be inferior to the existing levels, with improvements where specified. An example of an improvement in the level of service was in responsiveness to the public. The citizens of Sandy Springs placed a great value on responsiveness. The understanding was reached that the company would provide resources and related expenditures necessary to do a turnkey job in providing the services/functions. Whatever resources were needed to meet the service needs would be focused on getting the job done. This approach requires a level of trust that is above the norm, but is consistent with the partnership nature of the relationship. Further, it freed the company to be flexible and creative in the assignment of resources. Rather than tie down specific resources to provide a service, the company can move in and remove people as needed.

For those who may, on reading the preceding narrative, fear that the city has no control over the company's performance, remember that the ultimate "hammer" is written into the contract. The City Manager supervises the contract, and may terminate the agreement without cause. In the same manner, the City Manager may dictate the removal of key company personnel within the contract. This provision required a great deal of trust by the company.

The issues involving the provision of functional costs, in part, impacted the actual cost of the contract. From the city's viewpoint there was a need for as much cost information as possible. The team was sensitive to any concern by the community that we were over paying for services, and therefore sought cost details to support the contract. However, there were conflicting needs. The creation of a detailed cost accounting system is expensive, and would add to the total cost of the contract. The company's proposal had been based on a "Service" contract as discussed above. Further, it was a "Fixed Price" as opposed to a "Cost Plus" contract. The appliquéing of a detailed cost system would have significantly changed the costs.

One might ask why the city specified a fixed cost, rather than a cost plus arrangement. The primary reason was that with all of the uncertainties that the city faced in this massive startup, we did not want to be faced with the possibility of having an uncertain cost for the majority of our budget. The bid prices from private industry were clearly less than the cost under any other alternative that we had been able to discover, and we wanted to assure that those costs did not escalate. After many alternate proposals and much thought on both sides of the table, we returned to the Fixed Cost contract as the best for all concerned.

For those who might surmise that we left money on the table, let me relate a telephone interview with a reporter from the New York Times who wanted to question the merits of the contract. She was a nice young lady, but seemed to be very concerned that the company might actually be making a nice profit on the deal. She seemed astounded when I said that I not only did not care, but that I really hoped that there was a profit for them. Otherwise, it would, over time, be difficult for them to meet our service needs. I assured her that by virtue of competitive contracting, we were confident that this was the least-cost solution for obtaining the desired services. Her reply was, "but the company should not be allowed to profit from the public." After several further repetitions of our respective positions, I finally posed a hypothetical question to her. To wit: "If we project that to provide the services ourselves will cost $70 million but under the contract, the cost will be $50 million, Is it wrong for a company to make $10 million?" Her reply was: "Yes, it is the public's money." I followed with: "Then, should we spend $70 million of the public's money, $20 million more than necessary, to keep private industry from making a profit?" She said "no," but I am afraid she went away unsatisfied.

The Sandy Springs team is very satisfied that this was the right choice.

One of the products of contract negotiation which was very beneficial to the city was that as a result of the synergies generated by merging the two RFPs into one contract, there was a $2.3 million reduction in the contracts for each of the first two years. Originally CH2M HILL had proposed a price of $32 million for Year One and $27 million for Year Two. With the cost savings generated from the combined services, the prices were $29.7 and $24.7 million respectively.

The reason for the large reduction in price from Year One to Year Two may not be immediately obvious to the reader. It is not so much an actual drop-in cost, but is a reflection of the doubling up of implementation expenditures that the company was compelled to spend before the city started (2005), with the full year's expenditures for 2006. There were also anticipations of improved efficiencies in 2007, over 2006, which contributed further to the reduction.

As was pointed out in the chapter on "Legislative Deficiencies" The city could not actually offer the desired six-year contract. Each year the city council will have to vote to fund and extend the contract. However, if the extension is granted (as we are confident it will be), the price for Year Two is fixed. During the first 2 years, the city and the contractor will work together to identify measures of performance and concurrent costs. With this experience, the government/industry partnership will be in position to better determine contract terms for the following four years. Provisions were written into the contract to govern the future prices. Basically the potential future adjustments are described by a formula based on the CPI and ECI indices. The object is to maintain the contract at the Year Two level, with recognition of likely inflationary pressures (or deflation should it happen). There is a provision for re-basing the contract after Year Two to allow for changes in the service levels, and even the possibility of shifting to a cost plus basis, if both parties agree. (For more details see Appendix E, section 9.4)

An interesting segment of the contract negotiations was the opportunity to utilize the services of the two firms that had proposed on RFP #2 Technical, but had received lower overall rankings. In both cases, there were areas in which each firm had a superior ranking. The city's Negotiating Team raised the question as to whether CH2M HILL would consider partnering with the other firms in those areas. In the spirit of "partnership" with the city to obtain the best possible result, CH2M HILL responded in the affirmative. Side negotiations then took place between CH2M HILL and the other firms, which resulted in one of the firms receiving a substantial subcontract. Although there were significant and cordial talks with the third firm, no acceptable agreement was forged.

The contract negotiations over the "operating matters" such as scope of services, performance measures, organization, personnel and prices were completed in about three weeks. At that point the contracts were turned over to the legal representatives of both parties for what turned out to be even more protracted negotiations over issues such as liabilities and insurance.

Recognizing that those issues were beginning to drag out, the Negotiation Team decided to present the contracts as amended to the GCSS, with the recommendation that the GCSS accept the contracts in principle, subject to further legal review and amendment. On October 18, 2005, the GCSS did accept the contracts as offered and voted to recommend the contracts to the future city officials.

In hindsight, it was very fortunate that the decision was not made to wait for all the legal issues to be worked our before the GCSS made a recommendation. The legal issues and clarifications consumed almost two months. The December 1, start date appeared, and passed, without a contract. The new city council found it necessary to approve a

Memorandum of Agreement to reimburse CH2M HILL for the start-up expenses in case the contract could not be finalized. After all the months of creating, processing, evaluating and negotiating, the contract was finally signed on December 20, 2005, and the Memorandum of Agreement was never exercised.

J. LEGAL ISSUES

A close reading of the contracts in Appendix (E) and (F) will be required to identify all of the important points that the author has lumped together under the heading of Legal Issues. In general, these points include: Liability, Indemnification, Insurance, Conflicts of Interest, Rights to Data and Work Product Documents, and others.

Few of the above actually impact the workings of the city, but are very important to protect the interests of both parties to the contract.

There are two issues that are not directly addressed in the contracts that carry significant financial impact. These are Sovereign Immunity and Sales Tax Exemptions.

1. SOVEREIGN IMMUNITY

In Georgia, municipal governments have immunity from liability for claims for injuries or damages to members of the public. So, under sovereign immunity, in a traditional government there is not the necessity to carry major liability insurance for such occurrences. In a case such as in Sandy Springs, where private industry is the provider of the very same services that the city would have been providing, no such immunity exists. Therefore, there is the necessity of carrying a major liability insurance policy, either by the company or the city. Georgia also has a stronger than normal statute dealing with "Gratuities" which prohibited the city from carrying the liability insurance on behalf of the company. Other new cities need to consider this potential cost that can amount to several hundred thousand dollars.

New legislation may be possible that will extend immunity to private firms that can qualify as providing the majority of the city's services.

2. SALES TAX WAIVER

Another area of hidden cost is sales tax. Whereas, in Georgia, cities are exempt from state sales tax on purchases, private industry purchasing on behalf of the cities, is not. For any major expenditure, it will be advisable for the city to make its own purchases.

It is hoped that future legislation may be adopted that will extend the sales tax waiver to private industry acting on behalf of the city. The effect of such a waiver would be to eliminate roughly one million dollars in cost for Sandy Springs.

K. PARTNERSHIP and TRUST

From the outset, it was clear that to maximize the potential in utilizing the services of private industry, there had to be a sense of partnership. The traditional relationship in which the city is the boss and the company is just a subcontractor seeking to meet specific metrics would not optimize performance.

Sandy Springs was hiring more than just people and equipment. We needed and expected management and technical knowledge, coupled with innovation and creativity. It was important that the company that worked with us view this as an opportunity to exercise all their resources and experience to find new and better methods for providing the city's services. It was our view that treating this endeavor as a partnership was the only way to allow the desired behavior to blossom. The company of choice met us more than halfway. Even before the evaluation of their proposal had begun, they had chosen the motto "Our Community, Our Dream," and of greatest importance, began to act that way.

Throughout the contract negotiations there was a substantial need for trust on both sides. Many issues arose that could not have been resolved without a great deal of willingness to compromise and trust. Just a few examples of such behavior include:

> The resolution of the liability issue created by the lack of Sovereign Immunity. See the previous section (J), Legal Issues

The willingness of the company to be responsible for a five- year lease on a new city hall that was not included in the contract

The initiative of the company to provide, furnish and build out space for the temporary operating quarters for the city staff

Most significantly, the willingness of the company to spend millions on start-up without a contract

Only time will tell whether the partnership will deteriorate into an owner/worker mentality. The foundation for something better has been laid. The success of the initial year will be important in convincing the city officials that partnering is the best approach to maximizing the talent and experience that is potentially available from industry.

Certainly the first few months of operations have been an extraordinary example of the benefits to be enjoyed from giving a private company the freedom to innovate. The city started operating at one minute past midnight on Day One as if it had been running for years. Council meetings were efficient and orderly. Ordinances and building codes were approved. Contracts were let and key positions hired. Building inspectors were out inspecting and issuing citations that morning. Applications for building and zoning permits were accepted. Within a month, citizens were making positive comments about the changes. Streets were being cleaned, new street signs were up, illegal signs and graffiti were being removed or cited. Storm sewers were being cleaned. Traffic lights were being evaluated to determine why there was no synchronization. Parks and recreation programs continued to function without interruption. The police chief was hired to begin to organize the new and greatly expanded police force. Contracts for fire, E911, sewer, water and library services were secured. The municipal court was established. All this, and still no formal contract. That is trust and partnership!

CHAPTER XI

*"Be yourself and think for yourself, and while your
conclusions may not be infallible, they will be nearer
right than the conclusions forced on you"*
-Elbert Hubbard

CONCLUSION

This book has been intended to offer guidance to those who might be considering the establishment of a new city and to those who might be interested in the use of private industry in either, a new or existing city. The information and advice has been based on the author's very recent experience in implementing the city of Sandy Springs, Georgia. A unique experience, in that the city of almost 90,000 people was the seventh largest city in Georgia at birth, and the most broadly serviced by a private company in the country.

There are many who can criticize, but few who can create. This book is intended for those who have that creative gene. It offers encouragement and methods to those with the capability and the desire to be leaders.

If the reader lives in an unincorporated area that does not meet the needs of the citizens, then you may want to participate in the creation of a new municipal government. Remember the three words inscribed on the official seal of Sandy Springs: HONESTY, EFFICIENCY and

RESPONSIVENESS. If your current government fails in any of these areas, then go for it!

If you reside in an existing municipal government that fails the test, you may want to lead a movement to explore the benefits of the experience, innovativeness and resources offered by private industry. Go for it!

In either case, if you make the decision that employing private industry is the best option, I recommend these guidelines:

1. To obtain the best results, treat the company as your partner, not as a sub-contractor. The great benefit of private industry results from the new approaches that it can offer. Do not squelch that creativeness by over specifying the job to be done. Give the company the opportunity to "own" the service, and take pride in its contribution.

2. Make the ability to provide quality service the primary factor.

3. Do not try to squeeze the last dollar out of the contract. A company that makes a fair profit will do a better job over the long pull. After all, your responsibility is to obtain the service at a value that is better than could be obtained through any other source, not at some theoretical "perfect" price.

In conclusion, and based on the experiences described in this book, I offer the following seven general concepts for starting a city, or improving an existing municipality.

I. Make RESPONSIVENESS to the citizens the first priority.

II. HONESTRY and INTEGRITY must be givens.

III. Nothing is ever improved by continuing the same methods, so look for INNOVATIVE APPROACHES to providing services.

IV. Consider PRIVATE INDUSTRY as an option for all functions

V. Involve community VOLUNTEERS to the maximum extent possible.

VI. COOPERATE with other communities to derive economies of scale.

VII. Provide a structure in which elected officials are encouraged to represent the INTERESTS OF THE ENTIRE COMMUNITY rather than small districts or special interests.

Recognition of these concepts will lead you to a government by and for the people of the community. Good luck in you quest!

If you would like to talk about it, call me. I welcome your questions, comments or suggestions. I am in the book.

OLIVER W. PORTER
Sandy Springs, Georgia
Oliverporter1@comcast.net

APPENDICES

A P P E N D I X A

GEORGIA HOUSE BILL 36

A BILL TO BE ENTITLED
AN ACT

To revise provisions of law relating to creation of new municipal corporations; to amend Chapter 31 of Title 36 of the Official Code of Georgia Annotated, relating to incorporation of municipal corporations, so as to eliminate certain minimum distance requirements applicable to new incorporations; to provide that new municipal corporations shall have a minimum amount of time to arrange for service delivery; to change provisions relating to development requirements for areas to be incorporated; to provide that the Attorney General shall seek federal Voting Rights Act preclearances required in connection with new incorporations; to provide for the authorization and regulation of alcoholic beverage sales in new municipalities under certain circumstances; to provide for the orderly transition of responsibilities and functions to a new municipality from its county and provide for counties to retain certain functions and responsibilities for certain periods of time; to provide for intergovernmental relations; to provide for delayed application of certain laws; to authorize appointment of interim representatives; to provide that a chartering Act may specify any length or lengths for initial terms of office; to authorize the appropriation of funds to the Department of Community Affairs for loans or grants or both to new municipal corporations; to provide for effect with respect to certain

county special districts and provide certain protections for the residents
of such districts; to provide for the manner of expenditure of certain
county special district taxes, fees, and assessments under certain circumstances; to provide for certain auditing and reporting requirements with
respect to special district revenues and expenditures in certain counties; to amend Article 2 of Chapter 8 of Title 48 of the Official Code
of Georgia Annotated, relating to joint county and municipal local
option sales tax, so as to change provisions for distribution with respect
to certain newly incorporated municipalities and other local governments in the county; to provide for other related matters; to provide
for severability; to provide for effective dates and applicability; to repeal
conflicting laws; and for other purposes.

BE IT ENACTED BY THE GENERAL ASSEMBLY OF
GEORGIA:

SECTION 1.

Chapter 31 of Title 36 of the Official Code of Georgia Annotated, relating to incorporation of municipal corporations, is amended by striking
Code Section 36-31-2 thereof, relating to minimum distances between
corporate boundaries, and inserting in its place the following:

"36-31-2. Blank

SECTION 2.

Said Chapter 31 of Title 36 is further amended by striking Code section
36-31-4, relating to standards for areas to be incorporated, and inserting
in its place a new Code section to read as follows:

"36-31-4.
To be eligible for original incorporation as a municipal corporation, the
area embraced shall be so developed that at least 60 percent of the total
number of lots and tracts in the area at the time of incorporation are
used for residential, commercial, industrial, institutional, recreational,
or governmental purposes and shall be subdivided into lots and tracts
such that at least 60 percent of the total acreage, not counting the acreage used which at the time of incorporation is used for, held for future

use for, or subject to a contract for future use for commercial, industrial, governmental, recreational, or institutional purposes, consists of lots and tracts of five acres or less in size."

SECTION 3.

Said Chapter 31 of Title 36 is further amended by adding at its end new Code sections to read as follows:

"36-31-6.

When a new municipal corporation is created by local Act, the Attorney General shall be responsible for seeking any and all preclearances required in connection with such Act and incorporation under the federal Voting Rights Act of 1965, as amended, until such time as the new municipal corporation notifies the Attorney General that it has the ability to seek any further preclearances required.

36-31-7.

When a new municipal corporation is created by local Act, the governing authority of the municipal corporation shall have all the same powers to license and regulate alcoholic beverages within its territory as did the governing authority of the county when such territory was within the unincorporated area of the county. Without limiting the generality of the foregoing, it is specifically provided that no petition, election, or other condition precedent which might otherwise be required under Title 3 to authorize sales of any alcoholic beverages shall be required in order for the governing authority of the municipality to exercise such powers.

36-31-8.

(a) When a new municipal corporation is created by local Act, the local Act may provide for a transition period not to exceed 24 months for the orderly transition of governmental functions from the county to the new municipal corporation. The local Act may specify the time or times during the transition period (or the method or methods for determining the time or times during the transition period) at which:

(1) Various governmental functions, services, and responsibilities will be assumed by the new municipal corporation within its territory; and

(2) The municipal court of the new municipality shall begin to exercise its jurisdiction over various subject matters.

(b) When a chartering local Act so provides for a transition period, the county in which the new municipality is located shall continue to provide within the territory of the new city all government services and functions which it provided as of the date of enactment of the chartering local Act. The county shall continue to provide such services and functions until the end of the transition period; provided, however, that the new city may assume the provision of any service or function at such earlier time as may be specified in the chartering local Act or at such earlier time as may be agreed upon by the county and the new city.

(c) When a chartering local Act so provides for a transition period, on and after the first day the initial governing authority takes office, the governing authority may from time to time adopt appropriate measures to initiate collection within the territory of the new city during the transition period of all taxes, fees, assessments, fines and forfeitures, and other moneys. Where a particular tax, fee, assessment, fine, forfeiture, or other amount collected by the city during the transition period is specifically related to the provision of a particular government service or function by the county, the service or function shall continue to be provided by the county during the transition period contingent upon payment by the city of the actual cost of providing such service or function unless otherwise provided in a written agreement between the new city and the county.

(d) When a chartering local Act so provides for a transition period, the county in which the new city is located shall not from the time of enactment of the charter until the end of the transition period remove from the county road system any road within the territory of the new city except with the agreement of the new city.

(e) When a chartering local Act so provides for a transition period, the new municipality shall not be subject to the laws specified in this subsection during the transition period; provided, however, that the new city and other political subdivisions may during the transition period commence planning, negotiations, and other actions necessary or appropriate for compliance after the transition period. During the transition period, the new municipality shall not be subject to:

(1) Chapter 70 of this title, relating to planning and service delivery strategies;

(2) Provisions of Code Sections 12-8-31.1 and 12-8-39.2, relating to solid waste planning and solid waste management reporting;

(3) Provisions of Code Section 48-13-56, relating to reporting of excise taxes collected and expended pursuant to Article 3 of Chapter 13 of Title 48; and

(4) Provisions of Code Section 36-81-8, relating to reporting of local government finances, reporting of revenues derived from a tax levied pursuant to Article 3 of Chapter 13 of Title 48, and reporting of local government services and operations.

(f) When a chartering local Act so provides for a transition period, upon the termination of the transition period subsections (b) through (e) of this Code section shall cease to apply and the new city shall be a fully functioning municipal corporation and subject to all general laws of this state.

(g) As of the date a chartering local Act is approved by the Governor or becomes law without such approval, the Governor is authorized to appoint five persons to serve as interim representatives of the newly incorporated municipality until the election of the municipality's first governing authority. The interim representatives shall cease to serve as of the time the members of the first governing authority take office. The function of the interim representatives shall be to facilitate the provision of municipal services and facilities, the collection of taxes and fees, and the negotiation of intergovernmental agreements in preparation of the establishment of the new municipality. The interim representatives shall not have the ability to enter into any binding agreements, to expend public funds, or to incur any liability on behalf of the new municipality. Any person who is serving as or has served as an interim representative shall be ineligible to qualify for election as a member of the initial governing authority of the new municipality.

36-31-9.
When a new municipal corporation is created by local Act, the chartering local Act may provide for the initial terms of office of members of the governing authority to be of any length or lengths; and the provisions of this Code section shall control over any conflicting provisions of Code Sections 21-2-541.1 and 21-2-541.2.

36-31-10.
The General Assembly may, in connection with the incorporation of a new municipal corporation, at any time (before, after, or contemporaneously with the passage of the chartering Act) appropriate to the Department of Community Affairs funds for grants or loans or both to a specific existing or proposed municipal corporation. When funds are so appropriated, the department shall make grants as specified by recipient, amount, and purpose and loans as specified by recipient, amount, interest rate, term, and purpose in the appropriation unless the chartering Act fails to secure passage or otherwise fails to become effective.

36-31-11.
When a municipal corporation is created by local Act within a county which has a special district for the provision of local government services consisting of the unincorporated area of the county, the territory within the new municipal corporation shall be removed from the special district except to the extent otherwise provided by Code Section 36-31-8 during a transition period and except that the county may continue to levy within such territory any previously imposed tax for the purpose of retiring any special district debt until such time as such debt is retired.

36-31-12.
(a) The General Assembly finds that:

(1) The purpose of a special services district is to provide special services to a given geographic area and to finance the provision of those services from taxes, fees, and assessments levied in the geographic area which benefits from the services;

(2) The creation of a municipal corporation within a county which has a special services district for the unincorporated area of the county may result in the special services district being divided into noncontiguous areas or in existing noncontiguous areas of such district being even more remote from each other; and

(3) The purpose of a special services district is defeated if it becomes divided into noncontiguous areas which are remote from each other and one or more of such noncontiguous areas is subsidizing the provision of services in other such noncontiguous areas.

(b) When a municipal corporation is created by local Act within a county which has a special district for the provision of local government services consisting of the unincorporated area of the county and following the creation of said municipal corporation the special district is divided into two or more noncontiguous areas, any special district taxes, fees, and assessments collected in such a noncontiguous area shall be spent to provide services in that noncontiguous area.

(c) When a municipal corporation is created by local Act within a county subject to this Code section, the county shall for the fiscal year in which the municipal corporation is chartered and for each of the next two fiscal years have included in its annual audit detailed findings as to:

(1) The amount of any special district taxes, assessments, and fees collected in each noncontiguous area of the special district;

(2) The total amount of expenditures by the county for:

(A) The provision of services within each noncontiguous area of the special district, including only those services which are provided by the county only in the special district; and

(B) The construction and maintenance of facilities for the provision of services referred to in subparagraph (A) of this paragraph; and

(3) The amount by which expenditures stated in paragraph (2) of this subsection exceed or are less than the amount stated in paragraph (1) of this subsection.

(d) The party performing the audit required by subsection (c) of this Code section shall prepare as promptly as is practicable a brief informational summary of the audit findings required by that subsection. The informational summary shall also include a statement of the amount of proceeds collected by the county pursuant to any tax under Article 2 of Chapter 8 of Title 48 which would be allocated to each noncontiguous area of the special district if such area received an allocation equal on a per capita basis to the average per capita allocation to the cities in the county. After each year's summary becomes available, a copy of the summary shall be included with the next ad valorem tax bills mailed by the county to residents of the special district consisting of the unincorporated area of the county.

(e) For purposes of determining applicability of this Code section, a county shall be considered to have a special district for the provision of local government services when a county has created a special district for such purposes pursuant to Article IX, Section II, Paragraph VI of the Constitution or has created a similar district for the provision of services under any other provision of any past or present Constitution or law."

SECTION 4.

Article 2 of Chapter 8 of Title 48 of the Official Code of Georgia Annotated, relating to joint county and municipal local option sales tax, is amended by inserting a new subsection (f) at the end of Code Section 48-8-89.1, relating to distribution of the tax upon creation of a new municipal corporation in certain counties, to read as follows:

"(f)(1) This subsection shall apply only when:

(A) A municipal corporation is chartered by local Act within a county which has a special district for the provision of local government services consisting of the unincorporated area of the county; and

(B) The population of the unincorporated area of the county will, after removal of the population of the new municipality from the unincorporated area, constitute less than 20 percent of the population of the county according to the most recent decennial census.

(2) Notwithstanding any other provision of this Code section, if there exists within any special district in which the tax authorized by this article is imposed a qualified municipality described in paragraph (1) of this subsection which was not a qualified municipality on the date of filing with the commissioner of the most recently filed certificate under Code Section 48-8-89, such qualified municipality may request the commissioner to give notice of the qualified municipality's existence and status as a qualified municipality as provided in this subsection. Upon receipt of such a request, the commissioner shall, unless he or she determines that the requesting entity is not a qualified municipality, within 30 days give written notice of the qualified municipality's existence and status to the county which is conterminous with the special district in which the qualified municipality is located and to each other qualified municipality within the special district. Such written notice shall include the name of the new qualified municipality, the effective date of the notice, and a statement of the provisions of this subsection.

(3) Within 60 days after the effective date of the notice referred to in paragraph (2) of this subsection, a new distribution certificate shall be filed with the commissioner for the special district. This distribution certificate shall address only the proceeds of the tax available for distribution from the percentage allocated to the county in the current distribution certificate and shall specify as a percentage of the total proceeds of the tax what portion of the proceeds shall be received by the county in which the special district is located and by the new qualified municipality.

(4) Except as otherwise provided in this paragraph, a distribution certificate required by this subsection must be executed by the governing

authorities of the county within which the special district is located and each new qualified municipality located wholly or partially within the special district. If a new certificate is not filed within 60 days as required by paragraph (3) of this subsection, the commissioner shall distribute the proceeds of the tax available for distribution from the percentage allocated to the county in the current distribution certificate such that the new qualified municipality receives an allocation equal on a per capita basis to the average per capita allocation to the other qualified municipalities in the county (according to population), to be expended as provided in paragraph (2) of subsection (a) of Code Section 48-8-89. Every other qualified municipality shall continue to receive the share provided by the existing distribution certificate or otherwise provided by law. The county shall receive the remaining proceeds of the tax, to be expended as provided in paragraph (2) of subsection (a) of Code Section 48-8-89. For the purpose of determining the population of new qualified municipalities, only that portion of the population of each such municipality which is located within the special district shall be computed. For the purpose of determining population under this Code section, all calculations of population shall be according to the most recent decennial census.

(5) The commissioner shall begin to distribute the proceeds as specified in the certificate applicable to the county and the new qualified municipality or, if such a certificate is not filed, as specified in paragraph (4) of this subsection on the first day of the first month which begins more than 60 days after the effective date of the notice referred to in paragraph (2) of this subsection. The commissioner shall continue to distribute the proceeds of the tax according to the existing certificate and the certificate applicable to the county and the new qualified municipality or, if such a certificate is not filed, as specified in paragraph (4) of this subsection until a subsequent certificate is filed and becomes effective as provided in Code Section 48-8-89."

SECTION 5.

In the event any section, subsection, sentence, clause, or phrase of this Act shall be declared or adjudged invalid or unconstitutional, such adjudication shall in no manner affect the other sections, subsections, sentences, clauses, or phrases of this Act, which shall remain of full force and effect as if the section, subsection, sentence, clause, or phrase so declared or adjudged invalid or unconstitutional were not originally a part hereof. The General Assembly declares that it would have passed the remaining parts of this Act if it had known that such part or parts hereof would be declared or adjudged invalid or unconstitutional.

SECTION 6.

This Act shall become effective upon its approval by the Governor or upon its becoming law without such approval and shall apply with respect to any local Act enacted at the 2005 regular session of the General Assembly or any future session.

SECTION 7.

All laws and parts of laws in conflict with this Act are repealed.

A P P E N D I X   B

GEORGIA HOUSE BILL 37

A BILL TO BE ENTITLED AN ACT

To incorporate the City of Sandy Springs in Fulton County; to provide for a charter for the City of Sandy Springs; to provide for incorporation, boundaries, and powers of the city; to provide for general powers and limitations on powers; to provide for a governing authority of such city and the powers, duties, authority, election, terms, method of filling vacancies, compensation, expenses, qualifications, prohibitions, and districts relative to members of such governing authority; to provide for inquiries and investigations; to provide for organization and procedures: to provide for ordinances; to provide for the office of mayor and certain duties and powers relative to the office of mayor; to provide for administrative responsibilities; to provide for boards, commissions, and authorities; to provide for a city manager, a city attorney, a city clerk, a tax collector, a city accountant, and other personnel; to provide for a municipal court and the judge or judges thereof; to provide for practices and procedures; to provide for ethics and disclosures; to provide for taxation, licenses and fees; to provide for franchises, service charges, and assessments; to provide for bonded and other indebtedness; to provide for accounting and budgeting; to provide for purchases; to provide for homestead exemptions; to provide for bonds for officials; to provide for other matters relative to the foregoing; to provide for a referendum; to provide effective dates and transitional provisions governing the transfer of various functions and responsibilities from Fulton County to the City of Sandy Springs; to provide for severability; to repeal conflicting laws; and for other purposes.

BE IT ENACTED BY THE GENERAL ASSEMBLY OF GEORGIA:
INCORPORATION BOUNDARIES AND POWERS

SECTION 1.01.

Incorporation.
This Act shall constitute the charter of the City of Sandy Springs, Georgia. The City of Sandy Springs, Georgia, in the County of Fulton, and the inhabitants thereof, are constituted and declared a body politic and corporate under the same name and style of the "City of Sandy Springs" and by that name shall have perpetual succession, may sue and be sued, plead and be impleaded, in all courts of law and equity, and in all actions whatsoever, and may have and use a common seal.

SECTION 1.02.
Corporate boundaries.
The boundaries of the City of Sandy Springs shall be as set forth and described in Appendix A of this charter, and said Appendix A is incorporated into and made a part of this charter. The city manager shall maintain a current map and written legal description of the corporate boundaries of the city, and such map and description shall incorporate any changes which may hereafter be made in such corporate boundaries.

SECTION 1.03.
Powers and construction.
(a) This city shall have all powers possible for a city to have under the present or future Constitution and laws of this state as fully and completely as though they were specifically enumerated in this Act. This city shall have all the powers of self-government not otherwise prohibited by this Act or by general law.

(b) The powers of this city shall be construed liberally in favor of the city. The specific mention or failure to mention particular powers shall not be construed as limiting in any way the powers of this city. These powers shall include, but not be limited to, the following:

(1) Animal regulations. To regulate and license or to prohibit the keeping or running at-large of animals and fowl, and to provide for the impoundment of same if in violation of any ordinance or lawful order; to provide for the disposition by sale, gift, or humane destruction of animals and fowl when not redeemed as provided by ordinance; and to provide punishment for violation of ordinances enacted hereunder;

(2) Appropriations and expenditures. To make appropriations for the support of the government of the city; to authorize the expenditure of money for any purposes authorized by this charter and for any purpose for which a municipality is authorized by the laws of the State of Georgia; and to provide for the payment of expenses of the city;

(3) Building regulation. To regulate and to license the erection and construction of buildings and all other structures; to adopt building, housing, plumbing, electrical, gas, and heating and air conditioning codes; and to regulate all housing, and building trades to the extent permitted by general law;

(4) Business regulation and taxation. To levy and to provide for the collection of regulatory fees and taxes on privileges, occupations, trades and professions as authorized by Title 48 of the O.C.G.A., or other such applicable laws as are or may hereafter be enacted; to permit and regulate the same; to provide for the manner and method of payment of such regulatory fees and taxes; and to revoke such permits after due process for failure to pay any city taxes or fees;

(5) Condemnation. To condemn property, inside or outside the corporate limits of the city, for present or future use and for any corporate purpose deemed necessary by the city council, utilizing procedures enumerated in Title 22 of the O.C.G.A., or such other applicable laws as are or may hereafter be enacted;

(6) Contracts. To enter into contracts and agreements with other governmental entities and with private persons, firms and corporations;

(7) Emergencies. To establish procedures for determining and proclaiming that an emergency situation exists within or without the city, and to make and carry out all reasonable provisions deemed necessary to deal with or meet such an emergency for the protection, safety, health or well-being of the citizens of the city;

(8) Environmental protection. To protect and preserve the natural resources, environment and vital areas of the city, the region, and the state through the preservation and improvement of air quality, the restoration and maintenance of water resources, the control of erosion and sedimentation, the management of stormwater and establishment of a stormwater utility, the management of solid and hazardous waste, and other necessary actions for the protection of the environment;

(9) Ethics. To adopt ethics ordinances and regulations governing the conduct of municipal elected officials, appointed officials, and employees, establishing procedures for ethics complaints and setting forth penalties for violations of such rules and procedures;

(10) Fire regulations. To fix and establish fire limits and from time to time to extend, enlarge, or restrict the same; to prescribe fire safety regulations not inconsistent with general law, relating to both fire prevention and detection and to fire fighting; and to prescribe penalties and punishment for violations thereof;

(11) Garbage fees. To levy, fix, assess, and collect a garbage, refuse, and trash collection and disposal, and other sanitary service charge, tax, or fee for such services as may be necessary in the operation of the city from all individuals, firms, and corporations residing in or doing business therein benefiting from such services; to enforce the payment of such charges, taxes or fees; and to provide for the manner and method of collecting such service charges;

(12) General health, safety, and welfare. To define, regulate, and prohibit any act, practice, conduct, or use of property which is detrimental

to health, sanitation, cleanliness, welfare, and safety of the inhabitants of the city, and to provide for the enforcement of such standards;

(13) Gifts. To accept or refuse gifts, donations, bequests, or grants from any source for any purpose related to powers and duties of the city and the general welfare of its citizens, on such terms and conditions as the donor or grantor may impose;

(14) Health and sanitation. To prescribe standards of health and sanitation and to provide for the enforcement of such standards;

(15) Jail sentences. To provide that persons given jail sentences in the city's court may work out such sentences in any public works or on the streets, roads, drains, and other public property in the city, to provide for commitment of such persons to any jail, to provide for the use of pretrial diversion and any alternative sentencing allowed by law, or to provide for commitment of such persons to any county work camp or county jail by agreement with the appropriate county officials;

(16) Motor vehicles. To regulate the operation of motor vehicles and exercise control over all traffic, including parking upon or across the streets, roads, alleys, and walkways of the city;

(17) Municipal agencies and delegation of power. To create, alter, or abolish departments, boards, offices, commissions, and agencies of the city, and to confer upon such agencies the necessary and appropriate authority for carrying out all the powers conferred upon or delegated to the same;

(18) Municipal debts. To appropriate and borrow money for the payment of debts of the city and to issue bonds for the purpose of raising revenue to carry out any project, program, or venture authorized by this charter or the laws of the State of Georgia;

(19) Municipal property ownership. To acquire, dispose of, lease, and hold in trust or otherwise any real, personal, or mixed property, in fee simple or lesser interest, inside or outside the property limits of the city;

(20) Municipal property protection. To provide for the preservation and protection of property and equipment of the city and the administration and use of same by the public; and to prescribe penalties and punishment for violations thereof;

(21) Municipal utilities. To acquire, lease, construct, operate, maintain, sell, and dispose of public utilities, including but not limited to a system of waterworks, sewers and drains, sewage disposal, stormwater management, gas works, electric light plants, cable television and other telecommunications, transportation facilities, public airports, and any other public utility; to fix the taxes, charges, rates, fares, fees, assessments, regulations, and penalties; and to provide for the withdrawal of service for refusal or failure to pay the same;

(22) Nuisance. To define a nuisance and provide for its abatement whether on public or private property;

(23) Penalties. To provide penalties for violation of any ordinances adopted pursuant to the authority of this charter and the laws of the State of Georgia;

(24) Planning and zoning. To provide comprehensive city planning for development by zoning; and to provide subdivision regulation and the like as the city council deems necessary and reasonable to insure a safe, healthy, and aesthetically pleasing community;

(25) Police and fire protection. To exercise the power of arrest through duly appointed police officers, and to establish, operate, or contract for a police and a fire-fighting agency;

(26) Public hazards: removal. To provide for the destruction and removal of any building or other structure which is or may become dangerous or detrimental to the public;

(27) Public improvements. To provide for the acquisition, construction, building, operation, and maintenance of public ways, parks and playgrounds, recreational facilities, cemeteries, public buildings, libraries, public housing, parking facilities, or charitable, cultural, educational, recreational, conservation, sport, detentional, penal, and medical

institutions, agencies, and facilities; and to provide any other public improvements, inside or outside the corporate limits of the city and to regulate the use of public improvements; and for such purposes, property may be acquired by condemnation under Title 22 of the O.C.G.A., or such other applicable laws as are or may hereafter be enacted;

(28) Public peace. To provide for the prevention and punishment of loitering, disorderly conduct, drunkenness, riots, and public disturbances;

(29) Public transportation. To organize and operate such public transportation systems as are deemed beneficial;

(30) Public utilities and services. To grant franchises or make contracts for, or impose taxes on, public utilities and public service companies; and to prescribe the rates, fares, regulations, and standards and conditions of service applicable to the service to be provided by the franchise grantee or contractor, insofar as not in conflict with valid regulations of the Public Service Commission;

(31) Regulation of roadside areas. To prohibit or regulate and control the erection, removal, and maintenance of signs, billboards, trees, shrubs, fences, buildings, and any and all other structures or obstructions upon or adjacent to the rights of way of streets and roads or within view thereof, within or abutting the corporate limits of the city; and to prescribe penalties and punishment for violation of such ordinances;

(32) Retirement. To provide and maintain a retirement plan for officers and employees of the city;

(33) Roadways. To lay out, open, extend, widen, narrow, establish or change the grade of, abandon or close, construct, pave, curb, gutter, adorn with shade trees, or otherwise improve, maintain, repair, clean, prevent erosion of, and light the roads, alleys, and walkways within the corporate limits of the city; to grant franchises and rights of way throughout the streets and roads and over the bridges and viaducts for the use of public utilities; and to require real estate owners to repair and

maintain in a safe condition the sidewalks adjoining their lots or lands and to impose penalties for failure to do so;

(34) Sewer fees. To levy a fee, charge, or sewer tax as necessary to assure the acquiring, constructing, equipping, operating, maintaining, and extending of a sewage disposal plant and sewerage system, and to levy on those to whom sewers and sewerage systems are made available a sewer service fee, charge, or sewer tax for the availability or use of the sewers; to provide for the manner and method of collecting such service charges and for enforcing payment of the same; and to charge, impose, and collect a sewer connection fee or fees to those connected with the system;

(35) Solid waste disposal. To provide for the collection and disposal of garbage, rubbish, and refuse and to regulate the collection and disposal of garbage, rubbish, and refuse by others; and to provide for the separate collection of glass, tin, aluminum, cardboard, paper, and other recyclable materials and to provide for the sale of such items;

(36) Special assessments. To levy and provide for the collection of special assessments to cover the costs for any public improvements;

(37) Taxes: ad valorem. To levy and provide for the assessment, valuation, revaluation, and collection of taxes on all property subject to taxation; provided, however, that:

(A) For all years, the millage rate imposed for ad valorem taxes on real property shall not exceed 4.731 unless a higher limit is recommended by resolution of the city council and approved by the qualified voters of the City of Sandy Springs;

(B) For all years, the fair market value of all property subject to taxation shall be determined according to the tax digest of Fulton County, as provided in Code Section 48-5-352 of the O.C.G.A.; and

(C) For all years, the billing date or dates and due date or due dates for municipal ad valorem taxes shall be the same as for Fulton County ad valorem taxes;

(38) Taxes: other. To levy and collect such other taxes as may be allowed now or in the future by law;

(39) Taxicabs. To regulate and license vehicles operated for hire in the city; to limit the number of such vehicles; to require the operators thereof to be licensed; to require public liability insurance on such vehicles in the amounts to be prescribed by ordinance; and to regulate the parking of such vehicles;

(40) Urban redevelopment. To organize and operate an urban redevelopment program;

(41) Other powers. To exercise and enjoy all other powers, functions, rights, privileges, and immunities necessary or desirable to promote or protect the safety, health, peace, security, good order, comfort, convenience, or general welfare of the city and its inhabitants; to exercise all implied powers necessary or desirable to carry into execution all powers granted in this charter as fully and completely as if such powers were fully stated herein; and to exercise all powers now or in the future authorized to be exercised by other municipal governments under other laws of the State of Georgia; and any listing of particular powers in this charter shall not be held to be exclusive of others or restrictive of general words and phrases granting powers, but shall be held to be in addition to such powers unless expressly prohibited to municipalities under the Constitution or applicable laws of the State of Georgia.

SECTION 1.04.
Exercise of powers.

All powers, functions, rights, privileges, and immunities of the city, its officers, agencies, or employees shall be carried into execution as provided by this Act. If this charter makes no provision, such shall be carried into execution as provided by ordinance or as provided by pertinent laws of the State of Georgia.

ARTICLE II
GOVERNMENT STRUCTURE ELECTIONS AND
LEGISLATIVE BRANCH

SECTION 2.01.

City council creation; number; election.

a) The legislative authority of the government of Sandy Springs, except as otherwise specifically provided in this Act, shall be vested in a city council to be composed of a mayor and six council members.

(b) The mayor shall be elected by a majority vote of the qualified electors of the city at large voting at the elections of the city.

(c) Each councilmember shall be elected by a majority vote of the qualified electors of his or her respective council district voting at the elections of the city. For the purpose of electing the six councilmembers, there shall be six council districts, designated Council Districts 1 through 6, as described in Appendix B of this Act and the accompanying Redistricting Plan Components Report, which are attached to and made a part of the charter of the City of Sandy Springs. Each person desiring to offer as a candidate for councilmember shall designate the council district for which he or she is offering.

SECTION 2.02.

Mayor and city council members; election, terms, and qualifications for office.

(a) Except as otherwise provided in subsection (c) of this section, the mayor and members of the city council shall serve for terms of four years and until their respective successors are elected and qualified. No person shall be eligible to serve as mayor or councilmember unless that person shall have been a resident of the area comprising the corporate limits of the City of Sandy Springs for a continuous period of at least 12 months immediately prior to the date of the election for mayor or councilmember, shall continue to reside therein during that person's period of service, and shall continue to be registered and qualified to vote in municipal elections of the City of Sandy Springs. In addition to the above requirements, no person shall be eligible to serve as a councilmember representing a council district unless that person has been a resident of the district such person seeks to represent for a continuous period of at least six months immediately prior to the date of the election for councilmember and continues to reside in such district during that person's period of service.

(b) General municipal elections shall be held on the Tuesday next following the first Monday in November of 2005 and quadrennially thereafter.

(c) The first mayor and the initial councilmembers shall take office on December 1, 2005, and shall serve for terms which expire when their successors take office in January of 2010. Thereafter the mayor and councilmembers shall take office as provided in Code Section 21-2-541.1 of the O.C.G.A. and serve for terms of four years. The initial members and future members of the governing authority shall serve until their successors are elected and qualified.

SECTION 2.03.
Vacancy; filling of vacancies; suspensions.
The office of mayor or councilmember shall become vacant upon the incumbent's death, resignation, forfeiture of office, or removal from office in any manner authorized by this Act or the general laws of the State of Georgia. A vacancy in the office of mayor or councilmember shall be filled for the remainder of the unexpired term by a special election if such vacancy occurs 12 months or more prior to the expiration of the term of that office. If such vacancy occurs within 12 months of the expiration of the term of that office, the city council or those members remaining shall appoint a successor for the remainder of the term. This provision shall also apply to a temporary vacancy created by the suspension from office of the mayor or any councilmember.

SECTION 2.04.
Nonpartisan elections.
Political parties shall not conduct primaries for city offices and all names of candidates for city offices shall be listed without party designation.

SECTION 2.05.

Election by majority vote.

The candidates for mayor and councilmen who receive a majority of the votes cast in the applicable election shall be elected to a term of office. In the event no candidate receives a majority of the votes cast in said election, a run-off election shall be held between the two candidates receiving the highest number of votes. Such run-off shall be held at the time specified by state election law, unless such run-off date is postponed by court order.

SECTION 2.06.

Applicability of general laws; qualifying; other provisions.

All primaries and elections shall be held and conducted in accordance with Chapter 2 of Title 21 of the O.C.G.A., the "Georgia Election Code", as now or hereafter amended. Except as otherwise provided by this Act, the city council shall, by ordinance or resolution, prescribe such rules and regulations as it deems appropriate, including but not limited to the establishment of qualifying fees, to fulfill any options and duties under Chapter 2 of Title 21 of the O.C.G.A., the "Georgia Election Code", as now or hereafter amended.

SECTION 2.07.

Compensation and expenses.

The annual salary of the mayor shall be $25,000.00 and the annual salary for each councilmember shall be $12,000.00. Such salary shall be paid from municipal funds in monthly installments. The city council may provide by ordinance for the provision of insurance, retirement, workers' compensation, and other employee benefits to the mayor and members of the city council and may provide by ordinance for the reimbursement of expenses actually and necessarily incurred by the mayor and members of the city council in carrying out their official duties.

SECTION 2.08.

Inquiries and investigations.

The city council may make inquiries and investigations into the affairs of the city and conduct of any department, office, or agency thereof and for this purpose may subpoena witnesses, administer oaths, take testimony, and require the production of evidence. Any person who fails or refuses to obey a lawful order issued in the exercise of these powers by the city council shall be punished as may be provided by ordinance.

SECTION 2.09.

Meetings and mayor pro tempore.

(a) The city council shall meet on the first working day in January immediately following each regular municipal election. The meeting shall be called to order by the mayor-elect and the oath of office shall be administered to the newly elected mayor and councilmembers by a judicial officer authorized to administer oaths. The oath shall, to the extent that it comports with federal and state law, be as follows:

"I do solemnly swear or affirm that I will faithfully execute the office of [councilmember or mayor as the case may be] of the City of Sandy Springs, and will to the best of my ability support and defend the Constitution of the United States, the Constitution of Georgia, and the charter, ordinances, and regulations of the City of Sandy Springs. I am not the holder of any unaccounted for public money due this state or any political subdivision or authority thereof. I am not the holder of any office of trust under the government of the United States, any other state, or any foreign state which I by the laws of the State of Georgia am prohibited from holding. I am otherwise qualified to hold said office according to the Constitution and laws of Georgia. I have been a resident of my district and the City of Sandy Springs for the time required by the Constitution and laws of this state and by the municipal charter. I will perform the duties of my office in the best interest of the City of Sandy Springs to the best of my ability without fear, favor, affection, reward, or expectation thereof."

(b) Following the induction of the mayor and councilmembers, the city council, by a majority vote of the councilmembers, shall elect a councilmember to be mayor pro tempore, who shall serve for a term of four years and until a successor is elected and qualified. The mayor pro tempore shall assume the duties and powers of the mayor during the mayor's disability or absence, except that the mayor pro tempore shall continue to vote as a councilmember and may not exercise the mayor's prerogative to vote in the case of a tie. During the mayor's disability or absence, the mayor pro tempore may veto any action of council. If the mayor pro tempore is absent because of sickness or disqualification, any one of the remaining councilmembers, chosen by the members present, shall be clothed with all the rights and privileges of the mayor and shall perform the mayor's duties in the same manner as the mayor pro tempore.

(c) The city council shall, at least once a month, hold regular meetings at such times and places as prescribed by ordinance. The council may recess any regular meeting and continue such meeting on any weekday or hour it may fix and may transact any business at such continued meeting as may be transacted at any regular meeting.

(d) Special meetings of the council may be held on the call of the mayor or three members of the council. Notice of such special meetings shall be delivered to all members of the council and the mayor personally, by registered mail, or by electronic means, at least 24 hours in advance of the meeting. Such notice to councilmembers shall not be required if the mayor and all councilmembers are present when the special meeting is called. Such notice of any special meeting may be waived by the mayor or a councilmember in writing before or after such a meeting and attendance at the meeting shall also constitute a waiver of notice. The notice of such special meeting shall state what business is to be transacted at the special meeting. Only the business stated in the call may be transacted at the special meeting.

SECTION 2.10.

Quorum; voting.

Four council members shall constitute a quorum and shall be authorized to transact business for the council. Voting on the adoption of ordinances shall be taken by voice vote and the yeas and nays shall be recorded in the minutes, but on the request of any member there shall be a roll-call vote. In order for any ordinance, resolution, motion, or other action of the council to be adopted, the measure must receive at least three affirmative votes and must receive the affirmative votes of a majority of those voting. No member of the city council shall abstain from voting on any matter properly brought before the council for official action except when such member of council has a conflict of interest which is disclosed in writing prior to or at the meeting and made a part of the minutes. Any member of the city council present and eligible to vote on a matter and refusing to do so for any reason other than a properly disclosed and recorded conflict of interest shall be deemed to have acquiesced or concurred with the members of the majority who did vote on the question involved. The mayor shall vote only in the case of a tie or in the case where his or her vote will provide the third affirmative vote required for approval of a matter.

SECTION 2.11.

General power and authority of the council.

(a) Except as otherwise provided by law or by this charter, the council shall be vested with all the powers of government of the City of Sandy Springs as provided by state law and the provisions of this charter.

(b) In addition to all other powers conferred upon it by law, the council shall have the authority to adopt and provide for the execution of such ordinances, resolutions, rules, and regulations, not inconsistent with this charter and the Constitution and the laws of the State of Georgia, which it shall deem necessary, expedient, or helpful for the peace, good order, protection of life and property, health, welfare, sanitation, comfort, convenience, prosperity, or well-being of the inhabitants of the City of Sandy Springs and may enforce such ordinances by imposing penalties for violation thereof.

SECTION 2.12.

Administrative and service departments.

(a) Except for the office of city manager, the council, by ordinance, may establish, abolish, merge, or consolidate offices, positions of employment, departments, and agencies of the city as they shall deem necessary for the proper administration of the affairs and government of the city. The council shall prescribe the functions and duties of existing departments, offices, and agencies or of any departments, offices, and agencies hereinafter created or established; may provide that the same person shall fill any number of offices and positions of employment; and may transfer or change the functions and duties of offices, positions of employment, departments, and agencies of the city.

(b) The operations and responsibilities of each department now or hereafter established in the city shall be distributed among such divisions or bureaus as may be provided by ordinance of the council. Each department shall consist of such officers, employees, and positions as may be provided by this charter or by ordinance and shall be subject to the general supervision and guidance of the mayor and council.

SECTION 2.13.

Boards, commissions, and authorities.

(a) All members of boards, commissions, and authorities of the city shall be nominated by the mayor and be confirmed by the council for such terms of office and such manner of appointment as provided by ordinance, except where other appointing authority, term of office, or manner of appointment is prescribed by this charter or by applicable state law.

(b) No member of any board, commission, or authority of the city shall hold any elective office in the city. Councilmembers and the mayor, however, may serve as ex officio members of such boards, commissions, or authorities, without a vote.

(c) Any vacancy in office of any member of a board, commission, or authority of the city shall be filled for the unexpired term in the manner prescribed for original appointment, except as otherwise provided by this charter or any applicable state law.

(d) No member of any board, commission, or authority shall assume office until he or she shall have executed and filed with the designated officer of the city an oath obligating himself or herself to faithfully and impartially perform the duties of his or her office, such oath to be prescribed by ordinance of the council and administered by the mayor

(e) Any member of a board, commission, or authority may be removed from office for cause by a vote of a majority of the members of the council.

(f) Members of boards, commissions, and authorities may receive such compensation and expenses in the performance of their official duties as prescribed by ordinance.

(g) Except as otherwise provided by this charter or by applicable state law, each board, commission, or authority of the city government shall elect one of its members as chairperson and one member as vice chairperson for terms of one year and may elect as its secretary one of its own members or may appoint as secretary an employee of the city. Each board, commission, or authority of the city government may establish such bylaws, rules, and regulations not inconsistent with this charter, ordinances of the city, or applicable state law as it deems appropriate and necessary for the conduct of its affairs, copies of which shall be filed with the designated officer of the city.

SECTION 2.14.
Ordinance form; procedures.

(a) Every proposed ordinance and resolution shall be introduced in writing and the city council shall have the authority to approve, disapprove, or amend the same. A resolution may be passed at the time it is offered, but an ordinance shall not be adopted until the title of said ordinance shall have been read at two city council meetings, provided that the beginning of said meetings be not less than 24 hours nor more than 60 days apart. This requirement of two readings shall not apply to emergency ordinances or to ordinances adopted at the first business meeting of the city council in a calendar year.

(b) The catchlines of sections of this charter or any ordinance printed in boldface type, italics, or otherwise, are intended as mere catchwords to indicate the contents of the section, and:

(1) Shall not be deemed or taken to be titles of such sections or as any part of the section; and

(2) Shall not be so deemed when any of such sections, including the catchlines, are amended or reenacted unless expressly provided to the contrary.

Furthermore, the chapter, article, and section headings contained in this Act shall not be deemed to govern, limit, or modify or in any manner affect the scope, meaning, or intent of the provisions of any chapter, article, or section hereof.

(c) The city council may, by ordinance or resolution, adopt rules and bylaws to govern the conduct of its business, including procedures and penalties for compelling the attendance of absent members. Such rules may include punishment for contemptuous behavior conducted in the presence of the city council.

SECTION 2.15.

Submission of ordinances to the mayor.

(a) Every ordinance, resolution, and other action adopted by the council shall be presented promptly to the mayor. Except for council approval of appointments to committees, boards, and commissions, the employment of any appointed officer, internal affairs, or matters which must be approved by the voters, the mayor may veto Any action adopted by the city council.

(b) The veto must be exercised no later than the next regular city council meeting following the meeting at which the action was taken. If an action is disapproved, the mayor shall submit to the council a written statement of the reasons for the mayor's veto.

(c) An action vetoed by the mayor shall automatically be on the agenda at the next regular meeting of the city council for reconsideration. If the minimum number of council members necessary to vote on overriding the veto are not present, the action may be continued until the next meeting at which the minimum number of council members are present. Such action shall not become effective unless it is readopted by the affirmative votes of at least four members of council within 60 days of the veto.

(d) The mayor may disapprove or reduce any item or items of appropriation in any ordinance or resolution. The approved part or parts of any ordinance or resolution making appropriations shall become law, and the part or parts disapproved or reduced shall not become law unless subsequently passed by the city council over the mayor's Veto as provided in this charter.

(e) If an ordinance or resolution has been signed by the mayor, it shall become effective. If an ordinance or resolution is neither approved nor disapproved by the next regular meeting of the city council, it shall become effective.

ARTICLE III
EXECUTIVE BRANCH

SECTION 3.01.
Powers and duties of the mayor.

(a) The mayor shall be the chief executive officer of the city government, a member of and the presiding officer of the city council, and responsible for the efficient and orderly administration of the city's affairs. The mayor shall be responsible for the enforcement of laws, rules, regulations, ordinances, and franchises in the city. The mayor may conduct inquiries and investigations into the conduct of the city's affairs and shall have such powers and duties as specified in this charter or as may be provided by ordinance consistent with this charter.

(b) The mayor shall:

(1) Preside at all meetings of the city council;

(2) Be the head of the city for the purpose of service of process and for ceremonial purposes and be the official spokesperson for the city and the advocate of policy;

(3) Sign as a matter of course on behalf of the city all written and approved contracts, ordinances, resolutions, and other instruments executed by the city which by law are required to be in writing;

(4) See that all laws and ordinances of the city are faithfully executed;

(5) Vote on any motion, resolution, ordinance, or other question before the council only as provided in Section 2.10 of this charter and vote on any matter before a committee on which he or she serves;

(6) Obtain short term loans in the name of the city when authorized by the city council to do so;

(7) Appoint council members to oversee and report on the functions of the various departments of the city;

(8) Require the city manager to meet with him or her at a time and place designated for consultation and advice upon the affairs of the city;

(9) Name qualified residents of the city to boards and commissions with approval of the city council;

(10) Make recommendations with respect to the employment or termination of city employees;

(11) Prepare or have prepared an agenda for each meeting of the city council which shall include all business submitted by the mayor, any councilmember, the city manager, and the city attorney; and

(12) Fulfill and perform such other duties as are imposed by this charter and duly adopted ordinances.

SECTION 3.02.

City manager; appointment, qualification, and compensation.

The mayor shall appoint, subject to confirmation by the council, for an indefinite term an officer whose title shall be the "city manager" and the city manager shall serve at the pleasure of the council. The city manager shall be appointed without regard to political beliefs and solely on the basis of his or her executive and administrative qualifications with special reference to his or her educational background and actual experience in, and knowledge of, the duties of office as hereinafter prescribed.

SECTION 3.03.

City manager; chief administrative officer.

The city manager shall be the chief administrative officer of the government of the City of Sandy Springs. The city manager must devote all of his or her working time and attention to the affairs of the city and shall be responsible to the mayor and council for the proper and efficient administration of the affairs of the city over which said officer has jurisdiction.

SECTION 3.04.

City manager; powers and duties enumerated.

The city manager shall have the power, and it shall be his or her duty to:

(1) See that all laws and ordinances are enforced;

(2) Appoint and employ all necessary employees of the city, provided that excepted from the power of this appointment are those officers and employees who by this Act are appointed or elected by the council or departments not under the jurisdiction of the city manager;

(3) Remove employees employed by said officer without the consent of the council and without assigning any reason therefore;

(4) Exercise supervision and control of all departments and all divisions created in this charter or that may hereafter be created by the council except as otherwise provided in this Act;

(5) Attend all meetings of the council with a right to take part in the discussions, but having no vote. The city manager shall be entitled to notice of all special meetings;

(6) Recommend to the council, after prior review and comment by the mayor, for adoption such measures as the city manager may deem necessary or expedient;

(7) See that all terms and conditions imposed in favor of the city or its inhabitants in any public utility franchise are faithfully kept and performed and upon knowledge of any violation thereof to call the same to the attention of the city attorney, whose duty it shall be forthwith to take such steps as are necessary to protect and enforce the same;

(8) Make and execute all lawful contracts on behalf of the city as to matters within said officer's jurisdiction to the extent that such contracts are funded in the city's budget, except such as may be otherwise provided by law; provided, however, that no contract purchase or obligation requiring a budget amendment shall be valid and binding until after approval of the council;

(9) Act as budget officer to prepare and submit to the council, after review and comment by the mayor, prior to the beginning of each fiscal year a budget of proposed expenditures for the ensuing year, showing in as much detail as practicable the amounts allotted to each department of the city government and the reasons for such estimated expenditures;

(10) Keep the council at all times fully advised as to the financial condition and needs of the city;

(11) Make a full written report to the council on the first of each month showing the operations and expenditures of each department of the city government for the preceding month, and a synopsis of such reports shall be published by the clerk of the city;

(12) Fix all salaries and compensation of city employees in accordance with the city budget and the city pay and classification plan; and

(13) Perform such other duties as may be prescribed by this Act or required by ordinance or resolution of the council.

SECTION 3.05.
Council interference with administration.

Except for the purpose of inquiries and investigations under Section 2.08 of this charter, the city council or its members shall deal with city officers and employees who are subject to the direction or supervision of the manager solely through the manager, and neither the city council nor its members shall give orders to any such officer or employee, either publicly or privately.

SECTION 3.06.
City manager; removal.

(a) The mayor and council may remove the manager from office in accordance with the following procedures:

(1) The council shall adopt by affirmative vote of a majority of all its members a preliminary resolution removing the city manager and may suspend the city manager from duty for a period not to exceed 45 days. A copy of the resolution shall be delivered promptly to the city manager;

(2) Within five days after a copy of the resolution is delivered to the city manager, he or she may file with the council a written request for a public hearing. This hearing shall be held at a council meeting not earlier than 15 days nor later than 30 days after the request is filed. The city manager may file with the council a written reply not later than five days before the hearing; and

(3) The council may adopt a final resolution of removal, which may be made effective immediately, by affirmative vote of four of its members at any time after five days from the date when a copy of the preliminary resolution was delivered to the city manager, if he or she has not requested a public hearing, or at any time after the public hearing if he or she has requested one.

(b) The city manager shall continue to receive his or her salary until the effective date of a final resolution of removal and, unless he or she has been convicted of a felony at that time, he or she shall be given not less than 60 days' severance pay. The action of the council in suspending or removing the city manager shall not be subject to review by any court or agency.

(c) If the city manager becomes disabled and is unable to carry out the duties of the office or if the city manager dies, the acting city manager shall perform the duties of the city manager until the city manager's disability is removed or until the city manager is replaced. Removal of the city manager because of disability shall be carried out in accordance with the provisions of subsection (a) of this section.

SECTION 3.07.

Acting city manager.

(a) The city manager may designate in writing any administrative employee of the city who shall exercise all powers, duties, and functions of the city manager during the city manager's temporary absence from the city or during the city manager's disability. If such designation has not been made and the city manager is absent from the city or unable to perform the duties of the office or to make such designation, the council may, by resolution, appoint any qualified administrative employee of the city to perform the powers, duties, and functions of the city manager until the city manager shall return to the city, the disability ceases, or the council appoints a new city manager. (b) In the event of a vacancy in the office of city manager, the council may designate a person as acting city manager, who shall exercise all powers, duties, and functions of the city manager until a city manager is appointed.

SECTION 3.08.

City attorney.

The mayor shall nominate and the council shall confirm by majority vote of the council a city attorney, together with such assistant city attorneys as may be deemed appropriate, and shall provide for the payment of such attorney or attorneys for services rendered to the city. The city attorney shall be responsible for representing and defending the city in all litigation in which the city is a party; may be the prosecuting officer in the municipal court; shall attend the meetings of the council as directed; shall advise the council, mayor, other officers, and employees of the city concerning legal aspects of the city's affairs; and shall perform such other duties as may be required by virtue of his or her position as city attorney. The city attorney shall review all contracts of the city but shall not have the power to bind the city.

SECTION 3.09.

City clerk.

The mayor may appoint a city clerk, subject to confirmation by majority vote of the council, to keep a journal of the proceedings of the city council; to maintain in a safe place all records and documents pertaining to the affairs of the city; and to perform such duties as may be required by law or ordinance or as the mayor or city manager may direct.

SECTION 3.10.

Tax collector.

The mayor may appoint a tax collector, subject to confirmation by majority vote of the council, to collect all taxes, licenses, fees, and other moneys belonging to the city subject to the provisions of this charter and the ordinances of the city; and the tax collector shall diligently comply with and enforce all general laws of Georgia relating to the collection, sale, or foreclosure of taxes by municipalities.

SECTION 3.11.

City accountant.

The mayor may appoint a city accountant, subject to confirmation by majority vote of the council, to perform the duties of an accountant.

SECTION 3.12.

Consolidation of functions.

The city manager, with the approval of the council, may consolidate any two or more of the positions of city clerk, city tax collector, and city accountant, or any other positions or may assign the functions of any one or more of such positions to the holder or holders of any other positions. The city manager may also, with the approval of the city council, perform all or any part of the functions of any of the positions or offices in lieu of the appointment of other persons to perform the same.

SECTION 3.13.

Position classification and pay plans; employment at will.

The city manager shall be responsible for the preparation of a position classification and a pay plan which shall be submitted to the council for approval. Said plan may apply to all employees of the City of Sandy Springs and any of its agencies and offices. When a pay plan has been adopted by the council, neither the council nor the city manager shall increase or decrease the salaries of individual employees except in conformity with such pay plan or pursuant to an amendment of said pay plan duly adopted by the council. Except as otherwise provided in this charter, all employees of the city shall be subject to removal or discharge, with or without cause, at any time.

ARTICLE IV

MUNICIPAL COURT

SECTION 4.01.

Creation.

There is established a court to be known as the Municipal Court of the City of Sandy Springs which shall have jurisdiction and authority to try offenses against the laws and ordinances of said city and to punish for a violation of the same. Such court shall have the power to enforce its judgments by the imposition of such penalties as may be provided by law, including ordinances of the city; to punish witnesses for nonattendance and to punish also any person who may counsel or advise, aid, encourage, or persuade another whose testimony is desired or material in any proceeding before said court to go or move beyond the reach of the process of the court; to try all offenses within the territorial limits of the city constituting traffic cases which, under the laws of Georgia, are placed within the jurisdiction of municipal courts to the extent of, and in accordance with, the provisions of such laws and all laws subsequently enacted amendatory thereof. Said court shall be presided over by the judge of said court. In the absence or disqualification of the judge, the judge pro tem shall preside and shall exercise the same powers and duties as the judge when so acting.

SECTION 4.02.

Judge.

(a) No person shall be qualified or eligible to serve as judge unless he or she shall have attained the age of 21 years and shall have been a member of the State Bar of Georgia for a minimum of three years. The judge shall be appointed by resolution of the council. The compensation of the judge shall be fixed by the council. The position of judge created in this article shall not be a full-time position, and the person serving in said position may engage in the private practice of law.

(b) The judge pro tem shall serve as requested by the judge, shall have the same qualifications as the judge, shall be appointed by resolution of the council, and shall take the same oath as the judge.

(c) Before entering on duties of his or her office, the judge and judge pro tem shall take an oath before an officer duly authorized to administer oaths in this state declaring that he or she will truly, honestly, and faithfully discharge the duties of his or her office to the best of his or her ability without fear, favor, or partiality. The oath shall be entered upon the minutes of the council.

(d) The judge, or judge pro tem, shall serve for a term of four years but may be removed from the position by a two-thirds vote of the entire membership of the city council or upon action taken by the State Judicial Qualifications Commission for:

(1) Willful misconduct in office;

(2) Willful and persistent failure to perform duties;

(3) Habitual intemperance;

(4) Conduct prejudicial to the administration of justice which brings the judicial office into disrepute; or

(5) Disability seriously interfering with the performance of duties, which is, or is likely to become, of a permanent character.

SECTION 4.03.
Convening.
Said court shall be convened at such times as designated by ordinance or at such times as deemed necessary by the judge to keep current the dockets thereof.

SECTION 4.04.
Jurisdiction; powers.
(a) The municipal court shall try and punish for crimes against the City of Sandy Springs and for violation of its ordinances. The municipal court shall have authority to punish those in its presence for contempt, provided that such punishment shall not exceed $200.00 or imprisonment for 15 days. The municipal court may fix punishment for offenses within its jurisdiction to the full extent allowed by state law.

(b) The municipal court shall have authority to establish a schedule of fees to defray the Cost of operation.

(c) The municipal court shall have authority to establish bail and recognizances to insure the presence of those charged with violations before said court and shall have discretionary authority to accept cash or personal or real property as security for appearances of persons charged with violations. Whenever any person shall give bail for his or her appearance and shall fail to appear at the time fixed for trial, the bond shall be forfeited by the judge presiding at such time and an execution issued thereon by serving the defendant and his or her sureties with a rule nisi at least two days before a hearing on the rule nisi. In the event that cash or property is accepted in lieu of bond for security for the appearance of a defendant at trial, and if such defendant fails to appear at the time and place fixed for trial, the cash so deposited shall be on order of the judge declared forfeited to the City of Sandy Springs, or the property so deposited shall have a lien against it for the value forfeited.

(d) The municipal court shall have the authority to bind prisoners over to the appropriate court when it appears, by probable cause, that a state law has been violated.

(e) The municipal court shall have the authority to administer oaths and to perform all other acts necessary or proper to the conduct of said court.

(f) The municipal court may compel the presence of all parties necessary to a proper disposal of each case by the issuance of summons, subpoena, and warrants which may be served as executed by any officer as authorized by this charter or by state law.

(g) The municipal court is specifically vested with all of the judicial jurisdiction and judicial powers throughout the entire area of the City of Sandy Springs granted by state laws generally to municipal courts, and particularly by such laws as authorize the abatement of nuisances.

SECTION 4.05.
Certiorari.
The right of certiorari from the decision and judgment of the municipal court shall exist in all criminal cases and ordinance violation cases, and such certiorari shall be obtained under the sanction of a judge of the Superior Court of Fulton County under the laws of the State of Georgia regulating the granting and issuance of writs of certiorari.

SECTION 4.06.
Rules for court.
With the approval of the council, the judge shall have full power and authority to make reasonable rules and regulations necessary and proper

to secure the efficient and successful administration of the municipal court.

ARTICLE V
FINANCE AND FISCAL

SECTION 5.01.
Fiscal year.

The council shall set the fiscal year by ordinance. Said fiscal year shall constitute the budget year and the year for financial accounting and reporting of each and every office, department or institution, agency, and activity of the city go

SECTION 5.02.
Preparation of budgets.

The council shall provide, by ordinance, the procedures and requirements for the preparation and execution of an annual operating budget and a capital improvement program and a capital budget, including requirements as to the scope, content, and form of such budgets and programs.

SECTION 5.03.
Submission of operating budget to city council.

On or before a date fixed by the council, but not later than 30 days prior to the beginning of each fiscal year, the city manager shall, after review and comment by the mayor, submit to the council a proposed operating budget for the ensuing fiscal year. The budget shall be accompanied by a message from the city manager containing a statement of the general fiscal policies of the city, the important features of the budget, explanations of major changes recommended for the next fiscal year, a general summary of the budget, and such other comments and information as he or she may deem pertinent. The operating budget and the capital improvements budget hereinafter provided for, the budget message, and all supporting documents shall be filed in the office of the city manager and shall be open to public inspection.

SECTION 5.04.

Action by council on budget.

The council may amend the operating budget proposed by the city manager, except that the budget, as finally amended and adopted, must provide for all expenditures required by law, or by other provisions of this charter, and for all debt service requirements for the ensuing fiscal year and the total appropriations from any fund shall not exceed the estimated fund balance, reserves, and revenues, constituting the fund availability of such fund.

SECTION 5.05.

Audits.

(a) There shall be an annual independent audit of all city accounts, funds, and financial transactions by a certified public accountant selected by the city council. The audit shall be conducted according to generally accepted accounting principles. Any audit of any funds by the state or federal government may be accepted as satisfying the requirements of this charter. Copies of all audit reports shall be available at printing cost to the public.

(b) As a minimum, all audits and budgets of the city shall satisfy the requirements of Chapter 81 of Title 36 of the O.C.G.A., relating to local government audits and budgets.

SECTION 5.06.

Homestead exemptions.

Any homestead exemptions applicable to ad valorem taxes levied by the city shall be as provided by Act of the General Assembly pursuant to Article VII, Section II, Paragraph II of the Georgia Constitution.

ARTICLE VI
GENERAL PROVISIONS.

SECTION 6.01.

Referendum and initial election.

(a) Unless prohibited by the federal Voting Rights Act of 1965, as amended, the election superintendent of Fulton County shall call a special election for the purpose of submitting this Act to the qualified voters of the proposed City of Sandy Springs for approval or rejection. The superintendent shall set the date of such election for the third Tuesday in June, 2005. The superintendent shall issue the call for such election at least 30 days prior to the date thereof. The superintendent shall cause the date and purpose of the election to be published once a week for two weeks immediately preceding the date thereof in the official organ of Fulton County. The ballot shall have written or printed thereon the words:

"( ) YES   Shall the Act incorporating the City of Sandy Springs
 ( ) NO   in Fulton County according to the charter contained in
            the Act be approved?"

All persons desiring to vote for approval of the Act shall vote "Yes," and those persons desiring to vote for rejection of the Act shall vote "No." If more than one-half of the votes cast on such question are for approval of the Act, it shall become of full force and effect as provided in Section 6.02 of this charter, otherwise it shall be void and of no Force and effect.

The initial expense of such election shall be borne by Fulton County. Within two years after the elections if the incorporation is approved, the City of Sandy Springs shall reimburse Fulton County for the actual cost of printing and personnel services for such election and for the initial election of the mayor and members of the city council pursuant to subsection (b) of Section 2.02 of this charter. It shall be the duty of the superintendent to hold and conduct such election. It shall be his or her further duty to certify the result thereof to the Secretary of State.

(b) For the purposes of the referendum election provided for in this section and for the purposes of the election to be held on the Tuesday after the first Monday in November, 2005, the qualified electors of the City of Sandy Springs shall be those qualified electors of Fulton County residing within the corporate limits of the City of Sandy Springs as described by Appendix A of this charter. At subsequent municipal elections, the qualified electors of the City of Sandy Springs shall be determined pursuant to the authority of Chapter 2 of Title 21 of the O.C.G.A., known as the "Georgia Election Code."

(c) Only for the purposes of holding and conducting the referendum election provided for by this section and holding and conducting the election of the City of Sandy Springs to be held on the Tuesday after the first Monday in November, 2005, the election superintendent of Fulton County is vested with the powers and duties of the election superintendent of the City of Sandy Springs and the powers and duties of the governing authority of the City of Sandy Springs.

SECTION 6.02.

Effective dates.

(a) This Act shall become effective only if an amendment to Code Section 36-31-2 of the O.C.G.A., permitting incorporation of a municipal corporation less than three miles from another municipality's boundaries, is enacted at the 2005 regular session of the General Assembly, in which event this section and the provisions of this Act necessary for the election provided in Section 6.01 of this charter shall become effective upon the same date that such amendment to Code Section 36-31-2 of the O.C.G.A. becomes effective or as soon thereafter as this Act is approved by the Governor or becomes law without such approval if this Act is the later of the two to become law. The provisions of this Act necessary for the election to be held on the Tuesday after the first Monday in November, 2005, shall be effective upon the certification of the results of the referendum election provided for by Section 6.01 of this charter, if this Act is approved At such referendum election.

(b) A period of time will be needed for an orderly transition of various government functions from Fulton County to the City of Sandy Springs. Accordingly there shall be a transition period beginning December 1, 2005, and ending at midnight on December 31, 2006. During such transition period, all provisions of this charter shall be effective as law, but not all provisions of this charter shall be implemented.

(c) During such transition period, Fulton County shall continue to provide within the territorial limits of Sandy Springs all government services and functions which Fulton County provided in that area as of the date of enactment of this charter, except to the extent otherwise provided in this section; provided, however, that by agreement of Fulton

County and the City of Sandy Springs responsibility for any such service or function may be transferred to the City of Sandy Springs at such time as may be agreed upon by the parties. Effective December 1, 2005, the City of Sandy Springs shall collect taxes, fees, assessments, fines and forfeitures, and other moneys within the territorial limits of Sandy Springs. Where a particular tax, fee, assessment, fine, forfeiture, or other amount collected is specifically related to the provision of a particular government service or function by Fulton County, the service or function shall continue to be provided by the county contingent upon payment by the city of the actual cost of providing such service or function unless otherwise provided in a written agreement between the city and the county. Any existing contract for the performance of a governmental service with a private person residing or doing business within the city limits shall not be altered or adversely affected by the establishment of this Act of the city of Sandy Springs.

(d) During the transition period, the governing authority of the City of Sandy Springs:

(1) Shall hold regular meetings and may hold special meetings as provided in this charter;

(2) May enact ordinances and resolutions as provided in this charter;

(3) May amend this charter by home rule action as provided by general law;

(4) May accept gifts and grants;

(5) May borrow money and incur indebtedness to the extent authorized by this charter and general law;

(6) May levy and collect an ad valorem tax for calendar year 2006;

(7) May establish a fiscal year and budget;

(8) May create, alter, or abolish departments, boards, offices, commissions, and agencies of the city; appoint and remove officers and employees; and exercise all necessary or appropriate personnel and management functions;

(9) May generally exercise any power granted by this charter or general law, except to the extent that a power is specifically and integrally related to the provision of a governmental service, function, or responsibility not yet provided or carried out by the city.

(e) During the transition period, the Municipal Court of Sandy Springs shall exercise its jurisdiction to the extent appropriate with respect to the government services and functions performed by the City of Sandy Springs and the appropriate court or courts of Fulton County shall retain jurisdiction over the area incorporated as the City of Sandy Springs with respect to government services and functions performed by Fulton County. Any transfer of jurisdiction to the City of Sandy Springs at the beginning of, during, at the end of, or after the transition period shall not in and of itself abate any judicial proceeding pending in Fulton County or the pending prosecution of any violation of any ordinance of Fulton County.

(f) During the transition period, the governing authority of Sandy Springs may at any time, without the necessity of any agreement by Fulton County, commence to exercise its planning and zoning powers; provided, however, that the city shall give the county at least 30 days written notice of the date on which the city will assume the exercise of such powers. Upon the governing authority of Sandy Springs commencing to exercise its planning and zoning powers, the Municipal Court of Sandy Springs shall immediately have jurisdiction to enforce the planning and zoning ordinances of the city. The provisions of this subsection shall control over any conflicting provisions of any other subsection of this section.

(g) Effective upon the termination of the transition period, subsections (c) through (f) of this section shall cease to apply except for the last sentence of subsection (e) which shall remain effective. Effective upon the termination of the transition period, the City of Sandy Springs shall be a full functioning municipal corporation and subject to all general laws of this state.

SECTION 6.03.

Directory nature of dates.

It is the intention of the General Assembly that this Act be construed as directory rather than mandatory with respect to any date prescribed in this Act. If it is necessary to delay any action called for in this Act for providential cause, delay in securing approval under the federal Voting Rights Act, or any other reason, it is the intention of the General Assembly that the action be delayed rather than abandoned. Any delay in performing any action under this Act, whether for cause or otherwise, shall not operate to frustrate the overall intent of this Act. Without limiting the generality of the foregoing it is specifically provided that:

(1) If it is not possible to hold the referendum election provided for in Section 6.01 of this Act on the date specified in that section, then such referendum shall be held as soon thereafter as is reasonably practicable; and

(2) If it is not possible to hold the first regular municipal election provided for in Section 2.02 of this Act on the date specified in that section, then there shall be a special election for the initial members of the governing authority to be held as soon thereafter as is reasonably practicable, and the commencement of the initial terms of office shall be delayed accordingly.

SECTION 6.04.

Charter commission.

At the first regularly scheduled city council meeting, five years after the inception of the City of Sandy Springs, the mayor and city council shall call for a charter commission to review the city's experience and recommend to the General Assembly any changes to the city charter. Members of the charter commission shall be appointed as follows: one by the mayor, one by the city council, and one by each member of the Georgia House of Representatives and Senate whose district lies wholly or partially within the corporate boundaries of Sandy Springs. All members of the charter commission must reside in Sandy Springs. The commission must complete the recommendations within six months of its creation.

SECTION 6.05.
Severability.
In the event any section, subsection, sentence, clause, or phrase of this Act shall be declared or adjudged invalid or unconstitutional, such adjudication shall in no manner affect the other sections, subsections, sentences, clauses, or phrases of this Act, which shall remain of full force and effect, as if the section, subsection, sentence, clause, or phrase so declared or adjudged invalid or unconstitutional were not originally a part hereof. The General Assembly hereby declares that it would have passed the remaining parts of this Act if it had known that such part or parts hereof would be declared or adjudged invalid or unconstitutional.

SECTION 6.06.
Repealer.
All laws and parts of laws in conflict with this Act are repealed.

APPENDIX A
The corporate limits of the City of Sandy Springs shall consist of the following described territory of Fulton County:

Beginning at the northwest corner of the City of Atlanta, as the boundaries of said city existed on January 1, 2005, at the point where the northerly city limit line of said city intersects the westerly county line of Fulton County and the Chattahoochee River, running thence generally easterly along the said northerly city limit line of the City of Atlanta, following the meanderings thereof, to the point where said line intersects the Fulton-DeKalb County line; run thence northerly, generally easterly, and generally northerly along the easterly county line of Fulton County to the point where the Fulton-Gwinnett County line intersects the Chattahoochee River; run thence generally west and southwest along the southern bank of said river, following the meanderings thereof, to the point of beginning.

APPENDIX B
Council Districts 1 through 6 shall consist of the described territory of the City of Sandy Springs attached to this Act and made a part thereof and further identified as "Plan Name: sterling1R

Plan Type: Local User: Gina Administrator: Sandy Springs." When used in such attachment, the terms "Tract" and "BG" (Block Group) shall mean and describe the same geographical boundaries as provided in the report of the Bureau of the Census for the United States decennial census of 2000 for the State of Georgia. The separate numeric designations in a Tract description which are underneath a "BG" heading shall mean and describe individual Blocks within a Block Group as provided in the report of the Bureau of the Census for the United States decennial census of 2000 for the State of Georgia. Any part of the City of Sandy Springs which is not included in any such district described in that attachment shall be included within that district contiguous to such part which contains the least population according to the United States decennial census of 2000 for the State of Georgia. Any part of the City of Sandy Springs which is described in that attachment as being in a particular district shall nevertheless not be included within such district if such part is not contiguous to such district. Such noncontiguous part shall instead be included with that district contiguous to such part which contains the least population according to the United States decennial census of 2000 for the State of Georgia.

A P P E N D I X   C

REQUEST FOR PROPOSAL

FOR

PROVISION OF ADMINISTRATIVE, FINANCIAL COMMUNITY SERVICES, EMERGENCY 911, PHYSICAL PLANT, MOTOR VEHICLE, STAFFING, AND PURCHASING, PROCUREMENT AND CONTRACTING SERVICES

TO THE

CITY OF SANDY SPRINGS

PROPOSALS OPENED: (time)   (date)

INSTRUCTIONS TO PROPOSERS

All the spaces below and in the attached Proposal Signature and Certification form are to be filled in with signatures supplied where indicated. Failure to sign Proposal will cause rejection of your proposal.

PROPOSAL OF:

COMPANY NAME:
ADDRESS:

SUBMIT PROPOSAL TO:

Mr. Oliver Porter, Commissioner
150 Habersham Waters Court
Dunwoody, GA 30350

PROPOSAL MAILED:
CARRIER USED:

NOTE: **PLEASE ENSURE THAT ALL REQUIRED SIGNATURE BLOCKS ARE COMPLETED. FAILURE TO SIGN THIS FORM WILL CAUSE REJECTION OF YOUR PROPOSAL.**

Commission for
The City of Sandy Springs

PROPOSAL

We propose to furnish and deliver any and all of the services named in the attached Request for Proposal (RFP). The price or prices offered herein shall apply for the period of time stated in the RFP.

This offer is being made in with knowledge that the Commission for the City of Sandy Springs is promulgating this RFP in accordance with its authority granted by virtue of O.C.G.A. § 36-31-8(g). We understand that pursuant to said section, and the provisions of 05 HB 36 and 05 HB 37, the Commission has no authority to enter into binding agreements, to expend public funds, or to incur any liability on behalf of the City of Sandy Springs.

It is understood and agreed that this proposal constitutes an offer, which if accepted in writing by the City of Sandy Springs, Georgia, City Council, and subject to the terms and conditions of such acceptance, will constitute a valid and binding contract between the undersigned and the City of Sandy Springs, Georgia.

It is understood and agreed that we have read the specification shown or referenced in the RFP and that this proposal is made in accordance with the provisions of such specifications. By our written signature on this proposal, we guarantee and certify that all items included in this proposal meet or exceed any and all such specifications. We further agree if awarded a contract, to deliver services, which meet or exceed the specifications.

It is understood and agreed that any proposals shall be valid and held open for a period of sixty (60) days from the date of the first meeting of a quorum of the newly elected City Council of the City of Sandy Springs.

_____	_____
Authorized Signature	Date

_____	_____
Print/Type Name	Print/Type Company Name

PROPOSAL SIGNATURE AND CERTIFICATION

(Bidder must sign and return with proposal)

I certify that this proposal was made without prior understanding, agreement, or connection with any corporation, firm, or person submitting a proposal for the same materials, supplies, equipment, or services and is in all respects fair and without collusion or fraud. I understand collusive bidding is a violation of State and Federal Law and can result in fines, prison sentences, and civil damage awards. I agree to abide by all conditions of the proposal and certify I am authorized to sign this proposal for the proposer.

_____	_____
Authorized Signature	Date

_____	_____
Print/Type Name	Print/Type Company Name

1.0   GENERAL INFORMATION

1.1   Introduction

Pursuant to its authority granted by virtue of O.C.G.A. § 36-31-8(g), the Commission for the City of Sandy Springs (the "Commission") is requesting proposals for Provision of Services to the City of Sandy Springs, Georgia (the "City") to implement, manage and operate a wide range of services/functions for the new city to be incorporated December 1, 2005. This RFP is issued pursuant to its authority granted by virtue of O.C.G.A. § 36-31-8(g) and subject to all of the terms, limitations, and conditions as set forth in House Bill 36 and House Bill 37 as passed during the 2005 Georgia Legislative Session. Competitive sealed proposals shall be submitted in response hereto. All proposals submitted pursuant to the request shall be made in accordance with the provisions of these instructions.

As set forth herein, there shall be mandatory pre-proposal conference of all bidders. Further, packaging of bid services is allowed for the purposes of this Request for Proposal ("RFP"), provided however, that each component of said packaged services must be individually detailed in said response. Offerors may, and are encouraged, to form partnerships regarding the provisions of any particular services set forth herein to insure that the City has benefit of the best possible team to provide the required services.

The proposals shall be evaluated in accordance with the evaluation criteria set forth in this RFP. Subsequent to the opening of the sealed proposals, discussions may be conducted by the Commission for City of Sandy Springs with responsible offerors who submit proposals for the purpose of clarification to assure full understanding of and responsiveness to the solicitation requirements. Offerors shall be accorded fair and equal treatment with respect to any opportunity for discussion and revision of proposals.

In conducting any such discussion, there shall be no disclosure of any information derived from proposals submitted by competing offerors. All such discussions shall be conducted by a committee comprising some or all of the Commission Members.

In accordance with O.C.G.A. § 36-31-8(g), if determined advantageous to the City, recommendation of acceptance to the incoming City Council shall be made regarding the responsible offeror whose proposal is determined in writing to be the most advantageous to the City, taking into consideration qualifications, experience in provision of similar services, price, identification of potential needs, thoroughness of proposals, and all other evaluation factors set forth in this RFP. No other factors or criteria shall be used in the evaluation. The Commission reserves the right to reject any and all proposals submitted in response to this request and to withdraw this RFP at any time.

2.2 Background

The City will be incorporated on December 1, 2005, with almost 90,000 residents and the Commission is soliciting these proposals to evaluate the most cost effective, efficient, and reliable method of meeting a broad range of needs for the City.

With a "clean sheet of paper," the City has the remarkable opportunity to build the most effective, efficient and responsive local government in the State of Georgia. The Commission believes that creative solutions are available that can produce the model government for the 21st century.

Foremost among these solutions is tapping the resources of private industry through contracting for services and functions. Our desire is to identify firms that can provide a wide variety of services allowing the city to deal with a limited number of contracts. Further, we are seeking firms that have had experience in providing services/functions to other municipalities, or as a minimum, to similar entities.

While it may be necessary to contract with the existing county government for some services, the intent is to keep that to a minimum. A successful contractor will have the opportunity to showcase the firm's capability in serving the needs of municipal governments.

With the aforementioned restrictions on contracts and spending, the Commission must establish a relationship of trust with potential contract firms. The recommended firms must be financially able and willing to, in the months preceding the start date, establish the infrastructure, hire and train staff, and undertake any functions that will be necessary for the city to operate from its inception.

2.3   Timetable

The following timetable is anticipated for this RFP:

June 29, 2005	Release of RFP
July 14, 2005	Mandatory Pre-Proposal Conference
Aug. 3, 2005 12:00 p.m.	Proposals due
Aug. 17, 2005	Oral Presentations if required)
December 1, 2005	Commission Recommendation, if any (on or about)

Proposals will be received at the date and time set forth above in the following location:

Mr. Oliver Porter, Commissioner
150 Habersham Waters Court
Dunwoody, GA 30350

2.4   Restrictions on Communications with Commission Staff

1.4.1   From the issue date of this RFP until a provider is selected and the selection is announced, offerors are not allowed to communicate for any reason with any Commissioner, staff member, or representative concerning this RFP except through the Officer named herein, or during the pre-bid conference. For violations of this provision, the Commission shall reserve the right to reject the proposal of the offending offeror.

2.5   **RFP Amendments**

1.5.1   The Commission reserves the right to amend the RFP prior to the deadline for proposal submission, August 3, 2005. Amendments will be sent to all offerors who originally received a copy of the RFP. If an RFP amendment will impact the timeline contained in Section 1.3, all offerors will be promptly provided information concerning any timeline revisions.

1.6   **Proposal Withdrawal**

1.6.1   A written proposal is not subject to withdrawal except that, prior to the proposal due date, a submitted proposal may be withdrawn by the offeror submitting a written request to the Officer named herein. Any such request must be signed by a person authorized to sign for the offeror.

1.7   **Costs for Preparing Proposal**

1.7.1   The cost for developing the proposal is the sole responsibility of the offeror. The Commission and/or the City will not provide reimbursement for such costs.

1.8   **Contract Term**

1.8.1   The contract will be a multi-party contract between the service provider and the City. The term, if any, of the contract shall commence on January 1, 2006, and shall terminate on December 31, 2006, except that the Contract shall automatically renew for five (5) additional twelve (12) month periods unless affirmative written notice of non-renewal is given by the City not less than thirty (30) days prior to the expiration of the instant term. The terms and construction of the Contract shall be governed by applicable Georgia law.

1.9   **Contract**

1.9.1   The Contract, which the Commission intends to use with the successful offeror, is attached as Attachment "A" to this RFP. Prospective offerors are urged to carefully read the Contract prior to making their offers. The Contract and any exceptions to the provisions of the Contract must be submitted with the offeror's proposal. The Commission reserves the right to negotiate with the successful offeror other additions to, deletions from and/or changes in the language in the Contract, provided that no such addition, deletion or change in the contract language would, in the sole discretion of the Commission, affect the evaluation criteria set forth herein or give the successful offeror a competitive advantage.

The offeror shall confirm acceptance of the provisions of the Contract or, in the alternative, shall state explicitly which provisions are not acceptable and propose alternative wording or any additional wording or any additional provisions that the offeror believes to be necessary. Any exception to the Contract must be clearly identified, accompany the offeror's proposal, and be attached to the Contract. Offerors are cautioned that any exception submitted that would give the offeror a competitive advantage over another offeror or that would cause a failure to meet a mandatory requirement of the RFP will not be accepted.

Prior to a determination of recommedation, the apparent winning offeror will be required to enter into discussions with the Commission to resolve any contractual differences before a recommendation is made. These exceptions are to be finalized and all exceptions resolved within one (1) week of notification. If not, this could lead to rejection of the offeror's proposal. No exception to the Contract will be deemed to have been accepted by the Commission unless the exception is incorporated by reference into the final executed Contract. The Commission reserves the right to make non-material revisions to the form of the Contract as necessary at any time.

1.10   Offers by One or More Partners

1.10.1   Offerors may, and are encouraged, to form partnerships regarding the provisions of any particular services set forth herein to insure that the City has benefit of the best possible team to provide the required services. If more than one partner is participating in any response, however, each partner shall respond separately regarding their individual businesses, including but not limited to all responses to the RFQ portion of this request. All responses will further clearly delineate the specific responsibilities and duties of each partner regarding the requested services.

1.11   Format for Responses

1.11.1   Proposals should correspond with and satisfy the requirements set forth in this RFP. The offeror must submit the original proposal plus fifteen (15) copies of its proposal to the Commission. Proposals should be in one sealed package marked clearly on the front, "Sandy Springs RFP (A)"

1.12   Additional Information

1.12.1   An offeror that submits a proposal that meets the requirements set forth in this RFP may be requested to provide additional information or to meet with representatives of the Commission to discuss the specifics of the proposal in greater detail.

1.13   Retention of Proposals

1.13.1   All material submitted in response to this RFP will become the property of the Commission and may be returned at the option of the Commission. One copy shall be retained by the Commission for official files.

1.14   Waiver of Irregularities

1.14.1   The Commission reserves the right to waive any irregularities of any proposal submitted for this RFP.

1.15   Questions about this RFP

1.15.1   Questions regarding the requirements or technical criteria set forth in this RFP should be directed in writing to the individual listed below. The response and the question will then be shared with other offerors who are responding to this RFP.

Name: Mr. Oliver Porter
Address: 150 Habersham Waters Court
               Dunwoody, Georgia 30350
Telephone: 770-393-8898
E-mail: oliverporter1@comcast.net

The deadline for the submission of these questions is 12:00 P.M. EDT, July 25, 2005. Questions should reference the appropriate RFP section and may be submitted by email. Any files attached to e-mails must be MS Word format.

2.0 REQUEST FOR OFFEROR QUALIFICATIONS/ASSURANCES

2.1 Required Qualifications and Information

The Commission deems that it is in its best interest to work with offerors that have proven capabilities with a well-established record of success in the provision of the type of services being requested hereunder. To that end, the offeror shall include in a separate envelope as set forth herein, the following:

1.1.1   Offeror's name, address, and telephone number.

1.1.2   Primary local contact person(s) and telephone number(s).

1.1.3   Total number of offerors's full-time employees designating the geographic location of said employees with representative numbers regarding said location.

1.1.4   Year established.

1.1.5   Provide a listing and description of all current litigation involving the offeror.

1.1.6   Provide a listing and description of all litigation history for the offeror with any claim in excess of Twenty Thousand and 00/100 Dollars ($20,000.00) since and including the year 1990.

1.1.7   Provide a copy of the most recent completed year's financial statements (Income Statement and Balance Sheet) for the offeror.

1.1.8   List of all projects similar in quality and/or scope to that set forth in this RFP– Include: size, cost, total fee, implementation time, scope of services, awards received, and brief description of project.

1.1.9   Provide a description of the offeror's special capabilities, techniques or resources that can be contributed to this assignment. A minimum of three (3) references from projects of a similar scope and type shall be submitted with each proposal by offeror. Particular emphasis should be placed on demonstrating previous experience with projects for municipalities. Describe the offeror's, and/or proposed team's, qualifications to complete the work. The planning and/or expertise required to accomplish the complete scope-of-work must be represented either within the offerror's in-house staff, or by a partnership of offerors. A partnership submission must be made by an offeror. If the submission is a partnership submission, describe the previous experience that the offeror has had working with the various partners. Identify and provide resume information for the project manager and the key personnel who will be involved in implementing the project.

1.1.10   Statement of offeror's capability to absorb additional workload, availability of personnel, and commitment to provide services on a timely basis.

1.1.11   Conflict of Interest Statement.

As a duly authorized representative of _____ I, _____ with the title _____, certify that to the best of my knowledge that no circumstance exist which will cause a conflict of interest in performing services for the City of Sandy Springs, that no employee of _____, nor any public agency official or employee affected by this Request for Qualifications has any pecuniary interest in the business of this firm, associates or consultants of this firm, or the firm's parent firm, subsidiary, or other legal entity of which this firm is a part, and that no person associated with or employed by this firm has any interest that would conflict in any way, manner or degree with the performance of services for the City of Sandy Springs.

Date: _____

Company Name: _____

Authorized Representative Name: _____

Title: _____

Signature: _____

1.1.12   Provide a proposed Organizational Chart which identifies individual names and areas of responsibility regarding the implementation and responsibilities of the duties hereunder.

1.1.13   Provide a comprehensive outline of the steps you propose in order to meet the services required by this RFP. This detail should indicated what is to be done, who individually, and by name is responsible to do it, and when it is to be completed.

1.1.14   At your option, you may provide any additional supporting documentation or information which would be helpful in evaluating your qualifications and commitment.

1.1.15   The proposal should contain any documents pertaining to the requirements mentioned above and any other information the offeror deems necessary to fully demonstrate the offeror's qualifications so as to allow the Commission to evaluate the offeror's ability to provide the services requested herein.

2.2   **Proposal Guaranty**

2.2.1   No proposal will be considered unless it is accompanied by a proposal guaranty in the form of a cashier's check, a certified check, a savings and loan secured check, or a bid bond payable to the City of Sandy Springs in the amount of five percent (5%) of the total bid to ensure that the successful offeror will execute the contract which it has been recommended and ultimately awarded by the City. The proposal guaranty shall be forfeited by an offeror who fails to execute promptly and properly the contract it has been awarded, or who fails to furnish the required performance security and certificate of insurance in their proper forms within the time requirements indicated in this RFP. **ALL PROPOSAL GUARANTY SHALL BE RETAINED UNTIL FINAL CONTRACT AWARD.**

2.3   **Bonds**

2.3.1   Upon notification of the Commission's intent to recommend a proposal to the City, the apparent successful offeror shall furnish, within ten (10) days, a performance bond in the amount of one-hundred ten percent (110%) of the proposal amount on a form prescribed by the Commission. Failure to furnish a bond within ten (10) days may result in rejection of the proposal, forfeiture of the proposal guaranty, and awards of the contract to another offeror. Additionally, for a performance bond surety to be acceptable to the Commissions as surety for performance bonds, a surety company shall comply with the following provisions:

2.3.2   The surety company shall be authorized by law to do business in the State of Georgia pursuant to a current certificate of authority to transact business issued by the Commissioner of Insurance.

3.3.3.   The surety company shall be on the United States Department of Treasury's list of approved bond sureties.

3.3.4.   All bonds shall be signed by a Georgia Licensed Resident Agent who holds a current power of attorney from the surety company issuing the bond.

3.3.5.   PERFORMANCE SECURITY SHALL BE RETAINED BY THE CITY OF SANDY SPRINGS FOR A MINIMUM OF 150 CALENDAR DAYS FROM THE DATE OF CONTRACT COMPLETION.

4.4   Financial History

2.4.1   The Commission reserves the right to evaluate the financial integrity of the offeror. Prior to the award of the contracts, all offerors shall be required to submit the following items:

1.1.1.1   Audited Financial Statement or 10K Report for the most recent two (2) years, including at minimum:

2.4.1.1.1   statements of income and related earnings;

2.4.1.1.2   cash flow statement;

2.4.1.1.3   balance sheet;

2.4.1.1.4   opinion concerning financial statements from a CPA.

2.4.1.1.5   Primary banking source letter of reference.

2.5   Customer Reference

2.5.1   The offeror must provide the names of customer references, including a specific contact name and phone number of any entity to whom the provider has ever provided the proposed service or a similar service.

3.0   REQUIRED SERVICES

3.1   General

3.1.1   The services required for which this RFP is being issued shall include but not be limited to those outlined in Sections 4.0 et seq. through 9.0 et seq. hereof. The intent of the Contract is that the offeror firm assumes full responsibility for the structure, planning, and implementation necessary to provide the required services to the City. Where the offeror anticipates needs that may occur which are not specifically set forth hereunder, the offeror is expected to identify with specificity those needs as part of its proposal. The intent of the Contracts is that the offeror firm assumes full responsibility for the structure, planning, and implementation necessary to provide the required services to the City. Where the offeror anticipates needs that may occur which are not specifically set forth hereunder, the offeror is expected to identify with specificity those needs as part of its proposal.

3.1.2   It is anticipated that the proposal submitted hereunder shall, if awarded, be incorporated as an addendum to Exhibit "A" of the Contract between the offeror and the City to further define the scope of the offeror's services thereunder. Accordingly, all responses should be in a format suitable for incorporation into said Contract as an exhibit.

3.1.3   All services and duties must be operational as of the date of the award of the Contract by the City, should the City decide to make such award.

4.0   CITY ADMINISTRATIVE, FINANCIAL, AND COMMUNITY SERVICE REQUIREMENTS

4.1   ADMINISTRATIVE SERVICES

4.1.1   Administrative services shall include, but not be limited to the following.

4.1.2   **Contract Administration**

4.1.2.1   Assist the City Manager in negotiating City contracts, as directed by the City Manager.

4.1.2.2   Advise the City Manager on the status of negotiations as well as contract provisions and their impacts on the City.

4.1.2.3   Make recommendations on contract approval, rejection, amendment, renewal, and cancellation, as directed by the City Manager

4.1.2.4   Provide contract administration and supervision of all contracts, as directed by the City Manager.

4.1.2.5   Ensure ongoing protection of City interests.

4.1.2.6   Ensure compliance with all laws related to bidding, contracting and purchasing as set forth in the State of Georgia.

4.1.2.7   Assist and coordinate any necessary grant applications and submissions as directed by the City Manager.

4.1.3   **Policy Implementation**

4.1.3.1   Research current and likely future trends impacting the City.

4.1.3.2   Prepare administrative and financial analysis of all available options.

4.1.3.3   Attend all City Council meetings, hearing and agenda meetings, as directed by the City Manager.

4.1.3.4   Assist City Manager with identification of significant policies and analyze their administrative and financial impacts.

4.1.3.5   Prepare plans and procedures to ensure implementation of the City Council policies and directives, as directed by the City Manager.

4.1.3.6   Prepare status reports to advise the City Manager of the progress and results of public policy implementation.

4.1.4   **Daily Communications**

4.1.4.1   Respond to all inquires as directed.

4.1.4.2　　Prepare correspondence regarding City affairs for the City Manager and City Clerk, as requested.

4.1.4.3　　Ensure compliance with all Open Records and Open Meetings laws as set forth in O.C.G.A. § 50-14-1 et seq. and O.C.G.A. § 50-18-70 et seq. respectively.

4.1.5　　Customer Service

4.1.5.1　　Provide first-tier response to customer inquiries.

4.1.5.2　　Establish response protocols and direct customers to the appropriate party.

4.1.6　　Departmental Support

4.1.6.1　　Provide overall administrative support of all City Functions and departments.

4.1.7　　Clerking Support

4.1.7.1　　Record and transcribe all City Council meetings, hearing and agenda meetings.

4.1.7.2　　Assist City Clerk during Council meetings, take attendance, record motions and votes taken, and swear in witnesses of others presenting testimony to the Council.

4.1.7.3　　Assist in the review of documents to be presented to the Council, as directed by the City Manager.

4.1.7.4　　Upon City Clerk's absence, authenticate all City documents by appropriate signatures and City Seal.

4.1.7.5　　Retain public records and make them available for inspection by the public, in conformance with Georgia Law.

4.1.7.6　　Prepare all Council meeting agendas.

4.1.7.7　　Publish all appropriate public notices.

4.1.7.8　　Serve administrative needs of any and all Boards, Authorities or other entities established by the City for the furtherance of City objectives.

4.1.8   Records Management

4.1.8.1   Implement and maintain a custom-designed, state-of-the-art Document Management System to facilitate creating and saving all documents into the system (Word & Excel), then archiving these documents.

4.1.8.2   Improve employee productivity, collaboration, and document security by allowing the users to search for documents by profile information, content, person who created them, or even last person to edit the document. Users may also modify a previously created document for their use while leaving the original document unmodified.

4.1.8.3   Provide sufficient document scanning stations in City Hall so that any and all paper documents such as signed contracts, ordinances, resolutions, and other important City documents may be imported into the Document Management System using the Document Scanning Station.

4.1.8.4   Protect integrity of all public records in accordance with the requirements of State law.

4.1.8.5   Promote sharing of information and collaborative work between all City staff.

4.1.8.6   Provide an application server that will store and manage required data.

4.1.8.7   Provide and maintain access to data to other City contract providers as necessary.

4.1.8.8   Design state-of-the-art storage strategies and systems for all public records. Implement and coordinate the transfer of any and all necessary data, records, or other materials from Fulton County, Georgia as necessary for the operation of the City. This requirement must be met at the time of the award of the Contract by the City, if any.

4.1.9   Public Relations

4.1.9.1   Maintain continuous dialog and communications with City residents with timely updates, as directed by the City Manager.

4.1.9.2   Promote City policy, programs and achievements.

4.1.9.3 Serve as a liaison with residents, civic groups and other governments, as directed by the City Manager.

4.1.9.4 Document important City events for future use in City-developed publications.

4.1.10 Annual Reports

4.1.10.1 Develop a graphical and thematic design theme for the Annual Report, for approval by the City Manager.

4.1.10.2 Coordinate with the graphic designers, photographers, editors and others as necessary.

4.1.10.3 Provide effective written and non-written communications to reflect the year's message and inform residents of the City's actions and achievements.

4.1.10.4 Produce, print and deliver the annual reports to City residents.

4.1.11 City Website

4.1.11.1 Design and host the City website containing City contact information, statistics, history, departmental and facility description, Council meeting schedule, meeting agendas, agenda packages, minutes, City Codes, notices, and City in pictures and multimedia.

4.1.11.2 Update the site daily to post latest agendas, packages and minutes, notices, etc. and redesign the site annually.

4.1.11.3 Publish City-provided GIS database interface on the website.

4.1.12 City Newsletter

4.1.12.1 Provide text, pictures, graphics, maps, exhibits, etc. as necessary for the quarterly newsletter.

4.1.12.2 Coordinate with the publishers to produce a useful, informative, timely and attractive publication.

4.1.12.3 Produce, print and deliver a quality newsletter to all City residents.

4.1.13   Program Presentation

4.1.13.1   Publish studies, reports and analysis for staff and public presentation, as directed by the City Manager.

4.1.13.2   Prepare various media presentations of City programs to the staff and general public, as directed by the City Manager.

4.1.14   Information Technologies and Telephone Systems

4.1.14.1   Provide, install and maintain state-of-the-art information technology, software and hardware sufficient to efficiently satisfy all City needs.

4.1.14.2   Provide a state-of-the-art domain network to account for handling future growth and technologies.

4.1.14.3   Provide, install, configure and maintain a state-of-the-art server at City Hall and all City offices to improve performance ensure against data loss and minimize potential down time.

4.1.14.4   Provide centralized management of all network resources and a central location for the storage of the City's documents.

4.1.14.5   Ensure data security and integrity with a nightly backup (with offsite storage) and the ability to restore from a central location.

4.1.14.6   Provide, configure and maintain eight (10) state-of-the-art laptop computers to the members of the City Council (7), City Manager (2), and City Clerk (1).

4.1.14.7   Provide, install, configure and maintain state-of-the-art computer workstations, as needed.

4.1.14.8   Provide digital phones and remote connections for park sites.

4.1.14.9   Maintain software and hardware uniformity and interchangeability among users.

4.1.14.10   Provide, install and maintain sufficient network laser printers to efficiently conduct all City business.

4.1.14.11   Maintain a three-year replacement program for all computers and equipment.

4.1.14.12   Provide, install and maintain state-of-the-art network cabling/ data line system for communications, networking and data sharing.

4.1.14.13   Provide, install, configure and maintain servers in support of utility functions.

4.1.14.14   Provide all users with Internet and e-mail connections on a separate server for internal and external communications and common contact lists and scheduling.

4.1.14.15   Archive all e-mails in compliance with State retention requirements.

4.1.14.16   Provide, install and maintain a state-of-the-art telephone system in all City facilities with sufficient lines and features to satisfy all needs of the City.

4.1.15.   Databases – Municipal Management Software

4.1.15.1   Provide, install, configure and maintain a state-of-the-art database program to manage the City's occupational and business license functions

4.1.15.2   Coordinate the procurement, installation, configuration and maintenance of all databases required of municipalities in the State of Georgia by any governmental agencies.

4.1.16   Court Services

4.1.16.1   Provide all aspects of court record keeping and reporting as required by law and sound practices including but not limited to maintenance of calendars, recording of sentences and dispositions, coordination with probation services, coordination of collection of fees, fines and surcharges.

4.1.16.2   Provide adequate administrative personnel for Court hearings.

4.1.16.3   Oversee and maintain all systems required for fee, fine and surcharge accounting, reporting and remittance.

4.1.17   Police

4.1.17   Provide administrative and clerical assistance in all aspects of police department record keeping and reporting as required by law and sound practices in coordination with City authorities.

4.1.18   **Fire**

4.1.18   Provide administrative and clerical assistance in all aspects of fire department record keeping and reporting as required by law and sound practices in coordination with City authorities.

4.1.19   **Election Support**

4.1.19.1   Coordinate municipal and special elections as required, including but not limited to addressing polling station issues, preparation of ballot questions, or other related issues arising from election matters.

4.1.20   **Solid Waste**

4.1.20.1   Manage and coordinate all aspects of agreements with solid waste providers.

4.2   **FINANCIAL SERVICES**

4.2.1   Financial Services shall include, but not be limited to the following.

4.2.1   **Revenue Collection**

4.2.1.1   Coordinate with local, state and federal agencies charged with collection and disbursement of taxes, assessments, fees, charges and other impositions.

4.2.1.2   Administer the fees, charges and their miscellaneous revenues pertaining to utilities, private enterprises and individuals as they interface with the City programs.

4.2.1.3   Recommend enforcement actions to the City Manager to induce payment in accordance with the City's policies and procedures.

4.2.1.4   Prepare monthly financial reports showing revenues and expenses to date in comparison with budget projections and submit the reports to the City Manager no later than the tenth day of the following month.

4.2.1.5   Maintain a City address list for the Department of Revenue to ensure that the City obtains all shared revenues to which it is entitled.

4.2.2   **Capital Program Administration:**

4.2.2.1   Coordinate with the designated city representatives the capital needs of the City.

4.2.2.2   Obtain financing if necessary and maintain proper fund accounting procedures.

4.2.2.3   Administer and implement capital program financing.

4.2.3   **Investment Services**

4.2.3.1   Recommend investment policies and procedures pursuant to State law.

4.2.3.2   Invest City funds per approved policies.

4.2.3.3   Produce timely investment reports stating the effectiveness of the chosen investment policy.

4.2.4   **Fund Accounting**

4.2.4.1   Establish Fund Accounting System in accordance with Governmental Accounting Standards Board (GASB), the Uniform Accounting System prescribed by Department of Community Affairs and the rules of the Georgia Department of Audits and Accounts.

4.2.4.2   Prepare reports for Department of Community Affairs and State Revenue Department and distributions.

4.2.4.3   Prepare all other financial reports as required by applicable law and accounting standards.

4.2.5   **Accounts payable/receivable**

4.2.5.1   Administer the purchase order system and make timely payment of all invoices.

4.2.5.2   Coordinate tax collection, franchise fees, utility taxes and all other receivables.

4.2.6   **General fixed asset accounting**

4.2.6.1   Account for assets constructed by or donated to the City for maintenance.

4.2.6.2   Inventory City property in accordance with GASB and the Georgia Department of Audits and Accounts.

4.2.7   Budgeting:

4.2.7.1   Prepare and submit to the City Manager annual budgets per GASB standards.

4.2.7.2   Liaison with all City departments for annual budget categories.

4.2.7.3   Provide material for and attend all budget meetings, hearing and agenda meetings.

4.2.7.4   Coordinate with other departments and governmental entities as necessary.

4.2.7.5   Present findings in oral, print, multimedia, and web-based forms.

4.2.8   Forecasting:

4.2.8.1   Prepare detailed financial forecasts and analysis.

4.2.8.2   Identify trends and analyze their impact upon City's finances, operations and capital.

4.2.8.3   Develop policy and action recommendations.

4.2.8.4   Coordinate with other departments and governments.

4.2.8.5   Present findings in oral, print, multimedia, and web- based forms.

4.2.9   Comprehensive Annual Financial Report (CAFR):

4.2.9.1   Prepare the Annual Financial Report for Units of Local Government, in accordance with Generally Accepted Accounting Principals as defined by the Government Finance Officers Association.

4.2.10   Risk Management:

4.2.10.1   Recommend and advise the City Manager of the appropriate amounts and types of insurance and be responsible for procuring all necessary insurance.

4.2.10.2	Process and assist in the investigation of insurance claims, in coordination with the City Attorney.
4.2.10.3	Develop and maintain a risk management claims review procedure, in coordination with the City Manager and City Attorney.
4.2.10.4	Review insurance policies and coverage amounts of City vendors.

4.2.11 Human Resources:

4.2.11.1	Ensure proper functioning of payroll, fringe benefit, insurance tax and other City-specific and general law-provided human resources functions.
4.2.11.2	Establish a Code of Conduct for personnel that emphasize the responsibility of the staff to be professional, patient and responsive under all circumstances. The Code should emphasize that rudeness and impoliteness toward any person is unacceptable conduct and will not be tolerated.
4.2.11.3	Establish and implement with all employees an Employee Policies and Procedures Manual, which shall include, but not be limited to, policies and procedures on carrying out duties to the City, consequences of non-compliance to policies, and functions and roles of the employees.

4.2.12 Purchasing:

4.2.12.1	Recommend to the City Manager and assist in the implementation of procurement policies and procedures.
4.2.12.2	Assist in selection of vendors.
4.2.12.3	Participate in county and state level purchase plans.
4.2.12.4	Prepare RFP's, as directed by the City Manager.
4.2.12.5	Prepare and process requisitions.

4.2.13 HIPAA

4.2.13.1	Ensure that all City systems and procedures meet the requirements of HIPAA.

4.3   COMMUNITY SERVICES

4.3.1   Water Management and Utilities:

4.3.1.1   Manage and coordinate all aspects of intergovernmental relation-
              ship regarding water and sewer issues.

4.3.2   Animal Control

4.3.2.1   Provide field staff for the daily maintenance of animal control
              issues in the City.

5.0   EMERGENCY 911 SERVICE

5.1   Emergency 911 Infrastructure and Staffing

5.1.1   The offeror shall be responsible for implementing and staffing
              an emergency 911 system for the City in accordance with state
              law and in conjunction with any necessary vendors and local
              governmental entities. This proposal should include a detailed
              listing of any vendors which the offeror intends to use regarding
              the implementation of this system.

6.0   PHYSICAL PLANT REQUIREMENTS

6.1   Office, Administrative and Facilities Space

6.1.1   The offeror shall be responsible for providing facilities sufficient
              for the operations of all departments and functions the City on
              the date of acceptance of the proposal, whether or not offeror
              is responsible for said operations or function, if the Contract
              is awarded to offeror by the City. Said space should include
              but not be limited to All space shall meet all minimum GSA
              requirements, and exhibit a level of finish customary for a local
              government. Should offeror be the lessee of such space, offeror
              must have complied with all requirements for leasing said space
              as required by local governments under Georgia law, the lease
              shall be at a fair market value rental rate, and such lease shall
              provide for an unconditional assignment of such lease to the City
              of Sandy Springs exercisable by the unilateral determination of
              the City. Should offeror be the owner of such space, offeror shall
              allow the City of Sandy Springs the option to purchase said
              property at fair market value, with such option exercisable by the
              unilateral determination of the City. Should the City assume any

lease, or purchase any property as contemplated hereunder, there shall be no rent required of the offeror for the use of the space hereunder so long as said space is being devoted to purposes of the City. It is anticipated that the successful offeror will consult with the Commission pursuant to the terms set forth in this RFP, including at the Mandatory Pre-Proposal Conference, to coordinate the most beneficial space taking into consideration, cost effectiveness, location in the City, and other relevant factors.

6.2 Facilities Maintenance, Repair and Contracts

6.2.1 The offeror shall be responsible for providing personnel to maintain, repair, clean, and keep in good working order all facilities commensurate with local governmental standards all facilities occupied by the City. This provision, however, shall not apply to landscaping maintenance of any City rights-of-way or land.

6.3 Furniture, Fixtures, Equipment and Supplies

6.3.1 The offeror shall be responsible for providing Furniture, Fixtures, Equipment and Supplies in an amount sufficient for the reasonable operation of all departments and functions the City on the date of acceptance of the proposal, whether or not offeror is responsible for said operations or function, if the Contract is awarded to offeror by the City.

7.0 MOTOR VEHICLE REQUIREMENTS

7.1 The offeror shall be responsible for providing Motor Vehicles sufficient for the operations of all departments and functions the City on the date of acceptance of the proposal, whether or not offeror is responsible for said operations or function, if the Contract is awarded to offeror by the City. This requirement shall exclude any specialized service related emergency vehicles such as Police and/or Fire Emergency Vehicles; however the requirement will include sufficient vehicles for administrative necessities of said police and fire personnel.

7.2 The offeror shall submit a detailed Motor Vehicle Use and Safety Policy for the use of such vehicles by any staff of offeror sufficient to ensure that the City is protected regarding the use of said vehicles.

7.3   The offeror shall further be responsible for all maintenance, inspections, and other necessary service regarding said motor vehicles.

8.0   STAFFING REQUIREMENTS

8.1   General

8.1.1   Offeror shall provide with the Proposal a list of the proposed staffing requirements necessary to meet the needs for each of the services, duties, and/or functions outlined in Sections 4.0 et seq. through 9.0 et seq.. Offeror shall not, however, be responsible for staffing the City Parks and Recreation Department.

8.2   Key Positions

8.2.1   Regarding key positions, which shall include the proposed director of any department, the offeror shall provide a brief summary of said proposed key personnel's experience and qualifications for said position, provided, however that it shall be the duty of the offeror to assess the qualifications and skills of any proposed personnel and their suitability for the proposed positions. Offeror shall consider staffing recommendations of the Commission and subsequently the City, should the offer ultimately be accepted by the City. In addition, the proposal shall provide for the following position(s) setting out in detail the qualifications of the candidates for the following position(s):

1.1.1   Assistant City Manager

8.2.1.1   The Assistant City Manager shall have the responsibility working with the City Manager to coordinate and direct all of the activities set out in this RFP should it be accepted by the City. The Assistant City Manager will be a work closely with the City Manager and the City Council regarding all aspects of the offeror's activities should the offer be accepted by the City. Said Assistant City Manager   shall be the primary coordinator of all communications between the City and the offeror.

8.3   Subcontractors

8.3.1   Should the offeror intend to engage the services of any subcontractors regarding the delivery of services set forth herein, the name, address, and qualifications of such subcontractor shall be included in the proposal. Should the offeror include any subcontractors as potentially performing any of the services hereunder, the offeror shall affirmatively acknowledge as part of its proposal that the offeror shall be the sole entity to which the City shall look to for performance of the required services.

8.4	**Personnel**

8.4.1   The offeror shall include an affirmative statement in its proposal that it shall not knowingly engage in employment of, on any basis, any Commission member or committee members involved in the preparation of this RFP or in the selection and/or award process of this contract during the period of this contract. Once an offeror has been selected and a service contract negotiated, the names of those staff members who participated in this RFP process shall be provided to the service provider so that the requirements of this section can be implemented.

8.5	**Employment Practices**

8.5.1   The offeror shall include an affirmative statement in its proposal shall not discriminate against any employee or applicant for employment because of race, color, religion, sex, national origin, age, marital status, political affiliations, or disability. Such action shall include, but is not limited to the following: employment, promotion, demotion, transfer, recruitment or recruitment advertising, layoff or termination, rates of pay or other forms of compensation, and selection for training, including apprenticeship. Offeror agrees to post in conspicuous places, available to employees and applicants for employment, notices setting forth the provisions of this clause.

9.0	**PURCHASING, PROCUREMENT AND CONTRACTING**

9.1   The offeror shall include an affirmative statement in its proposal regarding the purchasing and/or procurement of any of the items set forth or required in the course of fulfilling the duties set forth in RFP, the offeror shall meet or exceed all laws and requirements regarding the same as set forth by the State of Georgia. Offeror shall also meet or exceed all laws and requirements regarding the same as set forth by the State of Georgia regarding any contracting required in the course of fulfilling the duties set forth in RFP.

10.0   PRICE QUOTATION

10.1   Each proposal shall include a price quote (Budget) for the required services as set forth herein for the year 2006, and a price for the year 2007. Each year shall be a separate quote and meet the requirements set forth herein. The price quotation for each year shall have two parts: (1) the quote shall break down with specificity the price for each general group of duties and obligations hereunder, by department and/or duty, and provide a total price for each delineated area of services, and (2) the quote shall further provide a summary page containing a total quote for all of the services requested in this RFP and a detail of the quote summarizing the components thereof in a succinct fashion. Said quote shall include a statement of the maximum percentage increase per year for any price escalation for the agreement for the years 2008, 2009 and 2010. This Quotation shall become Exhibit "C" to the Contract attached hereto, if awarded.

11.0   FORMAT OF RESPONSE

11.1   General

11.1.1   A responsive proposal shall be in accordance with Section 3.0 hereof and address each item as set forth in this RFP with specificity.

11.2   Required Sections

11.2.1   The response, shall generally follow the format as set forth below, however, the Commission shall, at its discretion, waive any deviation from this format should the offeror present an alternate format which provides sufficient detail and addresses all of the requirements as set forth in this RFP:

1.1.1.1   Response to Section 2.0 et seq. Request for Offeror Qualifications/ Assurances.

11.2.1.2   Presentation of proposed scope of services to conduct City Administrative, Financial and Community Service Requirements as set forth in Section 4.0 et seq.

11.2.1.3   Presentation of proposed scope of services to implement and conduct Emergency 911 Service Requirements as set forth in Section 5.0 et seq.

11.2.1.4   Proposed scope of services to conduct Physical Plant Requirements as set forth in Section 6.0 et seq.

11.2.2.5   Proposed scope of services to conduct Motor Vehicle Requirements as set forth in Section 7.0 et seq.

11.2.1.6   Proposed staffing requirements as set forth in Section 8.0 Et.seq. The response should include a proposed organizational chart setting out the structure of the offeror's staffing plan and all other requirements as set forth in said section in detail.

11.2.1.7   Proposed scope of services and statement of methodologies to conduct procurement, purchasing and contracting in conformance with Section 9.0 et seq.

11.2.1.8   A detailed start-up plan setting forth steps the offeror would take in order to meet all of the requirements for services and duties as set forth in this RFP on the date of the Award of the Contract by the City, should the City determine to award the same. The start-up plan should discuss with specificity how the proposal will meet the needs of the City. The plan should describe how the transition from Fulton County, Georgia to the offeror would be accomplished. The offeror should include start-up costs when calculating the prices submitted in the Price Quotation.

11.2.2   Of the 15 copies of the complete proposal, the proposal letter on one should contain the original manual signature of the person submitting the proposal on behalf of the offeror. All 15 copies should also contain the signer's name and title typed. The proposal letter shall clearly identify the complete legal name of the offeror. Each person signing a proposal certifies that he/she is the person in the offeror's organization authorized to make the proposal. The signer shall provide his/her affiliation with the offeror, address, telephone and fax numbers.

12.0   EVALUATION AND SELECTION PROCEDURE

12.1   General

12.1.1   The Commission will evaluate and select between the offerors in accordance with Georgia law.

12.2   Method of Evaluation

12.2.1   The Commission will rank the proposals by virtue of a points system with points being awarded in four (4) categories as follows: (1) Qualifications and Experience, (2) Previous Experience with Similar Services and Duties, (3) Start-up and Implementation Plan, and (4) Financial.

12.2.2   The Commission will award One Hundred (100) potential points based on the offeror's previous qualifications and experience including a review of all of the information and documentation requested in Section 2.0 et seq. above.

12.2.3   The Commission will award One Hundred (100) potential points based on the offeror's previous experience in providing similar services and duties including a review of all of the information and documentation requested in Section 2.0 et seq. above.

Service/Function	Point Scale
Administration	0 to 10
Accounting	0 to 20
Courts	0 to 5
Finance	0 to 10
Human Resources	0 to 10
IT	0 to 25
Police	0 to 10
Fire	0 to 10
Total	0 to 100

12.2.4   The Commission will award One Hundred (100) potential points based on the quality, detail and sufficiency of the offeror's start-up and implementation plan to have all of the required duties and services operational on the date of Contract Award by the City should the City decide to award the same. This analysis will also include an overall review of the entire proposal submitted by the offeror for quality, content, and detail.

12.2.5   The Commission will award One Hundred (100) points to the low bidder of the submitting offerors. Points for offerors submitting higher bids will be awarded in the following manner:

A ratio of the low bid dollars to the higher bid dollars will be calculated and multiplied by 100.

$$\frac{\text{Low Bid}}{\text{Higher Bid}} \times 100 \text{ Points} = \text{Higher Bid points}$$

12.3   Composite Score

12.3.1   The sum of the points for (1) Qualifications and Experience, (2) Previous Experience with Similar Services and Duties, (3) Start-up and Implementation Plan, and (4) Financial, will comprise the Composite Score. The maximum Composite Score is 400 Points.

APPENDIX C

SCOPE OF SERVICES
EXHIBIT "A"

AGREEMENT BY AND BETWEEN

CITY OF SANDY SPRINGS, GEORGIA

AND

FOR PROVISION OF

ADMINISTRATIVE, FINANCIAL COMMUNITY SERVICES, EMERGENCY 911, PHYSICAL PLANT, MOTOR VEHICLE, STAFFING, AND PURCHASING, PROCUREMENT AND CONTRACTING SERVICES

THIS AGREEMENT is made and entered into this _____ day of _____, 200__, by and between the CITY OF SANDY SPRINGS, a Georgia municipal corporation, (the "CITY"), and _____, a Georgia corporation ("Corporation").

WHEREAS, the City is desirous of maintaining a high level of competent professional and economically feasible contract administrative, finance and community services in conjunction and harmony with its fiscal policies of sound, economical management, and

WHEREAS, Corporation has agreed to render to the City a continuing high level of professional contract services and the City is desirous of contracting for such services upon the terms and conditions hereinafter set forth, and

WHEREAS the City is desirous of providing these daily services through a contractual relationship with Corporation,

NOW THEREFORE, in consideration of the sums hereinafter set forth and for other good and valuable considerations, the receipt and legal sufficiency of which are hereby acknowledged, it is hereby agreed as follows:

Section 1. PRIOR AGREEMENTS

As of the effective date hereof, all prior agreements between the City and Corporation are terminated and replaced by the terms hereof.

Section 2. GENERAL SERVICES

2.1   Corporation shall provide to City for the term hereinafter set forth, as the same may be extended in accordance with the provisions hereof, competent services, within and throughout the corporate limits of City to the extent and in the manner hereinafter described

2.2   The City hereby engages Corporation to provide, and Corporation hereby agrees to provide, all of the services described herein and in the "Scope of Services," attached hereto as Exhibit A and incorporated herein by reference.

2.3   The parties recognize that this Agreement is intended to provide flexibility to the City in order to meet its evolving challenges. Therefore, the Corporation shall provide any and all staffing to a level necessary to all said personnel to provide professional, competent services to the City as required under this Agreement.

2.4   Corporation agrees to provide City all services and personnel necessary to fulfill the obligations of Corporation under this contract.

2.5   Except as otherwise hereinafter specifically set forth, such professional services shall encompass all those duties and functions of the type coming within the jurisdiction of and customarily rendered by municipal departments (other than those provided by other contract providers) in accordance with the Charter of the City, and the Statutes of the State of Georgia.

2.6   Corporation shall, at all times, foster and maintain harmonious relationships with the members of the City Council, all employees of the City, all employees of the City's contract services providers and all City's residents, and shall represent the city in the best light possible.

2.7   All communications to the Mayor, City Council and press shall be through the City Manager. All mass communications to residents shall be reviewed and approved by the City Manager prior to printing and dissemination.

2.8   The President and/or Chief Executive Officer of Corporation shall be available to meet with the City Manager at City Hall on an annual basis and at any other times at the request of the City Manager.

Section 3.   FINANCIAL SERVICES

3.1   Corporation shall follow the procedures established by the City Manager for withdrawal, transfer and disbursement of City funds.

3.2   Corporation shall maintain all financial records in accordance with all applicable laws and guidelines for municipal accounting, including GAAP, GASB and GFOA standards, and shall produce and deliver to the City Manager any and all financial information and reports requested by the City Manager.

3.3   Corporation shall ensure that the City complies with all requirements regarding audits, and shall assist the City in procuring an auditor in compliance with all applicable laws and procedures.

3.4   All investments shall be made pursuant to any and all investment policies approved by the City Council in accordance with Georgia Statutes.

3.5   Corporation shall prepare and follow risk management policies and procedures, as adopted by the City Council.

3.6   Corporation shall take advantage of all available discounts on purchases and invoices for City purchases except when Corporation deems it is more favorable to the City based upon cash management practices.

3.7   Corporation shall promptly pay all City bills in accordance with Georgia law and sound business practices.

3.8   Corporation shall assist the City in finding and applying for various grants and in fulfilling all obligations that accompany such grants.

3.9   On or before the fifteenth day of each month, Corporation shall prepare and deliver to the City Manager a monthly financial statement for the prior month.

3.10   On or before October 1 of every year, Corporation shall prepare and deliver to the City Manager an annual inventory of all City owned tangible personal property and equipment in accordance with all applicable rules and standards.

Section 4.   ADDITIONAL SERVICES

4.1   Corporation shall provide to the City, upon the request of the City Manager and the availability of resources, such additional services as may from time to time be needed at the discretion of the City.

4.2   The cost of such additional services shall not be borne by the City and shall be payable in such amounts and in such a manner as may be determined by mutual agreement, upon each occurrence.

Section 5.   HOURS OF OPERATION

5.1   Corporation shall maintain fully staffed business hours equal to, but not less than, the City's business hours of 8 AM to 5 PM, Monday through Friday, with the exception of the following holidays:

New Year's Day
Martin Luther King Birthday
President's Day
Memorial Day

Independence Day
Labor Day
Veteran's Day
Thanksgiving Day
Day After Thanksgiving Day
Christmas

5.2   For all City related matters, Corporation shall use the address of Sandy Springs City Hall, including both incoming and outgoing mail.

Section 6. EQUIPMENT AND LABOR

6.1   Corporation shall furnish to and maintain for the benefit of the City, without additional cost, all necessary labor, supervision, equipment (including motor vehicles excluding, however, any specialized service related emergency vehicles such as Police and/or Fire Emergency Vehicles) necessary and proper for the purpose of performing the services, duties and responsibilities set forth and contemplated herein and as necessary to maintain the level of service to be rendered hereunder. In the event of emergencies or natural disasters, Corporation shall, immediately and on and on-going basis, supply its usual and customary personnel to ensure continuing operation of all services provided by Corporation and to satisfy all County, State and Federal administrative requirements.

6.2   All City owned equipment shall be used only for City purposes in performance of this Agreement, and shall not be used for any Corporation or personal purposes.

6.3   All City owned vehicles and equipment utilized by Corporation employees shall be maintained in strict accordance with manufacturer's recommended maintenance, and Corporation shall keep full records of all maintenance. All City vehicles shall be kept clean, free of damages and in safe operating condition. All City vehicles shall be used in strict conformance with the Vehicle Use Policy attached hereto as Exhibit B.

6.4   Corporation shall comply with all OSHA and other applicable standards for work place safety. Corporation shall comply with all applicable laws regarding hazardous materials and maintain all required Manufacturer's Safety Data Sheets (MSDS) forms on site in the City.

6.5   During regular business hours, all telephones at Corporation shall be answered by human, not automated, attendants.

Section 7.   CORPORATION EMPLOYEES

7.1   All personnel employed by Corporation in the performance of such services, functions and responsibilities as described and contemplated herein for the City shall be and remain Corporation employees (the "Corporation Employees").

7.2   Corporation shall be solely responsible for all compensation benefits, insurance and rights of the Corporation employees during the course of employment with Corporation. Accordingly, the City shall not be called upon to assume any liability for or direct payment of any salaries, wages, contribution to pension funds, insurance premiums or payments, workers compensation benefits under O.C.G.A. §34-9-1 et seq., or any other amenities of employment to any of the Corporation Employees or any other liabilities whatsoever, unless otherwise specifically provided herein.

7.3   In conformance with standards established by City, Corporation shall have and maintain the responsibility for and control of the rendition of the services, the standards of performance, the discipline of the Corporation Employees and other matters incident to the performance of the services, duties and responsibilities as described and contemplated herein.

7.4   In order to perform its obligations hereunder, certain Corporation Employees will be assigned to work full-time for the City (the "Designated Employees"). The Designated Employees shall work for the City full-time and shall perform no work for other Corporation clients. Prior to assigning any Designated Employees to the City, Corporation shall subject each prospective Designated Employee to a full background check, including a driver's license review.

7.5   The Corporation Employees shall wear attire with the logo of the City when, and only when, they are performing services for the City, except as otherwise directed by the City Manager.

7.6   The City Manager shall have the right to require Corporation to transfer any of the Designated Employees out of the City, for any reason or no reason. Other than the Assistant City Manager (which is governed by Section 8 below), Corporation agrees to transfer any of the Designated Employees immediately upon notification by the City Manager. The City Manager shall have the right to prohibit any Corporation Employee that is not a Designated Employee from performing any work for the City, and shall also have the right to limit, in any manner, the work done for the City by and Corporation Employee that is not a Designated Employee.

7.7   Corporation shall have the discretion to transfer or reassign any personnel out of the City for the following reasons:

   a.   Situations where an employee requests a transfer in order to accept a promotion or special assignment, which has been offered to him or her by Corporation upon his or her special education qualifications or career path;

   b.   Disciplinary reasons;

   c.   Failure of an employee to meet Corporation performance standards;

   d.   At the request of the employee.

In the event Corporation transfers or reassigns any employee for the above stated reasons, Corporation shall provide the City Manager with prompt written notice of such transfer or reassignment and explain the basis of the reassignment. Corporation shall not transfer or reassign any of the Corporation Employees for any other reason unless the City Manager concurs prior to any transfer, which concurrence shall not be unreasonably withheld. Any personnel, transferred or reassigned out of the City, pursuant to this subsection, shall not occur without first filling the vacated position as authorized by the City Manager, which shall not be unreasonably withheld.

Section 8.   ASSISTANT CITY MANAGER

8.1   The Assistant City Manager shall, among other duties specified by the City Manager:

a. Act as liaison between the City and Corporation;

b. Attend staff meetings, City Council meetings and any agenda meetings, at which attendance by the Assistant City Manager is deemed necessary by the City Manager. Attend other County and State agency meetings and forums as required by the City Manager;

c. Provide information to City Manager and City Council on all relevant and applicable issues;

d. Assist the City in all relations with other Contractors;

e. Serve as the Acting City Manager, at no additional cost to the City, when so designated by the City Manager.

8.2   In the event of a vacancy in the position of the Assistant City Manager, Corporation agrees to make such selections in good faith and in the best interest of the City. The City Manager shall have the opportunity to interview each of the candidates, and no person may be appointed Assistant City Manager without the City Manager's consent, which may be withheld for any reason or no reason, in City Manager's sole discretion.

8.3   In the event the City Manager becomes dissatisfied with the performance of the Assistant City Manager, the City Manager may, in its sole discretion, provide notification to Corporation. Thereafter, representatives of Corporation and the City Manager shall meet to discuss possible remedies of the problems experienced by the City. Corporation agrees to act in good faith in resolving any problems experienced by the City.

Section 9. CONSIDERATION

9.1   The City shall, on a monthly basis, no later than thirty (30) days following the completion of the month, pay to Corporation, in consideration for the stated services and responsibilities, 1/12th of the total amount of yearly compensation for the instant year contained in the Compensation Schedule attached hereto as Exhibit B, including any amendment to said schedule for subsequent years as provided for herein (The "Compensation Amount").

9.2   For each Fiscal Year, beginning January 1, 2008, the Compensation Amount payable to Corporation under the Terms and Conditions of this Agreement shall be in an amount agreed to by the City Manager and Corporation, and approved by the City Council, provided, however, under no circumstances shall the price increase more than _____ percent (_____ %) over the price of the prior year. Corporation shall provide to the City Manager a proposed new Exhibit B each year along with the proposed budget.

9.3   If, during any fiscal year, there is a reduction in the scope of services as directed by the City Manager, the Compensation Amount shall be reduced by an amount agreeable to the City Manager and Corporation, but in no event shall the reduction be an amount less than the actual cost, allocated overhead and profit to Corporation of providing the eliminated service. If the City Manager and Corporation are unable to agree upon an amount, the reduction in the Compensation Amount shall be equal to the actual cost, allocated overhead and profit to Corporation of providing the eliminated service. The Compensation Amount may not be increased in any fiscal year without the approval of the City Council.

Section 10. TERM

This Service Agreement shall remain in full force and effect commencing on January 1, 2006 and shall terminate on December 31, 2006.

Section 11. OPTION TO RENEW

This Agreement shall be automatically renewed for a period of five (5) one (1) year terms at the expiration of the initial term, unless the City furnishes Corporation affirmative written notice of its intent not to renew this Agreement not less than thirty (30) days prior to the expiration of this Agreement.

Section 12. TERMINATION

12.1   Corporation may terminate this Service Agreement at its discretion either with or without cause, by giving written notice thereof to City; provided, however, that such termination shall not be effective until the one hundred and eightieth (180th) day after receipt thereof by City.

12.2   City may terminate this Service Agreement in its entirety at its
           discretion either with or without cause, by giving written notice
           thereof to Corporation; provided, however, that such termina-
           tion shall not be effective until the one hundred and eightieth
           (180th) day after receipt thereof by Corporation. City may also
           terminate this Service Agreement in its entirety, at its discretion
           with no advance notice, in the event of a transfer of a controlling
           interest in Corporation (which shall be defined to mean more
           than 50% of the ownership interest) to a non-related entity.
           Corporation shall notify the City Manager immediately upon
           the transfer of a controlling interest in Corporation.

12.3   City may partially terminate this Service Agreement as to any
           specific service or services provided by Corporation hereunder
           by giving at least sixty (60) days advance written notice thereof
           to Corporation specifying the specific service or services that the
           City desires Corporation to cease performing. Upon a partial
           termination, the Compensation Amount shall be reduced pursu-
           ant to Section 9.3 of this Agreement.

12.4   In the event of termination by either party, the other party
           shall render such aid, coordination and cooperation as might be
           required for an expeditious and efficient termination of service.

Section 13. DEFAULT

13.1   An event of default shall mean a breach of this Agreement.
           Without limiting the generality of the foregoing and in addition
           to those instances referred to as a breach, an event of default shall
           include the following:

           a. Corporation has not performed services on a timely basis;

           b. Corporation has refused or failed, except in the case for
               which an extension of time is provided, to supply enough
               properly skilled Staff personnel;

           c. Corporation has failed to obtain the approval of the City
               where required by this Agreement;

           d. Corporation has refused or failed, except in the case for
               which an extension of time is provided, to provide the
               Services as defined in this Agreement.

13.2   In the event Corporation fails to comply with the provisions of this Agreement, the City may declare Corporation in default, notify Corporation in writing, and give Corporation fifteen (15) calendar days to cure the default. If Corporation fails to cure the default, compensation will only be for any completed professional services minus any damages pursuant to Section 13.3. In the event payment has been made for such professional services not completed, Corporation shall return these sums to the City within ten (10) days after notice that these sums are due. Nothing in this Article shall limit the City's right to terminate, at any time, pursuant to Sections 11 and 12, its right for damages under Section 13.3, and its right to assign pursuant to Section 38.

13.3   In an Event of Default by Corporation, it shall be liable for all damages resulting from the default.

13.4   The City may take advantage of each and every remedy specifically existing at law or in equity. Each and every remedy shall be in addition to every other remedy specifically given or otherwise existing and may be exercised from time to time as often and in such order as may be deemed expedient by the City. The exercise or the beginning of the exercise of one remedy shall not be deemed to be a waiver of the right to exercise any other remedy. The City's rights and remedies as set forth in this Agreement are not exclusive and are in addition to any other rights and remedies available to the City in law or in equity.

Section 14. TRANSITION

14.1   In the event of the full termination, partial termination or expiration of this Agreement, Corporation and City shall cooperate in good faith in order to effectuate a smooth and harmonious transition from Corporation to City, or to any other person or entity City may designate, and to maintain during such period of transition the same high quality services otherwise afforded to the residents of the City pursuant to the terms hereof.

14.2   In the event of the full termination, partial termination or expiration of this Agreement, the City shall have the absolute right to hire any of the Corporation Employees, without the consent of, or any liability, to Corporation.

14.3   In the event of the full termination, partial termination or expiration of this Agreement, and in the further event that the City is unable to provide the same level of services at the time of such termination or expiration, the then pending term of this Agreement may be extended by the City for a period of ninety (90) days or until City is capable, in its sole discretion, of rendering such service, whichever occurs sooner. The remuneration to be paid to Corporation during the transition period shall be based upon the actual cost of providing such services during the transition period.

Section 15. INDEMNIFICATION

15.1   Corporation shall indemnify, defend and hold harmless the City, its officers, agents, servants and employees from and against any and all liability, suits, actions, damages, costs, losses and expenses, including attorneys' fees, demands and claims for personal injury, bodily injury, sickness, diseases or death or damage or destruction of tangible property, arising out of any errors, omissions, misconduct or negligent acts, errors, or omissions of Corporation, its officials, agents, employees or subcontractors in the performance of the services of Corporation under this Agreement, whether direct or indirect and from and against any orders, judgments, or decrees which may be entered thereon and from and against all costs, damages of every kind and nature, attorneys' fees, expenses and liabilities incurred in and about the defense of any such claim and investigation thereof.

15.2   Corporation acknowledges that specific consideration has bee paid or will be paid under this Agreement for this hold harmless and indemnification provision, and further agrees with the foregoing provisions of indemnity and with the collateral obligation of insuring said indemnity as set forth In Section 16, Insurance.

Section 16. INSURANCE

16.1   Corporation shall not commence work under this contract until Corporation has obtained all insurance required under this paragraph and such insurance has been approved by the City Manager.

16.2   Corporation shall at all times carry professional liability insur-
            ance, workers' compensation insurance, comprehensive general
            liability insurance, and automotive liability insurance with policy
            limits and deductibles for each coverage at amounts reasonably
            approved by the City Manager, with such coverages specifying
            reasonable amounts of per occurrence, single limit, for prop-
            erty damage and bodily injury, including death, except that the
            dollar amount of workers compensation coverage shall be as
            provided by O.C.G.A. § 34-9-1 et. seq. Corporation shall be
            responsible for maintaining this professional liability insurance
            for a minimum of three (3) years from the date of expiration of
            this Agreement. Upon request of City, Corporation shall make
            available for inspection copies of any claims filed or made against
            any policy during the policy term. Corporation shall addition-
            ally notify City, in writing, within thirty (30) calendar days, of
            any claims filed or made against any policy in excess of $5,000
            during the policy term.

16.3   Certificates of insurance, reflecting evidence of the required
            insurance, shall be filed with the City Manager or designee
            prior to the commencement of the work. Policies shall be issued
            by companies authorized to do business under the laws of the
            State of Georgia, with financial ratings acceptable to the City
            Manager. The City shall be named as an additional insured on
            all insurance policies. Corporation agrees to furnish City with
            at least thirty (30) days prior written notice of any cancellation
            of any insurance policy required under this Agreement.

16.4   In the event the insurance certificate provided indicates that the
            insurance shall terminate and lapse during the period of this
            contract, then in that event, Corporation shall furnish, at least
            ten (10) days prior to the expiration of the date of such insur-
            ance, a renewed certificate of insurance as proof that equal and
            like coverage for the balance of the period of the contract and
            extension hereunder is in effect. Corporation shall not continue
            to work pursuant to this contract unless all required insurance
            remains in full force and effect.

16.5   The costs of all policies of insurance required hereunder shall be
            the obligation of Corporation and the City shall in no way be
            responsible therefore.

16.6   City shall pay for and maintain its own comprehensive general liability insurance or maintain a self-insuring fund for the term of this Agreement in the amount determined by City to adequately insure the City's liability assumed herein, but in no event shall coverage be less than the amount of statutory waiver of sovereign immunity. In the event such coverage is modified, in any regard, before the expiration date of this Agreement, and unless otherwise agreed, City will provide at least thirty (30) days prior written notice to Corporation.

Section 17. CONFLICTS OF INTEREST/COLLUSION/ CONTINGENT FEES

17.1   Corporation shall not review or perform any services regarding any application made to the City by any client of Corporation, unless the eservices Corporation performs for such client are unrelated to the City. In such instance, Corporation shall disclose the relationship immediately to the City Manager, who may retain an alternate to Corporation for those services. If the services relate to a fixed fee service, the fees for the alternate to Corporation shall be deducted from the fixed fee paid to Corporation.

17.2   Neither Corporation nor any of its employees shall have or hold any employment or contractual relationship that is antagonistic or incompatible with Corporation's loyal and conscientious exercise of judgment related to its performance under this Agreement.

17.3   Neither Corporation nor any of its officers or employees shall obtain any kickbacks or benefits for itself, themselves or other clients as a result of any City purchases or transactions.

17.4   Corporation shall not collude or enter into any business relationships with other City contract providers regarding City business or matters, without the approval of the City Manager, which may be withheld at the City Manager's sole discretion.

17.5   Corporation warrants that it has not employed or retained any company or person, other than a bona fide employee working solely for Corporation, to solicit or secure this Agreement, and that it has not paid or agreed to pay any person, company, corporation, individual or firm, other than a bona fide employee working solely for Corporation, any fee, commission, percentage, gift, or other consideration contingent upon or resulting from the award or making of this Agreement. For the breach or violation of this provision, the City shall have the right to terminate the Agreement without liability at its discretion, to deduct from the contract price, or otherwise recover the full amount of such fee, commission, percentage, gift or consideration.

Section 18. POLICY OF NON-DISCRIMINATION

Corporation shall not discriminate against any person in its operations, activities or delivery of services under this Agreement. Corporation shall affirmatively comply with all applicable provisions of federal, state and local equal employment laws and shall not engage in or commit any discriminatory practice against any person based on race, age, religion, color, gender, sexual orientation, national origin, marital status, physical or mental disability, political affiliation or any other factor which cannot be lawfully used as a basis for service delivery.

Section 19. DRUG FREE WORKPLACE

Corporation shall maintain a Drug Free Workplace.

Section 20. INDEPENDENT CONTRACTOR

Corporation, for the purposes of this Service Agreement, is and shall remain an independent contractor; not an employee, agent, or servant of the City. Personal services provided by Corporation shall be by employees of Corporation and subject to supervision by Corporation, and not as officers or employees of City. Personnel policies, tax responsibilities, social security and health insurance, employee benefits, and other similar administrative procedures applicable to services rendered under this Agreement shall be those of Corporation.

Section 21. COSTS AND ATTORNEY'S FEES

If the City is required to enforce the terms of this Agreement by court proceedings or otherwise, whether or not formal legal action is required, the Corporation shall pay the attorney's fees and costs of both the City and the Corporation.

Section 22. RIGHTS IN DATA; COPYRIGHTS; DISCLOSURE

22.1   Definition. The term "Data" as used in this Agreement includes written reports, studies, drawings, or other graphic, electronic, chemical or mechanical representation.

22.2   Rights in Data. Drawings, specifications, designs, models, photographs, computer CADD discs, reports, surveys and other data developed or provided in connection with this Agreement shall be the property of City and City shall have the full right to use such data for any official purpose permitted under Georgia Statutes, including making it available to the general public. Such use shall be without any additional payment to or approval by Corporation. City shall have unrestricted authority to publish, disclose, distribute and otherwise use, in whole or in part, any data developed or prepared under this Agreement.

22.3   Copyrights. No data developed or prepared in whole or in part under this Agreement shall be subject to copyright in the United States of America or other country, except to the extent such copyright protection is available for the City. Corporation shall not include in the data any copyrighted matter unless Corporation obtains the written approval of the City Manager and provides said City Manager with written permission of the copyright owner for Corporation to use such copyrighted matter in the manner provided herein.

22.4   If this Agreement is terminated for any reason prior to completion of the work, the City may, in its discretion, use any design and documents prepared hereunder.

Section 23. COMPLIANCE WITH LAWS; ADVICE OF OTHER PROFESSIONALS

23.1   Corporation shall fully obey and comply with all laws, ordinances and administrative regulations duly made in accordance therewith, which are or shall become applicable to the services performed under the terms of this Agreement.

23.2   Corporation acknowledges that the City is advised by its City Attorney and that, on all legal matters, Corporation shall abide by the advice and direction of the City Attorney in the performance of its duties as they relate to matters of the City.

23.3   Corporation acknowledges that the City is also advised by various other professionals (including, but not limited to, engineers, traffic engineers, planners, building officials, police officers and firefighters), and that, on all matters within their respective expertise, Corporation shall abide by their advice and direction in the performance of its duties as they relate to matters of the City.

Section 24. OWNERSHIP OF WORK PRODUCT DOCUMENTS

24.1   All work product prepared by Corporation for the City shall immediately become the property of the City.

24.2   Corporation understands and agrees that any information, document, report or any other material whatsoever which is given by the City to Corporation or which is otherwise obtained or prepared by Corporation under the terms of this Agreement is and shall at all times remain the property of the City.

Section 25. AUDIT AND INSPECTION RIGHTS

25.1   The City may, at reasonable times, and for a period of up to three (3) years following the date of final performance of Services by Corporation under this Agreement, audit, or cause to be audited, those books and records of Corporation that are related to Corporation's performance under this Agreement. Corporation agrees to maintain all such books and records at its principal place of business for a period of three (3) years after final payment is made under this Agreement. Corporation shall make all necessary books and records available for audit in Fulton County, Georgia.

25.2   The City may, at reasonable times during the term hereof, inspect Corporation's facilities and perform such inspections, as the City deems reasonably necessary, to determine whether the services required to be provided by Corporation under this Agreement conform to the terms of this Agreement. Corporation shall make available to the City all reasonable facilities and assistance to facilitate the performance of inspections by the City's representatives.

Section 26. WARRANTIES OF CORPORATION

Corporation hereby warrants and represents that at all times during the term of this Agreement it shall maintain in good standing all required licenses, certifications, and permits required under federal, state and local laws necessary to perform the Services.

Section 27. PUBLIC RECORDS

Corporation understands that the public shall have access, at all reasonable times, to all documents and information pertaining to the City, subject to the provision of O.C.G.A. §50-14-1 et seq., and agrees to allow access by the City and the public to all documents subject to disclosure under applicable law. Corporation's failure or refusal to comply with the provisions of this Section shall result in the immediate termination of this Agreement by the City. Corporation agrees to retain all public records in accordance with the City's records retention and disposal policies, O.C.G.A. 50-18-92 et. seq., and the Georgia Administrative Code.

Section 28. GOVERNING LAW; CONSENT TO JURISDICTION

This Agreement shall be construed in accordance with and governed by the laws of the State of Georgia. The parties submit to the jurisdiction of any Georgia state or federal court in any action or proceeding arising out of, or relating to, this Agreement. Venue of any action to enforce this Agreement shall be in Fulton County, Georgia.

Section 29. HEADINGS

Headings are for the convenience of reference only and shall not be considered in any interpretation of this Agreement.

Section 30. SEVERABILITY

If any provision of this Agreement or the application thereof to any person or situation shall, to any extent, be held invalid or unenforceable, the remainder of this Agreement, and the application of such provisions to persons or situations other than those as to which it shall have been held invalid or unenforceable, shall not be affected thereby, and shall continue in full force and effect, and be enforced to the fullest extent permitted by law.

Section 31. CONFLICT

In the event of a conflict between the terms of this Agreement and any terms or conditions contained in any attached documents, the terms in this Agreement shall prevail.

Section 32. SURVIVAL OF PROVISIONS

Any terms or conditions of this Agreement that require acts beyond the date of its termination shall survive the termination of this Agreement, shall remain in full force and effect unless and until the terms of conditions are completed, and shall be fully enforceable by either party.

Section 33. ENTIRE AGREEMENT

33.1 This Agreement and its attachments constitute the entire agreement between Corporation and City, and all negotiations and oral understandings between the parties are merged herein.

33.2 No modification, amendment or alteration in the terms or conditions of this Agreement shall be effective unless contained in a written document executed with the same formality as this Agreement.

Section 34. WAIVER

The waiver by either party of any failure on the part of the other party to perform in accordance with any of the terms or conditions of this Agreement shall not be construed as a waiver of any future or continuing similar or dissimilar failure.

Section 35. EQUIPMENT APPRAISAL AND TRANSFER

35.1 In the event of full termination, partial termination or expiration of this Agreement, City shall have the option to purchase from Corporation any piece of equipment, directly attributable to or in use by Corporation in the City at the time of such termination or expiration in connection with the services contemplated herein, or, as to a partial termination, in connection with the eliminated services.

35.2 The purchase price for such equipment shall be determined by mutual agreement of the parties as to the fair market value of such equipment.

35.3 Upon the exercise by the City of its option to possess the subject equipment, Corporation shall convey within ten (10) days or upon such other mutually agreed time, all of its rights, title and interest, thereto, to the City by Bill of Sale Absolute or Certificate of Title, as applicable.

Section 36. AUTHORITY TO EXECUTE: NO CONFLICT CREATED

36.1   Corporation by execution hereof does hereby represent to City that Corporation has full power and authority to make and execute this Service Agreement, to the effect that:

a.   The making and execution hereof shall create a legal obligation upon Corporation, which shall be legally binding upon Corporation.

b.   The same shall be enforceable by the City according and to the extent of the provisions hereof.

36.2   Nothing contained or any obligation on the part of Corporation to be performed hereunder shall in any way be contrary to or in contravention of any policy of insurance or surety bond required of Corporation pursuant to the laws of the State of Georgia.

36.3   Corporation shall perform this Agreement only under the name of _____.

36.4   The City Manager, Mayor and City Clerk, by their respective executions hereof, do each represent to Corporation that they, collectively, have full power and authority to make and execute this Service Agreement on behalf of the City, pursuant to the Resolution of the City Council of the City.

36.5   Nothing herein contained is intended in any way to be contrary to or in contravention of the Charter of the City and the Laws of the State of Georgia, and to the extent such conflict exists; the City and Corporation shall be mutually relieved of any obligations of such conflict.

36.6   In the event of any litigation arising from this Agreement, venue shall be in Fulton County, Georgia.

Section 37. NOTICES

Whenever either party desires to give notice to the other, it must be given by written notice, sent by certified United States mail, with return receipt requested, hand delivered or by facsimile transmission with proof of receipt, addressed to the party for whom it is intended, at the place last specified, and the place for giving of notice in compliance with the provisions of this paragraph. Notice shall be deemed given upon receipt by any method of delivery authorized above. For the present, the parties designate the following as the respective places for giving of notice:

For Corporation

For City:

Section 38. ASSIGNABILITY

Corporation shall not assign any of the obligations or benefits imposed hereby or contained herein, without the written consent of the City Council of the City, which consent must be evidenced by a duly passed Resolution. This contract for services is partially and/or fully assignable by the City on sixty (60) days notice to Corporation. Notice of Assignment shall be mailed via U.S. Mail, return receipt requested and any notice required hereunder shall be addressed to the party intended to receive the same at the addresses noted in Section 38. In the event that the City exercises its option to assign this agreement pursuant to this section, the City is not obligated to provide the Notice of Termination identified in Section 12 of this contract. However, Corporation shall coordinate and cooperate with the City as may be required for expeditious and efficient assignment of service pursuant to this article. In addition, Corporation shall transition this contract pursuant to this section in accordance with Section 14 of this Agreement.

Section 39. ENTIRE AGREEMENT; AMENDMENT

The parties acknowledge, one to the other, that the terms hereof constitute the entire understanding and agreement of the parties with respect hereof. No modification hereof shall be effective unless in writing, executed with the same formalities as this Agreement is executed.

Section 40. NEGOTIATION

The parties acknowledge that the terms of this Agreement were jointly negotiated between the parties, that both parties were represented by attorneys and that, in the case of any dispute regarding the terms of this Agreement, the terms should not be construed in favor of or against either party.

Section 41. BINDING EFFECT

This agreement shall inure to the benefit of and be binding upon the respective parties' successors.

AGREEMENT BY AND BETWEEN CORPORATION AND THE CITY OF SANDY SPRINGS FOR CONTRACT SERVICES AS SET FORTH HEREIN.

IN WITNESS WHEREOF, the parties hereto have caused their respective agents to execute this instrument on their behalf, at the times set forth below.

CORPORATION

_____   _____
By: DATE

ATTEST

_____   _____
                                     DATE

CITY OF SANDY SPRINGS

_____   _____
By: DATE
Mayor and Chair

_____   _____
By: DATE
City Manager

_____   _____
By: DATE
City Clerk

Approved as to form and legal
Sufficiency subject to execution
by the parties

_____   _____
By: DATE
City Attorney

AGREEMENT BY AND BETWEEN CORPORATION AND THE CITY OF SANDY SPRINGS.

INDEX TO EXHIBITS

Exhibit "A"   Scope of Services

Exhibit "B"   Vehicle Use Policy

Exhibit "C"   Compensation Amount

AGREEMENT BY AND BETWEEN CORPORATION AND THE CITY OF SANDY SPRINGS.

EXHIBIT "A"

SCOPE OF SERVICES

Services include, but are not limited to the following:

1.1   ADMINISTRATIVE SERVICES

Administrative services shall include, but not be limited to the following.

1.1.1   Contract Administration

1.1.1.1   Assist the City Manager in negotiating City contracts, as directed by the City Manager.

1.1.1.2   Advise the City Manager on the status of negotiations as well as contract provisions and their impacts on the City.

1.1.1.3   Make recommendations on contract approval, rejection, amendment, renewal, and cancellation, as directed by the City Manager

1.1.1.4   Provide contract administration and supervision of all contracts, as directed by the City Manager.

1.1.1.5   Ensure ongoing protection of City interests.

1.1.1.6   Ensure compliance with all laws related to bidding, contracting and purchasing as set forth in the State of Georgia.

1.1.1.7   Assist and coordinate any necessary grant applications and submissions as directed by the City Manager.

1.1.2   Policy Implementation

1.1.2.1   Research current and likely future trends impacting the City.

1.1.2.2   Prepare administrative and financial analysis of all available options.

1.1.2.3   Attend all City Council meetings, hearing and agenda meetings, as directed by the City Manager.

1.1.2.4   Assist City Manager with identification of significant policies and analyze their administrative and financial impacts.

1.1.2.5   Prepare plans and procedures to ensure implementation of the City Council policies and directives, as directed by the City Manager.

1.1.2.6   Prepare status reports to advise the City Manager of the progress and results of public policy implementation.

1.1.3   Daily Communications

1.1.3.1   Respond to all inquires as directed.

1.1.3.2   Prepare correspondence regarding City affairs for the City Manager and City Clerk, as requested.

1.1.3.3   Ensure compliance with all Open Records and Open Meetings laws as set forth in O.C.G.A. § 50-14-1 et seq. and O.C.G.A. § 50-18-70 et seq. respectively.

1.1.4   Customer Service

1.1.4.1   Provide first-tier response to customer inquiries.

1.1.4.2   Establish response protocols and direct customers to the appropriate party.

1.1.5   Departmental Support

1.1.5.1   Provide overall administrative support of all City functions and departments.

1.1.6   Clerking Support

1.1.6.1   Record and transcribe all City Council meetings, hearing and agenda meetings.

1.1.6.2   Assist City Clerk during Council meetings, take attendance, record motions and votes taken, and swear in witnesses of others presenting testimony to the Council.

1.1.6.3   Assist in the review of documents to be presented to the Council, as directed by the City Manager.

1.1.6.4   Upon City Clerk's absence, authenticate all City documents by appropriate signatures and City Seal.

1.1.6.5   Retain public records and make them available for inspection by the public, in conformance with Georgia Law.

1.1.6.6   Prepare all Council meeting agendas.

1.1.6.7   Publish all appropriate public notices.

1.1.6.8   Serve administrative needs of any and all Boards, Authorities or other entities established by the City for the furtherance of City objectives.

1.1.7   Records Management

1.1.7.1   Implement and maintain a custom-designed, state-of-the-art Document Management System to facilitate creating and saving all documents into the system (Word & Excel), then archiving these documents.

1.1.7.2   Improve employee productivity, collaboration, and document security by allowing the users to search for documents by profile information, content, person who created them, or even last person to edit the document. Users may also modify a previously created document for their use while leaving the original document unmodified.

1.1.7.3   Provide sufficient document scanning stations in City Hall so that any and all paper documents such as signed contracts, ordinances, resolutions, and other important City documents may be imported into the Document Management System using the Document Scanning Station.

1.1.7.4   Protect integrity of all public records in accordance with the requirements of State law.

1.1.7.5   Promote sharing of information and collaborative work between all City staff.

1.1.7.6   Provide an application server that will store and manage required data.

1.1.7.7   Provide and maintain access to data to other City contract providers as necessary.

1.1.7.8   Design state-of-the-art storage strategies and systems for all public records. Implement and coordinate the transfer of any and all necessary data, records, or other materials from Fulton County, Georgia as necessary for the operation of the City.

1.1.8   Public Relations

1.1.8.1   Maintain continuous dialog and communications with City residents with timely updates, as directed by the City Manager.

1.1.8.2   Promote City policy, programs and achievements.

1.1.8.3   Serve as a liaison with residents, civic groups and other governments, as directed by the City Manager.

1.1.8.4   Document important City events for future use in City-developed publications.

1.1.9   Annual Reports

1.1.9.1   Develop a graphical and thematic design theme for the Annual Report, for approval by the City Manager.

1.1.9.2   Coordinate with the graphic designers, photographers, editors and others as necessary.

1.1.9.3   Provide effective written and non-written communications to reflect the year's message and inform residents of the City's actions and achievements.

1.1.9.4   Produce, print and deliver the annual reports to City residents.

1.1.10   City Website

1.1.10.1   Design and host the City website containing City contact information, statistics, history, departmental and facility description, Council meeting schedule, meeting agendas, agenda packages, minutes, City Codes, notices, and City in pictures and multimedia.

1.1.10.2   Update the site daily to post latest agendas, packages and minutes, notices, etc. and redesign the site annually.

1.1.10.3   Publish City-provided GIS database interface on the website.

1.1.11   City Newsletter

1.1.11.1   Provide text, pictures, graphics, maps, exhibits, etc. as necessary for the quarterly newsletter.

1.1.11.2	Coordinate with the publishers to produce a useful, informative, timely and attractive publication.
1.1.11.3	Produce, print and deliver a quality newsletter to all City residents.

1.1.12   **Program Presentation**

1.1.12.1	Publish studies, reports and analysis for staff and public presentation, as directed by the City Manager.
1.1.12.2	Prepare various media presentations of City programs to the staff and general public, as directed by the City Manager.

1.1.13   **Information Technologies and Telephone Systems**

1.1.13.1	Provide, install and maintain state-of-the-art information technology, software and hardware sufficient to efficiently satisfy all City needs.
1.1.13.2	Provide a state-of-the-art domain network to account for handling future growth and technologies.
1.1.13.3	Provide, install, configure and maintain a state-of-the-art server at City Hall and all City offices to improve performance ensure against data loss and minimize potential down time.
1.1.13.4	Provide centralized management of all network resources and a central location for the storage of the City's documents.
1.1.13.5	Ensure data security and integrity with a nightly backup (with offsite storage) and the ability to restore from a central location.
1.1.13.6	Provide, configure and maintain eight (10) state-of-the-art laptop computers to the members of the City Council (7), City Manager (2), and City Clerk (1).
1.1.13.7	Provide, install, configure and maintain state-of-the-art computer workstations, as needed.
1.1.13.8	Provide digital phones and remote connections for park sites.
1.1.13.9	Maintain software and hardware uniformity and interchangeability among users.

1.1.13.10   Provide, install and maintain sufficient network laser printers to efficiently conduct all City business.

1.1.13.11   Maintain a three-year replacement program for all computers and equipment.

1.1.13.12   Provide, install and maintain state-of-the-art network cabling/data line system for communications, networking and data sharing.

1.1.13.13   Provide, install, configure and maintain servers in support of utility functions.

1.1.13.14   Provide all users with Internet and e-mail connections on a separate server for internal and external communications and common contact lists and scheduling.

1.1.13.15   Archive all e-mails in compliance with State retention requirements.

1.1.13.16   Provide, install and maintain a state-of-the-art telephone system in all City facilities with sufficient lines and features to satisfy all needs of the City.

1.1.14.   Databases – Municipal Management Software

1.1.14.1   Provide, install, configure and maintain a state-of-the-art database program to manage the City's occupational and business license functions

1.1.14.2   Coordinate the procurement, installation, configuration and maintenance of all databases required of municipalities in the State of Georgia by any governmental agencies.

1.1.15   Court Services

1.1.15.1   Provide all aspects of court record keeping and reporting as required by law and sound practices including but not limited to maintenance of calendars, recording of sentences and dispositions, coordination with probation services, coordination of collection of fees, fines and surcharges.

1.1.15.2   Provide adequate administrative personnel for Court hearings.

1.1.15.3   Oversee and maintain all systems required for fee, fine and surcharge accounting, reporting and remittance.

1.1.16   Police

1.1.16   Provide administrative and clerical assistance in all aspects of police department record keeping and reporting as required by law and sound practices in coordination with City authorities.

1.1.17   Fire

1.1.17   Provide administrative and clerical assistance in all aspects of fire department record keeping and reporting as required by law and sound practices in coordination with City authorities.

1.1.18   Election Support

1.1.18.1   Coordinate municipal and special elections as required, including but not limited to addressing polling station issues, preparation of ballot questions, or other related issues arising from election matters.

1.1.19   Solid Waste

1.1.19.1   Manage and coordinate all aspects of agreements with solid waste providers.

1.2   FINANCIAL SERVICES

Financial Services shall include, but not be limited to the following.

1.2.1   Revenue Collection

1.2.1.1   Coordinate with local, state and federal agencies charged with collection and disbursement of taxes, assessments, fees, charges and other impositions.

1.2.1.2   Administer the fees, charges and their miscellaneous revenues pertaining to utilities, private enterprises and individuals as they interface with the City programs.

1.2.1.3   Recommend enforcement actions to the City Manager to induce payment in accordance with the City's policies and procedures.

1.2.1.4   Prepare monthly financial reports showing revenues and expenses to date in comparison with budget projections and submit the reports to the City Manager no later than the tenth day of the following month.

1.2.1.5   Maintain a City address list for the Department of Revenue to ensure that the City obtains all shared revenues to which it is entitled.

1.2.2   Capital Program Administration:

1.2.2.1   Coordinate with the designated city representatives the capital needs of the City.

1.2.2.2   Obtain financing if necessary and maintain proper fund accounting procedures.

1.2.2.3   Administer and implement capital program financing.

1.2.3   Investment Services

1.2.3.1   Recommend investment policies and procedures pursuant to State law.

1.2.3.2   Invest City funds per approved policies.

1.2.3.3   Produce timely investment reports stating the effectiveness of the chosen investment policy.

1.2.4   Fund Accounting

1.2.4.1   Establish Fund Accounting System in accordance with Governmental Accounting Standards Board (GASB), the Uniform Accounting System prescribed by Department of Community Affairs and the rules of the Georgia Department of Audits and Accounts.

1.2.4.2   Prepare reports for Department of Community Affairs and State Revenue Department and distributions.

1.2.4.3   Prepare all other financial reports as required by applicable law and accounting standards.

1.2.5   Accounts payable/receivable

1.2.5.1   Administer the purchase order system and make timely payment of all invoices.

1.2.5.2   Coordinate tax collection, franchise fees, utility taxes and all other receivables.

1.2.6   **General fixed asset accounting**

1.2.6.1   Account for assets constructed by or donated to the City for maintenance.

1.2.6.2   Inventory City property in accordance with GASB and the Georgia Department of Audits and Accounts.

1.2.7   **Budgeting:**

1.2.7.1   Prepare and submit to the City Manager annual budgets per GASB standards.

1.2.7.2   Liaison with all City departments for annual budget categories.

1.2.7.3   Provide material for and attend all budget meetings, hearing and agenda meetings.

1.2.7.4   Coordinate with other departments and governmental entities as necessary.

1.2.7.5   Present findings in oral, print, multimedia, and web-based forms.

1.2.8   **Forecasting:**

1.2.8.1   Prepare detailed financial forecasts and analysis.

1.2.8.2   Identify trends and analyze their impact upon City's finances, operations and capital.

1.2.8.3   Develop policy and action recommendations.

1.2.8.4   Coordinate with other departments and governments.

1.2.8.5   Present findings in oral, print, multimedia, and web-based forms.

1.2.9   **Comprehensive Annual Financial Report (CAFR):**

1.2.9.1   Prepare the Annual Financial Report for Units of Local Government, in accordance with Generally Accepted Accounting Principals as defined by the Government Finance Officers Association.

1.2.10   Risk Management:

1.2.10.1   Recommend and advise the City Manager of the appropriate amounts and types of insurance and be responsible for procuring all necessary insurance.

1.2.10.2   Process and assist in the investigation of insurance claims, in coordination with the City Attorney.

1.2.10.3   Develop and maintain a risk management claims review procedure, in coordination with the City Manager and City Attorney.

1.2.10.4   Review insurance policies and coverage amounts of City vendors.

1.2.11   Human Resources:

1.2.11.1   Ensure proper functioning of payroll, fringe benefit, insurance tax and other City-specific and general law-provided human resources functions.

1.2.11.2   Establish a Code of Conduct for personnel that emphasize the responsibility of the staff to be professional, patient and responsive under all circumstances. The Code should emphasize that rudeness and impoliteness toward any person is unacceptable conduct and will not be tolerated.

1.2.11.3   Establish and implement with all employees an Employee Policies and Procedures Manual, which shall include, but not be limited to, policies and procedures on carrying out duties to the City, consequences of non-compliance to policies, and functions and roles of the employees.

1.2.12   Purchasing:

1.2.12.1   Recommend to the City Manager and assist in the implementation of procurement policies and procedures.

1.2.12.2   Assist in selection of vendors.

1.2.12.3   Participate in county and state level purchase plans.

1.2.12.4   Prepare RFP's, as directed by the City Manager.

1.2.12.5   Prepare and process requisitions.

1.2.13 HIPAA

1.2.13.1 Ensure that all City systems and procedures meet the requirements of HIPAA.

1.3 COMMUNITY SERVICES

1.3.1 Water Management and Utilities:

1.3.1.1 Manage and coordinate all aspects of intergovernmental relationship regarding water and sewer issues.

1.3.4 Animal Control

1.3.4.1 Provide field staff for the daily maintenance of animal control issues in the City.

2.0 EMERGENCY 911 SERVICE

2.1 Emergency 911 Infrastructure and Staffing

2.2 Implementing and staff emergency 911 system for the City in accordance with state law and in conjunction with any necessary vendors and local governmental entities.

3.0 PHYSICAL PLANT REQUIREMENTS

3.1 Office, Administrative and Facilities Space

3.1.1 Provide facilities sufficient for the operations of all departments and functions the City whether or not Corporation is responsible for said operations or function. All space shall meet all minimum GSA requirements, and exhibit a level of finish customary for a local government. Should the City assume any lease, or purchase the property, from the Corporation, the Corporation will be relieved of this obligation. In the event of a lease or purchase of space, the Corporation shall not have rent obligations for any personnel performing duties in behalf of the City.

3.2 Facilities Maintenance, Repair and Contracts

3.2.1 Provide personnel to maintain, repair, clean, and keep in good working order all facilities commensurate with local governmental standards all facilities occupied by the City. This provision, however, shall not apply to landscaping maintenance of any City rights-of-way or land.

3.3   Furniture, Fixtures, Equipment and Supplies

3.3.1   Provide Furniture, Fixtures, Equipment and Supplies in an amount sufficient for the reasonable operation of all departments and functions the City on the date of acceptance of the proposal, whether or not Corporation is responsible for said operations or function.

4.0   PURCHASING, PROCUREMENT AND CONTRACTING

4.1   Corporation shall meet or exceed all laws and requirements regarding purchasing, and procurement as set forth by the State of Georgia. Corporation shall also meet or exceed all laws and requirements regarding the same as set forth by the State of Georgia regarding any contracting required in the course of fulfilling the duties under this Agreement.

AGREEMENT BY AND BETWEEN CORPORATION AND
THE CITY OF SANDY SPRINGS.
EXHIBIT "A" ADDENDUM
RESERVED

AGREEMENT BY AND BETWEEN CORPORATION AND
THE CITY OF SANDY SPRINGS.
EXHIBIT "B"

VEHICLE USE POLICY

RESERVED

AGREEMENT BY AND BETWEEN CORPORATION AND THE CITY OF SANDY SPRINGS.
EXHIBIT "C"

COMPENSATION SCHEDULE – FISCAL YEAR 200--___

Services Compensation Schedule (as shown in the Fiscal Year 200___
Approved Budget

RESERVED

AGREEMENT BY AND BETWEEN CORPORATION AND THE CITY OF SANDY SPRINGS.
EXHIBIT "C"

COMPENSATION SCHEDULE – FISCAL YEAR 200--___

Services Compensation Schedule (as shown in the Fiscal Year 200___
Approved Budget

RESERVED .

APPENDIX D

COMMISSION FOR THE CITY OF
SANDY SPRINGS

REQUEST FOR PROPOSAL FOR PROVISION OF

PUBLIC WORKS, TRANSPORTATION, STREETS, RIGHT-
OF-WAY, FACILITIES, PARKS AND RECREATION,
CAPITAL IMPROVEMENTS, PLANNNING AND ZONING,
INSPECTIONS, CODE ENFORCEMENT, PERMITTING,
PURCHASING, PROCUREMENT, AND CONTRACTING
SERVICES

TO THE

CITY OF SANDY SPRINGS

PROPOSALS OPENED: **(time)** **(date)**

INSTRUCTIONS TO PROPOSERS

All the spaces below and in the attached Proposal Signature and Certification form are to be filled in with signatures supplied where indicated. Failure to sign Proposal will cause rejection of your proposal.

PROPOSAL OF:

COMPANY NAME:
ADDRESS:

SUBMIT PROPOSAL TO:

> **Mr. Oliver Porter, Commissioner**
> **150 Habersham Waters Court**
> **Dunwoody, GA 30350**

PROPOSAL MAILED:
CARRIER USED:

NOTE: **PLEASE ENSURE THAT ALL REQUIRED SIGNATURE BLOCKS ARE COMPLETED.   FAILURE TO SIGN THIS FORM WILL CAUSE REJECTION OF YOUR PROPOSAL.**

> **Commission for**
> **The City of Sandy Springs**

PROPOSAL

We propose to furnish and deliver any and all of the services named in the attached Request for Proposal (RFP). The price or prices offered herein shall apply for the period of time stated in the RFP.

This offer is being made in with knowledge that the Commission for the City of Sandy Springs is promulgating this RFP in accordance with its authority granted by virtue of O.C.G.A. § 36-31-8(g). We understand that pursuant to said section, and the provisions of 05 HB 36 and 05 HB 37, the Commission has no authority to enter into binding agreements, to expend public funds, or to incur any liability on behalf of the City of Sandy Springs.

It is understood and agreed that this proposal constitutes an offer, which if accepted in writing by the City of Sandy Springs, Georgia, City Council, and subject to the terms and conditions of such acceptance, will constitute a valid and binding contract between the undersigned and the City of Sandy Springs, Georgia.

It is understood and agreed that we have read the specification shown or referenced in the RFP and that this proposal is made in accordance with the provisions of such specifications. By our written signature on this proposal, we guarantee and certify that all items included in this proposal meet or exceed any and all such specifications. We further agree if awarded a contract, to deliver services, which meet or exceed the specifications.

It is understood and agreed that any proposals shall be valid and held open for a period of sixty (60) days from the date of the first meeting of a quorum of the newly elected City Council of the City of Sandy Springs.

_____   _____
Authorized Signature   Date

_____   _____
Print/Type Name   Print/Type Company Name

PROPOSAL SIGNATURE AND CERTIFICATION

(Bidder must sign and return with proposal)

I certify that this proposal was made without prior understanding, agreement, or connection with any corporation, firm, or person submitting a proposal for the same materials, supplies, equipment, or services and is in all respects fair and without collusion or fraud. I understand collusive bidding is a violation of State and Federal Law and can result in fines, prison sentences, and civil damage awards. I agree to abide by all conditions of the proposal and certify I am authorized to sign this proposal for the proposer.

_____   _____
Authorized Signature   Date

_____   _____
Print/Type Name   Print/Type Company Name

1.0   GENERAL INFORMATION

1.1   Introduction

Pursuant to its authority granted by virtue of O.C.G.A. § 36-31-8(g), the Commission for the City of Sandy Springs (the "Commission") is requesting proposals for Provision of Services to the City of Sandy Springs, Georgia (the "City") to implement, manage and operate a wide range of services/functions for the new city to be incorporated December 1, 2005. This RFP is issued pursuant to its authority granted by virtue of O.C.G.A. § 36-31-8(g) and subject to all of the terms, limitations, and conditions as set forth in House Bill 36 and House Bill 37 as passed during the 2005 Georgia Legislative Session. Competitive sealed proposals shall be submitted in response hereto. All proposals submitted pursuant to the request shall be made in accordance with the provisions of these instructions.

As set forth herein, there shall be mandatory pre-proposal conference of all bidders. Further, packaging of bid services is allowed for the purposes of this Request for Proposal ("RFP"), provided however, that each component of said packaged services must be individually detailed in said response. Offerors may, and are encouraged, to form partnerships regarding the provisions of any particular services set forth herein to insure that the City has benefit of the best possible team to provide the required services.

The proposals shall be evaluated in accordance with the evaluation criteria set forth in this RFP. Subsequent to the opening of the sealed proposals, discussions may be conducted by the Commission for City of Sandy Springs with responsible offerors who submit proposals for the purpose of clarification to assure full understanding of and responsiveness to the solicitation requirements. Offerors shall be accorded fair and equal treatment with respect to any opportunity for discussion and revision of proposals.

In conducting any such discussion, there shall be no disclosure of any information derived from proposals submitted by competing offerors. All such discussions shall be conducted by a committee comprising some or all of the Commission Members.

In accordance with O.C.G.A. § 36-31-8(g), if determined advantageous to the City, recommendation of acceptance to the incoming City Council shall be made regarding the responsible offeror whose proposal is determined in writing to be the most advantageous to the City, taking into consideration qualifications, experience in provision of similar services, price, identification of potential needs, thoroughness of proposals, and all other evaluation factors set forth in this RFP. No other factors or criteria shall be used in the evaluation. The Commission reserves the right to reject any and all proposals submitted in response to this request and to withdraw this RFP at any time.

2.2   Background

The City will be incorporated on December 1, 2005, with almost 90,000 residents and the Commission is soliciting these proposals to evaluate the most cost effective, efficient, and reliable method of meeting a broad range of needs for the City.

With a "clean sheet of paper," the City has the remarkable opportunity to build the most effective, efficient and responsive local government in the State of Georgia. The Commission believes that creative solutions are available that can produce the model government for the 21st century.

Foremost among these solutions is tapping the resources of private industry through contracting for services and functions. Our desire is to identify firms that can provide a wide variety of services allowing the city to deal with a limited number of contracts. Further, we are seeking firms that have had experience in providing services/functions to other municipalities, or as a minimum, to similar entities.

While it may be necessary to contract with the existing county government for some services, the intent is to keep that to a minimum. A successful contractor will have the opportunity to showcase the firm's capability in serving the needs of municipal governments.

With the aforementioned restrictions on contracts and spending, the Commission must establish a relationship of trust with potential contract firms. The recommended firms must be financially able and willing to, in the months preceding the start date, establish the infrastructure, hire and train staff, and undertake any functions that will be necessary for the city to operate from its inception.

2.3   Timetable

The following timetable is anticipated for this RFP:

June____, 2005	Release of RFP
July ____, 2005	Mandatory Pre-Proposal Conference
July ____, 2005 12:00 p.m.	Proposals due
July ____, 2005	Oral Presentations (if required)
December 1, 2005	Commission Recommendation, if any (on or about)

Proposals will be received at the date and time set forth above in the following location:

Mr. Oliver Porter, Commissioner
150 Habersham Waters Court
Dunwoody, GA 30350

2.4   Restrictions on Communications with Commission Staff

1.4.1   From the issue date of this RFP until a provider is selected and the selection is announced, offerors are not allowed to communicate for any reason with any Commissioner, staff member, or representative concerning this RFP except through the Officer named herein, or during the pre-bid conference. For violations of this provision, the Commission shall reserve the right to reject the proposal of the offending offeror.

2.5   RFP Amendments

1.5.1   The Commission reserves the right to amend the RFP prior to the deadline for proposal submission, July __, 2005. Amendments will be sent to all offerors who originally received a copy of the RFP. If an RFP amendment will impact the timeline contained in Section 1.3, all offerors will be promptly provided information concerning any timeline revisions.

1.6   Proposal Withdrawal

1.6.1   A written proposal is not subject to withdrawal except that, prior to the proposal due date, a submitted proposal may be withdrawn by the offeror submitting a written request to the Officer named herein. Any such request must be signed by a person authorized to sign for the offeror.

1.7   Costs for Preparing Proposal

1.7.1   The cost for developing the proposal is the sole responsibility of the offeror. The Commission and/or the City will not provide reimbursement for such costs.

1.8   Contract Term

1.8.1   The contract will be a multi-party contract between the service provider and the City. The term, if any, of the contract shall commence on January 1, 2006, and shall terminate on December 31, 2006, except that the Contract shall automatically renew for five (5) additional twelve (12) month periods unless affirmative written notice of non-renewal is given by the City not less than thirty (30) days prior to the expiration of the instant term. The terms and construction of the Contract shall be governed by applicable Georgia law.

1.9 **Contract**

1.9.1 The Contract, which the Commission intends to use with the successful offeror, is attached as Attachment "A" to this RFP. Prospective offerors are urged to carefully read the Contract prior to making their offers. The Contract and any exceptions to the provisions of the Contract must be submitted with the offeror's proposal. The Commission reserves the right to negotiate with the successful offeror other additions to, deletions from and/or changes in the language in the Contract, provided that no such addition, deletion or change in the contract language would, in the sole discretion of the Commission, affect the evaluation criteria set forth herein or give the successful offeror a competitive advantage.

The offeror shall confirm acceptance of the provisions of the Contract or, in the alternative, shall state explicitly which provisions are not acceptable and propose alternative wording or any additional wording or any additional provisions that the offeror believes to be necessary. Any exception to the Contract must be clearly identified, accompany the offeror's proposal, and be attached to the Contract. Offerors are cautioned that any exception submitted that would give the offeror a competitive advantage over another offeror or that would cause a failure to meet a mandatory requirement of the RFP will not be accepted.

Prior to a determination of recommedation, the apparent winning offeror will be required to enter into discussions with the Commission to resolve any contractual differences before a recommendation is made. These exceptions are to be finalized and all exceptions resolved within one (1) week of notification. If not, this could lead to rejection of the offeror's proposal. No exception to the Contract will be deemed to have been accepted by the Commission unless the exception is incorporated by reference into the final executed Contract. The Commission reserves the right to make non-material revisions to the form of the Contract as necessary at any time.

1.10 **Offers by One or More Partners**

1.10.1 Offerors may, and are encouraged, to form partnerships regarding the provisions of any particular services set forth herein to insure that the City has benefit of the best possible team to provide the required services. If more than one partner is participating in any response, however, each partner shall respond separately regarding their individual businesses, including but not limited to all responses to the RFQ portion of this request. All responses will further clearly delineate the specific responsibilities and duties of each partner regarding the requested services.

1.11   Format for Responses

1.11.1   Proposals should correspond with and satisfy the requirements set forth in this RFP. The offeror must submit the original proposal plus fifteen (15) copies of its proposal to the Commission. Proposals should be in one sealed package marked clearly on the front, "Sandy Springs RFP (B)"

1.12   Additional Information

1.12..1   An offeror that submits a proposal that meets the requirements set forth in this RFP may be requested to provide additional information or to meet with representatives of the Commission to discuss the specifics of the proposal in greater detail.

1.13   Retention of Proposals

1.13.1   All material submitted in response to this RFP will become the property of the Commission and may be returned at the option of the Commission. One copy shall be retained by the Commission for official files.

1.14   Waiver of Irregularities

1.14.1   The Commission reserves the right to waive any irregularities of any proposal submitted for this RFP.

1.15   Questions about this RFP

1.15.1   Questions regarding the requirements or technical criteria set forth in this RFP should be directed in writing to the individual listed below. The response and the question will then be shared with other offerors who are responding to this RFP.

Name: Mr. Oliver Porter
Address: 150 Habersham Waters Court
             Dunwoody, Georgia 30350

Telephone: 770-393-8898

E-mail: oliverporter1@comcast.net

The deadline for the submission of these questions is 12:00 P.M. EDT, July _____, 2005. Questions should reference the appropriate RFP section and may be submitted by email. Any files attached to e-mails must be MS Word format.

2.0   REQUEST FOR OFFEROR QUALIFICATIONS/ASSURANCES

2.1   Required Qualifications and Information

The Commission deems that it is in its best interest to work with offerors that have proven capabilities with a well-established record of success in the provision of the type of services being requested hereunder. To that end, the offeror shall include in a separate envelope as set forth herein, the following:

1.1.1   Offeror's name, address, and telephone number.

1.1.2   Primary local contact person(s) and telephone number(s).

1.1.3   Total number of offerors's full-time employees designating the geographic location of said employees with representative numbers regarding said location.

1.1.4   Year established.

1.1.5   Provide a listing and description of all current litigation involving the offeror.

1.1.6   Provide a listing and description of all litigation history for the offeror with any claim in excess of Twenty Thousand and 00/100 Dollars ($20,000.00) since and including the year 1990.

1.1.7   Provide a copy of the most recent completed year's financial statements (Income Statement and Balance Sheet) for the offeror.

1.1.8   List of all projects similar in quality and/or scope to that set forth in this RFP– Include: size, cost, total fee, implementation time, scope of services, awards received, and brief description of project.

1.1.9   Provide a description of the offeror's special capabilities, techniques or resources that can be contributed to this assignment. A minimum of three (3) references from projects of a similar scope and type shall be submitted with each proposal by offeror. Particular emphasis should be placed on demonstrating previous experience with projects for municipalities. Describe the offeror's, and/or proposed team's, qualifications to complete the work. The planning and/or expertise required to accomplish the complete scope-of-work must be represented either within the offerror's in-house staff, or by a partnership of offerors. A partnership submission must be made by an offeror. If the submission is a partnership submission, describe the previous experience that the offeror has had working with the various partners. Identify and provide resume information for the project manager and the key personnel who will be involved in implementing the project.

1.1.10   Statement of offeror's capability to absorb additional workload, availability of personnel, and commitment to provide services on a timely basis.

1.1.11   Conflict of Interest Statement.

As a duly authorized representative of _____ I, _____ with   the title _____, certify   that to the best of my knowledge that no circumstance exist which will cause a conflict of interest in performing services for the City of Sandy Springs, that no employee of _____, nor any public agency official or employee affected by this Request for Qualifications has any pecuniary interest in the business of this firm, associates or consultants of this firm, or the firm's parent firm, subsidiary, or other legal entity of which this firm is a part, and that no person associated with or employed by this firm has any interest that would conflict in any way, manner or degree with the performance of services for the City of Sandy Springs.

Date: _____

Company Name: _____

Authorized Representative Name: _____

Title: _____

Signature: _____

1.1.12   Provide a proposed Organizational Chart which identifies individual names and areas of responsibility regarding the implementation and responsibilities of the duties hereunder.

1.1.13   Provide a comprehensive outline of the steps you propose in order to meet the services required by this RFP. This detail should indicate what is to be done, who individually, and by name is responsible to do it, and when it is to be completed.

1.1.14   At your option, you may provide any additional supporting documentation or information which would be helpful in evaluating your qualifications and commitment.

1.1.15   The proposal should contain any documents pertaining to the requirements mentioned above and any other information the offeror deems necessary to fully demonstrate the offeror's qualifications so as to allow the Commission to evaluate the offeror's ability to provide the services requested herein.

2.2   Proposal Guaranty

2.2.1   No proposal will be considered unless it is accompanied by a proposal guaranty in the form of a cashier's check, a certified check, a savings and loan secured check, or a bid bond payable to the City of Sandy Springs in the amount of five percent (5%) of the total bid to ensure that the successful offeror will execute the contract which it has been recommended and ultimately awarded by the City. The proposal guaranty shall be forfeited by an offeror who fails to execute promptly and properly the contract it has been awarded, or who fails to furnish the required performance security and certificate of insurance in their proper forms within the time requirements indicated in this RFP. **ALL PROPOSAL GUARANTY SHALL BE RETAINED UNTIL FINAL CONTRACT AWARD.**

2.3   Bonds

2.3.1   Upon notification of the Commission's intent to recommend a proposal to the City, the apparent successful offeror shall furnish, within ten (10) days, a performance bond in the amount of one-hundred ten percent (110%) of the proposal amount on a form prescribed by the Commission. Failure to furnish a bond within ten (10) days may result in rejection of the proposal, forfeiture of the proposal guaranty, and awards of the contract to another offeror. Additionally, for a performance bond surety to be acceptable to the Commissions as surety for performance bonds, a surety company shall comply with the following provisions:

2.3.2   The surety company shall be authorized by law to do business in the State of Georgia pursuant to a current certificate of authority to transact business issued by the Commissioner of Insurance.

3.3.3   The surety company shall be on the United States Department of Treasury's list of approved bond sureties.

3.3.4   All bonds shall be signed by a Georgia Licensed Resident Agent who holds a current power of attorney from the surety company issuing the bond.

3.3.5   **PERFORMANCE SECURITY SHALL BE RETAINED BY THE CITY OF SANDY SPRINGS FOR A MINIMUM OF 150 CALENDAR DAYS FROM THE DATE OF CONTRACT COMPLETION.**

2.4   **Financial History**

2.4.1   The Commission reserves the right to evaluate the financial integrity of the offeror. Prior to the award of the contracts, all offerors shall be required to submit the following items:

1.1.1.1   Audited Financial Statement or 10K Report for the most recent two (2) years, including at minimum:

2.4.1.1.1   statements of income and related earnings;

2.4.1.1.2   cash flow statement;

2.4.1.1.3   balance sheet;

2.4.1.1.4   opinion concerning financial statements from a CPA.

2.4.1.1.5   Primary banking source letter of reference.

2.5   **Customer Reference**

2.5.1   The offeror must provide the names of customer references, including a specific contact name and phone number of any entity to whom the provider has ever provided the proposed service or a similar service.

3.0	**REQUIRED SERVICES**

3.1	**General**

3.1.1 The services required for which this RFP is being issued shall include but not be limited to those outlined in Sections 4.0 et seq. through 13.0 et seq. hereof. The intent of the Contract is that the offeror firm assumes full responsibility for the structure, planning, and implementation necessary to provide the required services to the City. Where the offeror anticipates needs that may occur which are not specifically set forth hereunder, the offeror is expected to identify with specificity those needs as part of its proposal. The intent of the Contracts is that the offeror firm assumes full responsibility for the structure, planning, and implementation necessary to provide the required services to the City. Where the offeror anticipates needs that may occur which are not specifically set forth hereunder, the offeror is expected to identify with specificity those needs as part of its proposal.

3.1.2 It is anticipated that the proposal submitted hereunder shall, if awarded, be incorporated as an addendum to Exhibit "A" of the Contract between the offeror and the City to further define the scope of the offeror's services thereunder. Accordingly, all responses should be in a format suitable for incorporation into said Contract as an exhibit.

3.1.3 All services and duties must be operational as of the date of the award of the Contract by the City, should the City decide to make such award.

3.1.4 Each of the following shall include as a material provision thereof the attendance as necessary and/or requested of any an all meetings of the City Council to either discuss and/or make recommendations regarding any matters within the purview of the requested services. Whenever the requirement calls for the offeror to develop and/or implement a policy, it shall be material provisions thereof that such policy shall be made in furtherance of the directives as provided to the offeror by the City Manager.

4.0	**PUBLIC WORKS**

4.1 Public Works services shall include, establishing, staffing (as needed to meet the requirements herein), and maintaining the

Public Works Department for the City. The areas of responsibility shall include, but not be limited to, the following:

4.1.1 Storm Water

4.1.1.1 Coordinate with all other City personnel and/or contractors the transfer maintenance, storage and retrieval of all documents and records from Fulton County, Georgia, necessary for the effective implementation and operation of the City's storm water requirements under applicable, federal, state, and local laws. The offeror shall be responsible for determining the documentation necessary for transfer as well as coordinating and implementing the physical retrieval, reproduction and storage of the transferred records.

4.1.1.2 Provide ongoing engineering, design and maintenance of storm water systems, as needed, to meet the needs of the City.

4.1.1.3 Develop and implement all necessary policies, protocols, rules and regulations necessary to meet or exceed the City's storm water requirements under applicable, federal, state, and local laws, including but not limited to federal clean water requirements.

4.1.1.4 Integrate activities as necessary with Planning/Zoning and other departments.

4.1.2 Emergency Preparedness

4.1.2.1 Establish policies and guidelines, and coordinate, operate and maintain the city's emergency preparedness program in accordance with all applicable, federal, state, and local laws, as well as prudent local government practices.

4.1.2.2 Integrate and coordinate all emergency preparedness operations in conjunction with Homeland Security, Emergency 911, FEMA, and GEMA.

4.1.3 Recycling

4.1.3.1 Establish policies and guidelines, and operate the city's Recycling program.

4.1.3.2 Coordinate implementation of program and all other activities with City personnel and/or contractors.

4.1.3.3   Fulfill all reporting duties as required by any federal, state or local laws.

4.1.4   Geographic Information System (GIS)

4.1.4.1   Coordinate with all other necessary City personnel and/or contractors the transfer, maintenance, storage and retrieval of all documents and records from Fulton County, Georgia, necessary for the effective implementation and operation of the City's GIS System. The offeror shall be responsible for determining the documentation necessary for transfer as well as coordinating and implementing the physical retrieval, reproduction and storage of the transferred records.

4.1.4.2   Service, update and maintain GIS data bases on not less than a monthly basis.

4.1.4.3   Provide any GIS related information and/or data in response to requests and needs of City personnel as well as any other contractors.

5.0   TRANSPORTATION

5.1   Transportation services shall include, establishing, staffing (as needed to meet the requirements herein), and maintaining the Transportation Department for the City. The areas of responsibility shall include, but not be limited to, the following:

5.1.1   Funding and Grant Applications

5.1.1.1   Conduct all activities necessary to identify, develop and prepare submissions for any federal, state or local funding and grant programs, and provide fund oversight as required by law. Coordinate all aspects of the above, as necessary with the Atlanta Regional Commission.

5.1.2   Traffic Engineering

5.1.2.1   Conduct all activities necessary to maintain a first quality traffic system, including but not limited to, conducting necessary studies and implementation of traffic control improvements.

5.1.3   Street Design

5.1.3.1   Conduct all activities necessary to maintain a first quality street system plan, including but not limited to, the coordination, review, and management of all contracts for streets, sidewalks and related projects.

5.1.4   Street Maintenance

5.1.4.1   Conduct all activities necessary to maintain a first quality roadway and bridge infrastructure system, including but not limited to providing necessary maintenance of all roadways and bridges, which shall include minor repairs, cleaning, and repairs necessitated by storm events. The offeror may provide this service by the use of subcontractors, provided however, when subcontracts are anticipated, the offeror should include as part of its proposal the same information regarding said subcontractor as required of offeror in Section 2.0 hereof. Offeror should further provide an estimate of annual costs for the services of said subcontractor as a separate section of the quotation submitted on this RFP.

5.1.5   Street lights, Sidewalks, Gutters and Related Street Areas

5.1.5.1   Conduct all activities necessary to maintain first quality street lights, sidewalks, gutters and related street areas including but not limited to providing a necessary maintenance and cleaning of the same. The offeror may provide this service by the use of subcontractors, provided however, when subcontracts are anticipated, the offeror should include as part of its proposal the same information regarding said subcontractor as required of offeror in Section 2.0 hereof. Offeror should further provide an estimate of annual costs for the services of said subcontractor as a separate section of the quotation submitted on this RFP.

6.0   STREETS, RIGHTS-OF-WAY, AND FACILITIES

6.1   General

6.1.1   Streets, Rights-of-Way, and Facilities services shall, in addition to the requirements set out in Section 6.2, include, but not be limited to, establishing, staffing (as needed to meet the requirements herein), to:

6.1.1.1 Coordinate the transfer of all City Rights-of-Way from Fulton County, Georgia The offeror shall be responsible for determining the documentation necessary for transfer.

6.1.1.2 Establish, operate and oversee all aspects of the City Rights-of-Way permitting process.

6.2   **Contract Administration.**

6.2.1   Establish, operate and oversee all aspects contract administration for daily maintenance of all public rights-of-way and property, including but not limited to landscaping and irrigation systems, in order to provide safe and comfortable common grounds for the residents of Sandy Springs.

6.2.2   Establish, operate and oversee all aspects contract administration for the construction, operation and maintenance of public facilities.

6.2.3   Establish, operate and oversee all aspects of emergency preparedness plan with local, state and federal agencies for debris removal, roadway access, flood prevention and safe, operable utilities.

7.0   **PARKS AND RECREATION**

7.1   Parks and Recreation services shall include, establishing, staffing (as needed to meet the requirements herein), and maintaining the Parks and Recreations for the City. The areas of responsibility shall include, but not be limited to, the following:

7.1.1   Plan, implement and coordinate staffing and contract administration for the daily maintenance and use of all public parks and recreational facilities.

7.1.2   Plan, implement and coordinate staffing for the planning, promoting, and supervising of recreation programs and special events.

7.1.3   Plan, implement and coordinate staffing for the managing, coordinating and scheduling of City athletic facilities as needed.

7.1.4   Develop and recommend to the City Manager short, mid, and long-range plans for capital improvements and implement plans as directed.

7.1.5   Establish, operate and oversee all aspects of emergency management procedures with local, state and federal agencies to ensure safe recreational system.

7.1.6   Conduct all activities necessary to identify, develop and prepare submissions for any federal, state or local funding and grant programs for improvements to the park and recreation system within Sandy Springs, and provide fund oversight as required by law.

8.0   CAPITAL IMPROVEMENTS

8.1   Develop and recommend to the City Manager short, mid, and long-range plans for capital improvements and implement plans as directed. Such plans should meet all requirements of the Department of Community Affairs and the Atlanta Regional Commission for adoption in the City's Comprehensive Land Use Plan.

9.0   PLANNING AND ZONING

9.1   Planning and Zoning services shall include, establishing, staffing (as needed to meet the requirements herein), and maintaining the Planning and Zoning Department for the City. The areas of responsibility shall include, but not be limited to, the following:

9.1.1   Provide information to the general public as it relates to all land development activities within the City.

9.1.2   Provide information to builders and developers regarding policies and procedures within the City related to land planning within the city.

9.1.3   Oversee the development, maintenance and updating of land use and zoning maps as required by state and local agencies.

9.1.4   Develop policies and procedures regarding all planning and zoning activities, and develop schedules and time frames for processing all land development activities (including, but not limited to, zoning).

9.1.5   Provide information to the City Manager, Mayor and Council, Planning and Zoning Boards, and any other City entities needing information regarding all relevant and applicable zoning and/or planning issues.

9.1.6   Develop, plan, recommend and implement, in coordination with all other City staff or contractors, a plan for the implementation and assessment impact fees by the City.

9.1.7   Conduct all activities necessary to maintain a first quality planning an zoning system for the City.

9.1.8   Develop, plan, recommend and implement, in coordination with all other City staff or contractors, a plan for the issuance of certificates of use and occupational licenses.

10.0   INSPECTIONS, CODE ENFORCEMENT, AND PERMITTING

10.1   Inspections, Code Enforcement and Permitting services shall include, establishing, staffing (as needed to meet the requirements herein), and maintaining the Inspections, Code Enforcement, Permitting Departments for the City. The areas of responsibility shall include, but not be limited to, the following:

10.1.1   Develop, plan, recommend and implement, in coordination with all other City staff or contractors, a plan review process for the City.

10.1.2   Develop, plan, recommend and implement, in coordination with all other City staff or contractors, a plan for the building permit process for the City.

10.1.3   Develop, plan, recommend and implement, in coordination with all other City staff or contractors, a plan for the code enforcement process for the City.

10.1.4   Develop, plan, recommend and implement, in coordination with all other City staff or contractors, a plan for the authorization and implementation plan for the City to conduct Soil Erosion and Sedimentation Control inspections for the City.

11.0   STAFFING REQUIREMENTS

11.1   General

11.1.1   Offeror shall provide with the Proposal a list of the proposed staffing requirements necessary to meet the needs for each of the services, duties, and/or functions outlined in Sections 4.0 et seq. through 11.0 et seq..

11.2   Key Positions

11.2.1   Regarding key positions, which shall include the proposed director of any department, the offeror shall provide a brief summary of said proposed key personnel's experience and qualifications for said position, provided, however that it shall be the duty of the offeror to assess the qualifications and skills of any proposed personnel and their suitability for the proposed positions. Offeror shall consider staffing recommendations of the Commission and subsequently the City, should the offer ultimately be accepted by the City. In addition, the proposal shall provide for the following position(s) setting out in detail the qualifications of the candidates for the following position(s):

11.2.1.1   Assistant City Manager

11.2.1.1.1   The Assistant City Manager shall have the responsibility working with the City Manager to coordinate and direct all of the activities set out in this RFP should it be accepted by the City. The Assistant City Manager will be a work closely with the City Manager and the City Council regarding all aspects of the offeror's activities should the offer be accepted by the City. Said Assistant City Manager shall be the primary coordinator of all communications between the City and the offeror.

11.2.1.2   Community Development Director

11.2.1.2.1   The Community Development Director shall have the responsibility working with the Assistant City Manager to coordinate and direct all of the activities set out in this RFP, should it be accepted by the City, as well as all other usual and customary duties for a city Community Development Director, including but not limited to:

11.2.1.2.2   Overseeing and ensuring the proper implementation and execution of all duties set forth in Section 9.0 <u>et seq.</u> and 10.0 <u>et seq.</u> hereof.

11.2.1.2.3   Attending all City Manager and/or Assistant City Manager staff meetings, council meetings and any other meetings deemed necessary by the City Manager and/or Assistant City Manager.

4.4.4.4.4   Acting as a liaison, with City Manager and Assistant City Manager approval, between the City, Fulton County, Georgia, the Atlanta Regional Council and necessary federal, state, and local officials and/or agencies.

11.3   Subcontractors

11.3.1   Should the offeror intend to engage the services of any subcontractors regarding the delivery of services set forth herein, subject to any more specific requirements herein, the name, address, and qualifications of such subcontractor shall be included in the proposal. Should the offeror include any subcontractors as potentially performing any of the services hereunder, the offeror shall affirmatively acknowledge as part of its proposal that the offeror shall be the sole entity to which the City shall look to for performance of the required services.

11.4   Personnel

11.4.1   The offeror shall include an affirmative statement in its proposal that it shall not knowingly engage in employment of, on any basis, any Commission member or committee members involved in the preparation of this RFP or in the selection and/or award process of this contract during the period of this contract. Once an offeror has been selected and a service contract negotiated, the names of those staff members who participated in this RFP process shall be provided to the service provider so that the requirements of this section can be implemented.

11.5   Employment Practices

11.5.1   The offeror shall include an affirmative statement in its proposal shall not discriminate against any employee or applicant for employment because of race, color, religion, sex, national origin, age, marital status, political affiliations, or disability. Such action shall include, but is not limited to the following: employment, promotion, demotion, transfer, recruitment or recruitment advertising, layoff or termination, rates of pay or other forms of compensation, and selection for training, including apprenticeship. Offeror agrees to post in conspicuous places, available to employees and applicants for employment, notices setting forth the provisions of this clause.

12.0   PURCHASING, PROCUREMENT AND CONTRACTING

12.1   The offeror shall include an affirmative statement in its proposal regarding the purchasing and/or procurement of any of the items set forth or required in the course of fulfilling the duties set forth in RFP, the offeror shall meet or exceed all laws and requirements regarding the same as set forth by the State of Georgia. Offeror shall also meet or exceed all laws and requirements regarding the same as set forth by the State of Georgia regarding any contracting required in the course of fulfilling the duties set forth in RFP.

13.0   PRICE QUOTATION

13.1   Each proposal shall include a price quote (Budget) for the required services as set forth herein for the year 2006, and a price for the year 2007. Each year shall be a separate quote and meet the requirements set forth herein. The price quotation for each year shall have two parts: (1) the quote shall break down with specificity the price for each general group of duties and obligations hereunder, by department and/or duty, and provide a total price for each delineated area of services, and (2) the quote shall further provide a summary page containing a total quote for all of the services requested in this RFP and a detail of the quote summarizing the components thereof in a succinct fashion. Said quote shall include a statement of the maximum percentage increase per year for any price escalation for the agreement for the years 2008, 2009 and 2010. This Quotation shall become Exhibit "C" to the Contract attached hereto, if awarded.

14.0 FORMAT OF RESPONSE

14.1 General

14.1.1 A responsive proposal shall be in accordance with Section 3.0 hereof and address each item as set forth in this RFP with specificity.

14.2 Required Sections

14.2.1 The response, shall generally follow the format as set forth below, however, the Commission shall, at its discretion, waive any deviation from this format should the offeror present an alternate format which provides sufficient detail and addresses all of the requirements as set forth in this RFP.

14.2.2 Response to Section 2.0 et seq. Request for Offeror Qualifications/ Assurances.

14.2.4 Presentation of proposed scope of services to conduct Public Works Requirements as set forth in Section 4.0 et seq.

14.2.4 Presentation of proposed scope of services to implement and conduct Transportation Requirements as set forth in Section 5.0 et seq.

14.2.5 Proposed scope of services to conduct Streets, Rights-Of-Way, and Facilities Requirements as set forth in Section 6.0 et seq.

14.2.6 Proposed scope of services to conduct Parks and Recreation Requirements as set forth in Section 7.0 et seq.

14.2.7 Proposed scope of services to conduct Capital Improvements Requirements as set forth in Section 8.0 et seq.

14.2.8 Proposed scope of services to conduct Planning and Zoning Requirements as set forth in Section 9.0 et seq.

14.2.9 Proposed scope of services to conduct Inspections, Code Enforcement, and Permitting Requirements as set forth in Section 10.0 et seq.

14.2.10 Proposed staffing requirements as set forth in Section 11.0 et seq. The response should include a proposed organizational chart setting out the structure of the offeror's staffing plan and all other requirements as set forth in said section in detail.

14.2.11   Proposed scope of services and statement of methodologies to conduct procurement, purchasing and contracting in conformance with Section 12.0 et seq.

14.2.12   A detailed start-up plan setting forth steps the offeror would take in order to meet all of the requirements for services and duties as set forth in this RFP on the date of the Award of the Contract by the City, should the City determine to award the same. The start-up plan should discuss with specificity how the proposal will meet the needs of the City. The plan should describe how the transition from Fulton County, Georgia to the offeror would be accomplished. The offeror should include start-up costs when calculating the prices submitted in the Price Quotation.

14.2.13   Of the 15 copies of the complete proposal, the proposal letter on one should contain the original manual signature of the person submitting the proposal on behalf of the offeror. All 15 copies should also contain the signer's name and title typed. The proposal letter shall clearly identify the complete legal name of the offeror. Each person signing a proposal certifies that he/she is the person in the offeror's organization authorized to make the proposal. The signer shall provide his/her affiliation with the offeror, address, telephone and fax numbers.

15.0   EVALUATION AND SELECTION PROCEDURE

15.1   General

15.1.1   The Commission will evaluate and select between the offerors in accordance with Georgia law.

15.2   Method of Evaluation

15.2.1   The Commission will rank the proposals by virtue of a points system with points being awarded in four (4) categories as follows: (1) Qualifications and Experience, (2) Previous Experience with Similar Services and Duties, (3) Start-up and Implementation Plan, and (4) Financial.

15.2.2   The Commission will award One Hundred (100) potential points based on the offeror's previous qualifications and experience including a review of all of the information and documentation requested in Section 2.0 et seq. above.

15.2.3   The Commission will award One Hundred (100) potential points based on the offeror's previous experience in providing similar services and duties including a review of all of the information and documentation requested in Section 2.0 et seq. above.

Service/Function	Point Scale
Public Works	0 to 15
Transportation	0 to 20
Streets, Rights-of-Way and Facilities	0 to 10
Parks and Recreation	0 to 10
Capital Improvement Plans	0 to 10
Planning and Zoning	0 to 20
Inspections, Code Enforcement and Permitting	0 to 15
Total	0 to 100

15.2.4   The Commission will award One Hundred (100) potential points based on the quality, detail and sufficiency of the offeror's start-up and implementation plan to have all of the required duties and services operational on the date of Contract Award by the City should the City decide to award the same. This analysis will also include an overall review of the entire proposal submitted by the offeror for quality, content, and detail.

15.2.5   The Commission will award One Hundred (100) points to the low bidder of the submitting offerors. Points for offerors submitting higher bids will be awarded in the following manner:

A ratio of the low bid dollars to the higher bid dollars will be calculated and multiplied by 100.

$$\frac{\text{Low Bid}}{\text{Higher Bid}} \times 100 \text{ Points} = \text{Higher Bid points}$$

15.3   Composite Score

15.3.1   The sum of the points for (1) Qualifications and Experience, (2) Previous Experience with Similar Services and Duties, (3) Start-up and Implementation Plan, and (4) Financial, will comprise the Composite Score. The maximum Composite Score is 400 Points.

APPENDIX D

SCOPE OF SERVICES

AGREEMENT BY AND BETWEEN CORPORATION AND
THE CITY OF SANDY SPRINGS

EXHIBIT "A"
RFP 2—PUBLIC WORKS
SCOPE OF SERVICES

Services described in this Exhibit A will be delivered in a manner that is consistent with reasonable municipal management practices as compared with municipalities of similar size in the State of Georgia.

The Corporation will provide sufficient staff, including contractor and subcontractor personnel, to provide the services described in this Exhibit A. It is recognized that the project staffing may fluctuate due to seasonal or other conditions to meet the service demands. It is envisioned that the average annual staffing levels will be approximately sixty-one (61) full-time equivalent (FTE) positions to deliver the intended services consistent with reasonable municipal management practices as compared with municipalities of similar size in the State of Georgia. If there are modifications to the scope of service that require significant additional staffing levels, such changes will be handled as per Section 8.2 of the Agreement.

Unless otherwise noted, the Corporation is not responsible for providing security services.

The services to be provided are described in the following sections.

1.0   PUBLIC WORKS

1.1   Public Works services shall include staffing and maintaining the Public Works Department for the City. The areas of responsibility shall include the following:

1.1.1   Stormwater

1.1.1.1   Under the direction of the City, coordinate with other City personnel and/or contractors for the transfer, maintenance, storage, and retrieval of available documents and records from Fulton County, Georgia, that are necessary for the effective implementation and operation of the City's stormwater requirements under applicable, federal, state, and local laws. The City shall facilitate the transfer of records. The Corporation shall be responsible for determining the documentation necessary for transfer, as well as coordinating and implementing the physical retrieval, reproduction, and storage of the transferred records.

1.1.1.2   Provide ongoing engineering, design and maintenance for the operation of stormwater system, as needed, to meet the needs of the City per Section 3.3 of the Agreement. Scope of services is limited to daily maintenance. Other services such as master planning and design services for capital program shall be handled per Section 3.3 of the agreement..

1.1.1.3   Develop and recommend to the City and upon approval implement the necessary policies, protocols, rules, and regulations to meet or exceed the City's stormwater requirements under applicable federal, state, and local laws, including, but not limited to, federal clean water requirements.

1.1.1.4   Integrate activities as necessary with Planning/Zoning and other departments by establishing department head planning sessions that incorporate integrated client service goals.

1.1.1.5   To accomplish the stormwater services, the Corporation will provide the following levels of effort consistent with reasonable municipal management practices:

a.   Furnish a level of effort consistent with 50 percent of one FTE position during startup and two FTEs ongoing for records transfer.

b. Furnish a level of effort consistent with 25 percent of one FTE for stormwater design.

c. Furnish a level of effort consistent with a crew of three FTE for stormwater maintenance.

d. Furnish a level of effort consistent with 25 percent of one FTE for policy development.

1.1.1.6   The scope does not include water sample collection, environmental testing, or reporting.

1.1.2   Emergency Preparedness

1.1.2.1   Develop and recommend policies and guidelines to the City, and upon approval, coordinate, operate, and maintain the City's emergency preparedness program in accordance with applicable federal, state, and local laws, as well as prudent local government practices.

1.1.2.2   Integrate and coordinate emergency preparedness operations in conjunction with Homeland Security, Emergency 911, Federal Emergency Management Agency (FEMA), and Georgia Emergency Management Agency (GEMA).

1.1.2.3   To accomplish emergency preparedness, the corporation will provide:

a. Baseline safety audit during transition

b. Recommended Emergency Preparedness Plan (EPP) policy during transition

c. Practice exercise during transition

d. Up to $50,000 for emergency cleanup (annually).

1.1.3   Recycling

1.1.3.1   Prepare and recommend policies and guidelines to the City, and operate the City's recycling program or a similar recycling program, which is defined presently as the City's proportionate share of the Keep Sandy Springs/North Fulton Beautiful Recycling Center (up to $81,000 annually).

1.1.3.2   Upon adoption, coordinate implementation of program and other activities with City personnel and/or contractors.

1.1.3.3 Fulfill reporting duties as required by applicable federal, state and local laws.

1.1.3.4 This scope of service does not include the hauling or disposing of yard waste or hazardous substances.

1.1.4 Geographic Information System (GIS)

1.1.4.1 Coordinate with the necessary City personnel and/or contractors for the transfer, maintenance, storage, and retrieval of available documents and records from Fulton County, Georgia, that are necessary for the effective implementation and operation of the City's geographic information system (GIS) database. The Corporation shall be responsible for determining the documentation necessary for transfer, as well as coordinating and implementing the physical retrieval, reproduction, and storage of the transferred records. Core elements of the GIS database will be in place to allow City staff to store and access GIS files and data obtained from Fulton County. The full implementation of the GIS database and interfaces will be complete on or around August 31, 2006.

1.1.4.2 Service, update, and maintain GIS databases on not less than a monthly basis.

1.1.4.3 Provide GIS-related information and/or data in response to requests and needs of City personnel.

1.1.4.4 To provide GIS services, the Corporation will provide levels of effort consistent with one (1) FTE during startup and two (2) FTEs for ongoing operations.

2.0 TRANSPORTATION

2.1 At the direction of the City, the transportation services shall include establishing, staffing, and maintaining the Transportation Department for the City. The areas of responsibility shall include the following:

2.1.1 Funding and Grant Applications

2.1.1.1 Conduct activities necessary to identify, develop, and prepare submissions for federal, state or local funding and grant programs, and provide fund oversight as required by law. Coordinate those aspects of the above, as necessary with the Atlanta Regional Commission and other local governmental entities as may be necessary. To accomplish the above service, Corporation will provide a level of effort consistent with 30 percent of a Transportation Planning Manager and 30 percent of a transportation planner.

2.1.2　　Traffic Engineering

1.1.1.1　　Conduct operational activities (maintenance, engineering, and planning services) necessary to maintain a traffic system, including conducting necessary studies and implementing traffic control improvements. To accomplish these services, the Corporation will provide a level of effort consistent with seventeen (17) FTEs under the direction of the Transportation Director, which includes up to $850,000 for the first year (2006) of traffic system operations and improvements, which includes street striping and signage. Design services for capital program projects and consulting services for master planning are not included in this scope of services and shall be handled per Section 3.3 of the Agreement.

1.1.1.2　　The scope does not include the purchase of Christmas decorations for the City.

2.1.3　　Street Design

2.1.3.1　　Conduct activities necessary to maintain a street system plan, including the coordination, review, and management of contracts for streets, sidewalks, and related projects. To accomplish these services, the Corporation will provide a level of effort consistent with 25 percent of one road engineer. In addition, in order to manage ongoing Capital Improvement Plan (CIP) projects, the Corporation will provide a level of effort consistent with 50 percent of one CIP manager and one CIP engineer.

2.1.4　　Street Maintenance

2.1.4.1　　Conduct activities necessary to maintain a roadway and bridge infrastructure system, including minor repairs, pothole repairs, cleaning, and minor repairs necessitated by storm events. At City request, Corporation may perform utility cuts to the roadway which will be repaired and inspected as per City specifications by the Corporation. Corporation may also perform, at the direction of the City, the non normal road and bridge repair (such as wash outs, sink holes and damage caused by vehicle accidents). The utility cuts and non normal repairs are not included within this Scope of Services and shall be handled as per Section 8.2 of the Agreement. In order to accomplish this service, a baseline condition of streets will need to be obtained from Fulton County and updated by the Corporation. The Corporation will then put into place a preventive and corrective maintenance system and a capital program list will be developed and prioritized for the City Council. For these services, the Corporation will provide a level of effort consistent with five (5) FTEs and maintenance sub-contractors. The scope does not include costs to procure, operate, or maintain street sweeping services or resurfacing City streets.

2.1.5   Street lights, Sidewalks, Gutters and Related Street Areas

2.1.5.1   Conduct activities necessary to maintain street lights, sidewalks, gutters, and related street areas.

3.0   STREETS, RIGHTS-OF-WAY, AND FACILITIES

3.1   General

3.1.1   Streets, rights-of-way, and facilities services shall.

3.1.1.1   Coordinate the transfer of City rights-of-way from Fulton County, Georgia. The Corporation shall be responsible for determining the documentation necessary for transfer. The City shall be responsible for facilitating this process.

3.1.1.2   Operate and oversee aspects of the City rights-of-way permitting process. Right-of-way permits are issued for curb-cuts and private use of the City-owned rights-of-way. To accomplish this process, the Corporation will provide a level of effort consistent with one (1) FTE and maintenance sub-contractors.

3.1.1.3   The Corporation shall be responsible for up to $1,000 per event and up to $10,000 per year invested in the planting and maintenance of City rights-of-way beautification.

3.1.1.4   The Corporation shall not be responsible for security at City facilities, including both staff and security apparatuses such as metal detectors.

3.1.1.5   The scope includes up to $456,000 for street light electricity. The Corporation shall not be responsible for other utility costs associated with facilities, streets, or rights-of-way, including, but not limited to, water and electricity other than noted here and in Section 4.1.1.

3.2   Contract Administration

3.2.1   Operate and oversee aspects of contract administration for the daily maintenance of public rights-of-way and property, including landscaping and irrigation systems, in order to provide safe and comfortable common grounds for the residents of Sandy Springs. The scope includes hiring a subcontractor, scheduling, inspecting contracted work, and reviewing and approving payment requests.

3.2.2   Operate and oversee aspects of contract administration for the construction (excluding CIP; refer to Section 3.3), operation, and maintenance of public facilities. The scope includes hiring a subcontractor, scheduling, inspecting contracted work, and reviewing and approving payment requests.

3.2.3   Operate and oversee aspects of the emergency preparedness plan for debris removal, roadway access, flood prevention, and safe, operable utilities. To accomplish this service, the Corporation will provide the elements listed in Section 1.1.2.3. The scope includes preparing the plan, setting up a practice session, distributing a contact list, and reviewing and implementing GEMA and FEMA requirements through Corporation employees and subcontractors, with local, state and federal agencies.

4.0   PARKS AND RECREATION

4.1   Parks and recreation services shall include staffing and maintaining the Parks and Recreation Department for the City. The areas of responsibility shall reasonably include the following:

4.1.1   Plan, recommend, and upon adoption, implement and coordinate staffing and contract administration for the daily maintenance and use of public parks and recreational facilities. The scope includes managing and procuring the services of subcontractors and temporary personnel on behalf of the City to administer recreation programs and manage subcontractors performing maintenance functions such as mowing, fence repair, and ballpark lining. The scope includes electrical costs of up to $240,000 for the lighting of the ballparks and associated fields.

4.1.2   Plan, recommend, and upon adoption, implement and coordinate staffing for the planning, promoting, and supervising of recreation programs and special events. Special events include festivals and parades but not field trips. The Corporation shall set up traffic barricades and provide cleanup services after an event is over, for up to two City events per year. The Corporation shall not provide security or transportation services for programs or events.

4.1.3   Plan, recommend, and upon adoption, implement and coordinate staffing for the managing, coordinating and scheduling of City athletic facilities, as needed. The Corporation shall set up traffic barricades and provide cleanup services after an event is over. The Corporation shall not provide security or transportation services for programs or events.

4.1.4   Develop and recommend to the City Manager short-, mid-, and long-range plans for capital improvements and implement the plans as directed by the City Manager. The scope does not include the development of a Park and Recreation Master Plan by the Corporation.

4.1.5   Operate and oversee aspects of emergency management procedures with local, state and federal agencies. To accomplish this service, the Corporation will provide those the elements listed in Section 1.1.2.3.

4.1.6   Conduct the activities necessary to identify, develop, and prepare submissions for federal, state or local funding and grant programs for improvements to the park and recreation system within Sandy Springs and provide fund oversight as required by law.

4.1.7   To accomplish the parks and recreation services, the Corporation will provide a level of effort consistent with three (3) FTEs, plus subcontractors, for programs and maintenance under the direction of the Parks and Recreation Director.

4.1.8   Under no circumstances shall the Corporation be directly involved in the distribution or sale of alcoholic beverages.

5.0   CAPITAL IMPROVEMENTS

5.1   Develop and recommend short-, mid-, and long-range plans for capital improvements and implement plans as directed by the City Manager. The plans should meet the requirements of the Department of Community Affairs and the Atlanta Regional Commission for adoption in the City's Comprehensive Land Use Plan. The Corporation has allotted a level of effort consistent with 10 percent of each of the following Director's positions to accomplish this service: Community Development, Public Works, Transportation, and Parks & Recreation, with support of one full-time planner and one full-time administrative assistant split between these areas. This scope of service does not include procurement services for the capital improvements, which will be handled per Section 3.3 of the Agreement.

6.0   PLANNING AND ZONING

6.1   Planning and zoning services shall include staffing as needed to meet the requirements herein and operating the Planning and Zoning Department for the City. The areas of responsibility shall include the following:

6.1.1   At the direction of the City, provide information to the general public as it relates to land development activities within the City.

6.1.2   At the direction of the City, provide information to builders and developers regarding policies and procedures related to land planning within the City.

3.3.3   Oversee the development, maintenance, and updating of land use and zoning maps as approved and required by State and local agencies.

6.1.4   Prepare and recommend policies and procedures regarding planning and zoning activities and prepare and recommend schedules and time frames for processing land development activities, including, but not limited to, zoning.

6.1.5 Provide information to the City Manager, Mayor, City Council, Planning and Zoning Boards, and other City entities needing information regarding relevant and applicable zoning and/or planning issues.

6.1.6 Develop and recommend a plan for the implementation and assessment of impact fees by the City. Upon adoption, implement the plan in coordination with City staff and/or contractors. The scope does not include an impact fee study.

6.1.7 Conduct activities necessary to maintain a planning and zoning system for the City. These include, but are not limited to, the following:

a. Receiving, processing, and approving building plans

b. Building inspection

c. Recommend enforcement of codes, including signs, landscape, and arborist

d. Preparing a comprehensive plan, including zoning ordinances

e. Reviewing land development plans

f. Inspecting land disturbances

6.1.8 Develop and recommend a plan for the issuance of certificates of use and certificates of occupancy (COs). Upon approval, implement the plan in coordination with other City staff or contractors.

6.1.9 To accomplish the planning and zoning services, the Corporation will provide a level of effort consistent with seven FTEs under the direction of one full-time Community Development Director.

7.0 INSPECTIONS, CODE ENFORCEMENT, AND PERMITTING

7.1 Inspections, code enforcement, and permitting services shall include staffing and operating the inspections, code enforcement, and permitting functions for the City. The areas of responsibility shall include the following:

7.1.1   Develop and recommend a plan for the review and inspection process for the City. Upon adoption, implement the plan in coordination with City staff or contractors.

7.1.2   Develop and recommend a plan for the buildi[...] and inspection process for the City. Upon adoption, i[...] plan in coordination with City staff or contractors.

7.1.3   Develop and recommend a plan for the code enforcem[...] [...]s for the City. Upon adoption, implement the plan in co[...] [...]on with City staff or contractors.

7.1.4   Develop and recommend a plan for the City to conduct Soil Erosion and Sedimentation Control inspections. Upon adoption, implement the plan in coordination with City staff or contractors.

7.1.5   To accomplish the inspections, code enforcement, and permitting services, the Corporation will supply a level of effort consistent with eleven (11) FTEs in Code Enforcement and six (6) FTEs, plus sub-contracting inspection services, in Permitting and Inspections under the direction of one full-time Community Development Director.

A P P E N D I X   E

AGREEMENT BY AND BETWEEN

CITY OF SANDY SPRINGS, GEORGIA

AND

CH2M HILL, INC

FOR PROVISION OF

ADMINISTRATIVE, FINANCIAL COMMUNITY SERVICES,
MOTOR VEHICLE, STAFFING, AND PURCHASING,
PROCUREMENT AND CONTRACTING SERVICES

THIS AGREEMENT is made and entered into this _____ day of _____
____, 200__, by and between the CITY OF SANDY SPRINGS, a Georgia
municipal corporation, (the "City"), and CH2M HILL, Inc., a Florida corporation. ("Corporation").

WHEREAS, the City is desirous of maintaining a level of competent professional and economically feasible contract administrative, finance and community services in conjunction and harmony with its fiscal policies of sound,
economical management, and

WHEREAS, Corporation has agreed to render to the City a continuing level
of professional contract services and the City is desirous of contracting for
such services upon the terms and conditions hereinafter set forth, and

WHEREAS, Corporation is licensed to do business within the state of Georgia as a foreign corporation, and

WHEREAS the City is desirous of providing these daily services to its constituents through a contractual relationship with Corporation,

WHEREAS the Governors Commission for the City of Sandy Springs, an entity created pursuant to O.C.G.A. § 36-31-8, followed a specific procedure, issued a request for proposals, and the proposals were reviewed by representatives of the Governor's Commission and the members of the Governor's Commission and were made available to the members of the public at large,

WHEREAS the City has the power to contract,

WHEREAS the City will have on-hand funds to pay for all obligations incurred hereunder,

NOW THEREFORE, in consideration of the sums hereinafter set forth and for other good and valuable considerations, the receipt and legal sufficiency of which are hereby acknowledged, it is hereby agreed as follows:

SECTION 1.   PRIOR AGREEMENTS

As of the effective date hereof, all prior agreements between the City and Corporation are terminated and replaced by the terms hereof.

SECTION 2.   GENERAL SERVICES

2.1   Corporation shall provide to City for the term hereinafter set forth, as the same may be extended in accordance with the provisions hereof, competent services, within and throughout the corporate limits of City to the extent and in the manner hereinafter described.

2.2   The City hereby engages Corporation to provide, and Corporation hereby agrees to provide, all of the services described herein and in the "Scope of Services," attached hereto as Exhibit A and incorporated herein by reference.

2.3   The parties recognize that this Agreement is intended to provide flexibility to the City in order to meet its evolving challenges. The Corporation reserves the right to reasonably allocate resources for the performance of services between this Agreement and the

Agreement for Public Works, Transportation, Streets, Right-Of-Way, Facilities, Parks And Recreation, Capital Improvements, Planning And Zoning, Inspections, Code Enforcement, Permitting, Purchasing, Procurement, and Contracting Services per the priorities agreed-to with the City Manager so long as such allocations do not adversely affect the City regarding either (1) cost of services under this Agreement, or (2) service quality to the public. Staff additions as agreed upon between the parties resulting from new services outside the Scope of Services in this contract, will be considered a change to this Agreement.

2.4   Corporation agrees to provide City all services and personnel necessary to fulfill the obligations of Corporation under this contract; provided, however, that to the extent that the City must cooperate and/or perform services in conjunction with a third party, excluding Corporation's second tier subcontractors which shall be defined as any individual or entity retained, employed, affiliated, or engaged by or under contract with Corporation to undertake any services performed hereunder, should the third party fail to fulfill their obligations or duties, any additional services performed or costs reasonably incurred by the Corporation in conjunction with compensating for the failure of the third party to fulfill its obligations shall be handled as a change to this Agreement as per Section 9.2.

2.5   Except as otherwise hereinafter specifically set forth, such professional services shall encompass all those duties and functions of the type coming within the jurisdiction of and customarily rendered by municipal departments (other than those provided by other contract providers) in accordance with the Charter of the City, and the Statutes of the State of Georgia.

2.6   Corporation shall, at all times, foster and maintain harmonious relationships with the members of the City Council, all employees of the City, all employees of the City's contract services providers and all City's residents, and shall represent the City in the best light possible.

2.7   All communications to the Mayor, City Council, and press, unless otherwise authorized, shall be through the City Manager. All mass communications to residents shall be reviewed and approved by the City Manager prior to printing and dissemination.

2.8   The President or Senior Executive Officer of Corporation shall be available to meet with the City Manager at City Hall on an annual basis, date to be determined by mutual agreement, and at any other times at the request of the City Manager after reasonable notice has been provided to President or Senior Executive Officer of Corporation.

SECTION 3.   FINANCIAL SERVICES

3.1   Corporation shall follow the procedures established by the City Manager for withdrawal, transfer and disbursement of City funds.

3.2   Corporation shall maintain all financial records in accordance with all applicable laws and guidelines for municipal accounting, including GAAP, GASB and GFOA standards, and shall produce and deliver to the City Manager any and all financial information and reports requested by the City Manager.

3.3   Corporation shall ensure that the City complies with all requirements regarding audits, and shall assist the City in procuring an independent auditor with experience in governmental auditing in compliance with all applicable laws and procedures.

3.4   All investments shall be made pursuant to any and all investment policies approved by the City Council in accordance with Georgia Statutes.

3.5   Corporation shall prepare and follow risk management policies and procedures, as adopted by the City Council.

3.6   Corporation shall take advantage of all available discounts on purchases and invoices for City purchases, unless, based upon best cash management practices, a more beneficial payment structure is available to the City.

3.7   Corporation shall promptly pay all City bills in accordance with Georgia law and sound business practices.

3.8   Corporation shall assist the City in finding and applying for various grants and in fulfilling all obligations that accompany such grants.

3.9   On or before the fifteenth day of each month, Corporation shall prepare and deliver to the City Manager a monthly financial statement for the prior month.

3.9.1   On or before October 1 of every year, Corporation shall prepare and deliver to the City Manager an annual inventory of all City owned tangible personal property and equipment in accordance with all applicable rules and standards.

SECTION 4.   ADDITIONAL SERVICES

4.1   Corporation shall provide to the City, upon the request of the City Manager and the availability of resources, such additional services as may from time to time be needed at the discretion of the City.

4.2   The cost of such additional services shall be borne by the City and shall be payable in such amounts and in such a manner as may be determined by mutual agreement, upon each occurrence in accordance with Section 9.2.

4.3   Corporation may provide management of capital improvements and engineering services (provided, however, Corporation acknowledges that it is responsible for certain engineering services encompassed in that certain Agreement for Public Works, Transportation, Streets, Right-Of-Way, Facilities, Parks And Recreation, Capital Improvements, Planning And Zoning, Inspections, Code Enforcement, Permitting, Purchasing, Procurement, and Contracting Services executed contemporaneously herewith) as set out in Section 1.2.2 of the Scope of Services attached hereto as Exhibit A. Both Parties agree that Corporation's duties under this Agreement are limited to the coordination for capital improvement programs and procurement and program management for small projects (i.e., estimated procurement contract value of under $50,000 although final decision will be based upon the complexity of said project), unless otherwise agreed upon between the Parties. Corporation's duties do not include the program management of the large or complex (those projects outside of the above definition of small projects) which would be outside the Scope of Services herein and, accordingly, handled through an additional services authorization and change to the Agreement as per Section 9.2

of this Agreement. Subject to all other requirements contained herein, the parties agree that if requested to conduct program management of the operations of a capital improvement project, Corporation may provide for such services to be completed by either Corporation, an affiliate of Corporation, or second tier subcontractor.

4.4   **MAINTENANCE. REPAIR AND CAPITAL IMPROVEMENTS**

4.4.1   Corporation shall provide for ordinary maintenance of City assets and infrastructure in the course of its duties under this Agreement as per Exhibit A, Scope of Services. Such ordinary maintenance shall be performed to the extent of the capabilities of the project staff during normal business hours. For the purposes of this Agreement, the definition of ordinary maintenance shall be: the routine/repetitive activities required for operational continuity, safety, and performance of City assets or infrastructure.

4.4.2   Corporation shall provide for repair of City assets and infrastructure in the course of its duties under this Agreement as per Exhibit A, Scope of Services. For the purposes of this Agreement, the definition of repair shall be: the cost of non-routine/non-repetitive activities required for operational continuity, safety, and performance generally resulting from the failure or to avert a failure of the equipment, vehicle, roadway, or facility or some component thereof. The parties agree that such repair work shall be limited $50,000 annually unless otherwise specified in the Scope of Services or unless and in the event Corporation is responsible for the needed repairs through its failure to perform routine maintenance or because of any intentional acts of the Corporation's employees. The parties further agree that Corporation is authorized pursuant to this agreement to immediately perform emergency repair services which may fall outside of the Scope of Services hereto to address unforeseen issues of safety and welfare which may arise, provided, however, Corporation and shall notify the City Manager of the existence of, and the scope of, any such emergency repair as soon as feasible based upon the circumstances, but in no event later than twenty-four (24) hours of receipt of notification of such emergency repairs.

4.4.3   A capital improvement is defined as, any work or materials applied to an existing asset that restores that asset or infrastructure to a "like new" condition and/or improves the performance and/or reliability levels of the asset beyond the capabilities of the original installation or performs a duty or service that was not previously provided. The Corporation's duties under this Agreement do not encompass payment for capital improvements to assets of the City unless so agreed to between the parties.

SECTION 5.   HOURS OF OPERATION

5.1   Corporation shall maintain for the purposes of City business, fully staffed business hours equal to, but not less than, the City's business hours of 8:00 a.m. to 5:00 p.m. and shall reasonably provide appropriate staff to perform the after hours requirements associated with court services, clerking support, public relations, and election support to fulfill the performance of the services as per Exhibit A, Monday through Friday, with the exception of the following holidays:

New Year's Day
Martin Luther King Birthday
President's Day
Memorial Day
Independence Day
Labor Day
Veteran's Day
Thanksgiving Day
Day After Thanksgiving Day
Christmas

5.2   For all City related matters, Corporation shall use the address of Sandy Springs City Hall, including both incoming and outgoing mail.

SECTION 6.   EQUIPMENT AND LABOR

6.1   Corporation shall furnish to and maintain, as per Section 3.3. of the Exhibit A, for the benefit of the City, without additional cost, all necessary labor, supervision, equipment (including motor vehicles excluding, however, any specialized service related emergency vehicles such as Police and/or Fire Emergency Vehicles) necessary and proper for the purpose of performing the services, duties and responsibilities set forth and contemplated herein and as necessary to maintain the level of service to be rendered hereunder. In the event of emergencies or natural disasters, Corporation shall, immediately and on and on-going basis, supply its usual and customary personnel to ensure continuing operation of all services provided by Corporation and to satisfy all County, State and Federal administrative and emergency requirements.

6.2   All City owned equipment shall be used only for City purposes in performance of this Agreement, and shall not be used for any purely corporate, non-governmental Corporation business or personal purposes.

6.3   All City owned vehicles and equipment utilized by Corporation employees shall be maintained in strict accordance with manufacturer's recommended maintenance, and Corporation shall keep full records of all maintenance. All City vehicles shall be kept clean, free of damages and in safe operating condition. All City vehicles shall be used in strict conformance with the Vehicle Use Policy attached hereto as Exhibit B.

6.4   Corporation shall comply with all OSHA and other applicable federal and state statutes, regulations and standards for work place safety. Corporation shall comply with all applicable laws regarding hazardous materials and maintain all required Manufacturer's Safety Data Sheets (MSDS) forms on site in the City.

6.5   During regular business hours, all telephones at Corporation shall be answered by human, not automated, attendants.

SECTION 7.   CORPORATION EMPLOYEES

7.1   All personnel employed by Corporation in the performance of such services, functions and responsibilities as described and contemplated herein for the City shall be and remain Corporation employees (the "Corporation Employees").

7.2   Corporation shall be solely responsible for all compensation benefits, insurance and rights of the Corporation employees during the course of or arising or accruing as a result of any employment, whether past or present, with Corporation, as well as all legal costs including attorney's fees incurred in the defense of any conflict or legal action resulting from such employment or related to the corporate amenities of such employment. Accordingly City shall not be called upon to assume any liability for or direct payment of any salaries, wages, contribution to pension funds, insurance premiums or payments, workers compensation benefits under O.C.G.A. §34-9-1 et seq., or any other amenities of employment to any of the Corporation Employees or any other liabilities whatsoever, unless otherwise specifically provided herein.

7.3 In conformance with standards established by City for achieving an acceptable level of customer service and delivery of municipal services to the City residents and constituents consistent with reasonable municipal management practices as compared with municipalities of similar size in the State of Georgia, Corporation shall have and maintain the responsibility for and control of the rendition of the services, the standards of performance, the discipline of the Corporation Employees and other matters incident to the performance of the services, duties and responsibilities as described and contemplated herein.

7.4 In order to perform its obligations hereunder, certain Corporation Employees will be assigned to work full-time for the City (the "Designated Employees"). Prior to assigning any Designated Employees to the City, Corporation shall subject each prospective Designated Employee to a full background check, including a driver's license review. Corporation retains the ability to discipline such Designated Employees as per Corporation's established guidelines, including termination.

7.5 The Corporation Employees shall wear attire with the logo of the City when, and only when, they are performing services for the City, except as otherwise directed by the City Manager.

7.6 The City Manager shall have the right utilizing an objective standard based upon job performance to require Corporation to transfer any of the Designated Employees out of the City or to a different position. Corporation agrees to transfer any of the Designated Employees immediately upon notification by the City Manager. Utilizing an objective standard based upon job performance, the City Manager shall have the right to prohibit any Corporation Employee that is not a Designated Employee from performing any work for the City, and shall also have the right to limit, in any manner, the work done for the City by any Corporation Employee that is not a Designated Employee.

7.7   Corporation shall have the discretion to transfer or reassign any personnel out of the City for the following reasons:

    a.   Situations where an employee requests a transfer in order to accept a promotion or special assignment, which has been offered to him or her by Corporation upon his or her special education qualifications or career path;

    b.   Disciplinary reasons;

    c.   Failure of an employee to meet Corporation performance standards;

    d.   At the request of the employee.

In the event Corporation transfers or reassigns any employee for the above stated reasons, Corporation shall provide the City Manager with prompt written notice of such transfer or reassignment and explain the basis of the reassignment. Corporation shall not transfer or reassign any of the Corporation Employees for any other reasons unless the City Manager concurs prior to any transfer, which concurrence shall not be unreasonably withheld. Any personnel, transferred or reassigned out of the City, pursuant to this subsection, shall not occur without first filling the vacated position with a Corporation employee approved and authorized by the City Manager, which approval and authorization shall not be unreasonably withheld.

SECTION 8.   ASSISTANT CITY MANAGER AND PROGRAM DIRECTOR

8.1   The Program Director assisted by the Assistant City Manager shall, among other duties specified by the City Manager:

    a.   Act as liaison between the City and Corporation;

    b.   Attend staff meetings, City Council meetings and any agenda meetings, at which attendance by the Program Director and Assistant City Manager is deemed necessary by the City

Manager. Attend other County and State agency meetings and forums as required by the City Manager;

c. Provide information to City Manager and City Council on all issues relevant and applicable to the City, its officials, its constituents or to its status as a municipal corporation;

d. Assist the City in all relations with other Contractors;

e. When so directed by the City Manager, carry out such other duties and responsibilities as are necessary to fulfill services under Exhibit A, but that are not inconsistent with Corporation's obligations under this Agreement, nor expand Corporation's obligations under this Agreement.

8.2   In the event of a vacancy in the position of the Program Director and/or Assistant City Manager, Corporation agrees to make such selections in good faith and in the best interest of the City. The City Manager shall have the opportunity to interview each of the candidates, and no person may be appointed Program Director or Assistant City Manager without the City Manager's consent, which may be withheld for any reason or no reason, in City Manager's sole discretion.

8.3   In the event the City Manager becomes dissatisfied with the performance of the Program Director or Assistant City Manager, utilizing an objective standard based upon job performance, the City Manager may, in its sole discretion, provide notification to Corporation. Thereafter, representatives of Corporation and the City Manager shall meet to discuss possible remedies of the problems experienced by the City. Corporation agrees to act in good faith in resolving any problems experienced by the City, including if necessary the removal of Al Crace as Assistant City Manager or Rick Hirsekorn as Program Director.

SECTION 9.   COMPENSATION

9.1   The City shall pay to Corporation as compensation for services performed under this Agreement a fixed price of $11,200,000 for the first year of this Agreement ("Compensation Amount"). One-twelfth (1/12) of the Compensation Amount shall invoiced by the first of the month in which services are to be performed and the invoice shall be due thirty (30) days from receipt. The

City shall budget an additional fifteen percent (15%) of the annual Compensation Amount for new services not defined in Exhibit A, Scope of Services. Access to these funds will be controlled by the City and authorized via the defined Change Order process outlined in Section 9.2 of this Service Agreement. **The Compensation Amount does not include Sales, Use or other taxes. Such applicable taxes will be added to the monthly invoice.** Such Compensation Amount shall be adjusted on an annual basis as per Section 9.4, to take effect on January 1st of the new calendar year in which Corporation is performing services. Corporation shall provide to City on a monthly basis the breakdown of monthly price per overall service in a format to be agreed upon between the parties.

9.1.1   The City from time-to-time may request the Corporation to perform services which are not included in Exhibit A, Scope of Services ("Change Order"). Upon request by the City, the Corporation will, within a reasonable time period (generally within 5 working days) provide to the City a price for the Change Order service(s) in writing. The estimate will be provided to the City for review and approval. If approved by the City in writing, the Corporation will proceed with the Change Order services. Unless otherwise stated in the estimate, the Corporation will invoice the City on the next billing cycle after completion of Change Order service(s). If the Change Order service request generates an on-going new service or will result in an on-going new service under the Scope of Services, the Corporation will include the associated adjustment for the Change Order to the monthly Compensation Amount invoice for City consideration.

9.1.2   City shall pay interest at an annual rate equal to Wells Fargo Bank, N.A.'s prime rate plus one and one-half percent (1-1/2%) (said amount of interest not to exceed any limitation provided by law) on payments not paid and received within thirty (30) calendar days from date of receipt by the City of Corporation's monthly invoice, such interest being calculated from the due date of the payment, so long as said delay is not caused by Corporation. City shall pay all undisputed amounts according to the terms of this Agreement. If City disputes any invoices issued, City shall notify Corporation in writing within five (5) days of receipt of invoice detailing out the invoice charge disputed and reasons why. Corporation shall respond within five (5) days to such notification. If such issue is not resolved within fifteen (15) days after notification, such issue shall be handled as per Section 42. Valid disputes on invoices shall not accrue interest until the date of resolution, and applicable interest, if any, shall be calculated from the date of resolution of the dispute.

9.4   For the fiscal year beginning January 1, 2007, the annual fee for the services pursuant to this Agreement will be $8,639,960. For years Fiscal Year 2008 and beyond, the Compensation Amount shall be an amount as determined by the following formula:

[CPI x (15% x Baseline Compensation Amount which is the current year compensation to be adjusted)] + [ECI x (85% x Baseline Compensation Amount which is the current year compensation to be adjusted)]

CPI = Consumer Price Index for all urban consumers as published by U.S. Department of Labor, Bureau of Labor Statistics in the CPI Detailed Report for the month October of the calendar year presently operating in, (South Urban region, Atlanta, GA)

ECI = Compensation for Civilians Workers, Not Seasonally Adjusted (Employment Cost Index) for the third quarter of the calendar year presently operating in as published by U.S. Department of Labor, Bureau of Labor Statistics in the Detailed Report.

Such adjustment formula does not take into consideration significant price increases related to gasoline, power, asphalt, fuel, and other commodities or services related to force majeure events. In the event Corporation can demonstrate that significant regional price increases have occurred, that are outside the reasonable control of Corporation, the City and Corporation will engage in good faith efforts to assess the relative impact on the respective variable to the Compensation Amount.

Subject to the foregoing paragraph regarding significant price increases, in no event shall the total upward adjustment of the Compensation Amount pursuant to this section exceed the sum of nine percent (9%) in any given annual period. Further, the Compensation Amount may not be increased in any fiscal year without the approval of the City Council. In addition, should any upward adjustment of the Compensation Amount be negotiated regarding the Agreement, City shall have a similar right to a proportional adjustment upwards of the amounts regarding Corporation's liability for costs, including but not limited to: (1) liability caps for damages and/or fines, (2) repair and maintenance costs, and (3) furniture, fixture and equipment expenditures under this Agreement, which shall all be set out in writing by way of addendum to this Agreement at the time of agreement upon any revised terms.

9.5   If, during any fiscal year, there is a reduction in the scope of services not related to default by Corporation as per Section 13, the Compensation Amount shall be reduced by an amount agreeable to the City Manager and Corporation, but in no event shall the reduced Compensation Amount be an amount less than the actual cost of said services, and the allocated overhead and profit for such services. If the City elects not to assume performance of the reduced or eliminated services as contemplated herein, and therefore the equipment, materials and staff procured or hired by Corporation for the provision to the City of said reduced services results in expense to the Corporation, Corporation may recover those expenses caused by such unassumed services including any demobilization costs, unamortized costs incurred by Corporation, and any applicable termination charges assessed by vendors or suppliers retained by Corporation to provide the eliminated service. If the City Manager and Corporation are unable to agree upon an amount, the reduced Compensation Amount shall be equal to the actual cost, allocated overhead and profit, less any allowed offsets as set forth in this Section.

9.6   The parties may agree to modify the baseline compensation amount for Fiscal Year 2008, provided, however, should Corporation seek to modify such baseline amount such request must be made in writing directed to the City Manager, setting forth all costs and justifications for such modification no less than six (6) months prior to the termination date under the Agreement. Any modification of the baseline compensation amount shall be subject to approval of the City Council.

SECTION 10. TERM

As per O.C.G.A. 36-60-13, this Service Agreement is effective January 1, 2006, and shall be effective for one year terms ending at the close of each calendar year. This Service Agreement shall be automatically renewed as per Section 11.

SECTION 11. OPTION TO RENEW

As per O.C.G.A. 36-60-13, this Agreement shall be automatically renewed for a period of five (5) one (1) year terms at the expiration of the initial term, upon the mutual agreement between the Parties, unless either party furnishes the other party written notice of its intent not to renew this Agreement not less than one hundred twenty (120) days prior to the expiration of this Agreement.

SECTION 12. TERMINATION

12.1   Corporation may terminate this Service Agreement at its discretion either with or without cause, by giving written notice thereof to City; provided, however, that such termination shall not be effective until the one hundred and eightieth (180th) day after receipt thereof by City.

12.2   City may terminate this Service Agreement in its entirety at its discretion either with or without cause, by giving written notice thereof to Corporation; provided, however, that such termination shall not be effective until the one hundred and eightieth (180th) day after receipt thereof by Corporation. City may also terminate this Service Agreement in its entirety, at its discretion with no advance notice, in the event of a vote by the Board of Directors, officers or employees to transfer of a controlling interest in Corporation (which shall be defined to mean more than 50% of the ownership interest) to a non-related entity. Corporation shall notify the City Manager immediately in the event of such a vote to so transfer of a controlling interest in Corporation.

12.3   City may partially terminate this Service Agreement as to any specific service or services provided by Corporation hereunder by giving at least sixty (60) days advance written notice thereof to Corporation specifying the specific service or services that the City desires Corporation to cease performing. Upon a partial termination, the Compensation Amount shall be reduced pursuant to Section 9.5 of this Agreement.

12.4   In the event of termination by either party, the other party shall render such aid, coordination and cooperation as might be required for an expeditious and efficient termination of service.

12.4.1   In the event of termination by City for reasons other than default as per Section 13, and if the City elects not to assume performance of some or all of the reduced services Corporation may recover costs as set forth in Section 9.5 of this Agreement.

12.4.2   This Service Agreement is contingent upon sufficient appropriation and authorization being made annually by the City Council, at least one hundred and twenty (120) days prior to renewal period, for the performance of the services provided in this contract. If sufficient appropriations and authorizations are not so made, this Contract shall terminate pursuant to the terms of this Section 12 upon written notice being given by the City to Corporation.

SECTION 13. DEFAULT

13.1   An event of default shall mean a material breach of this Agreement. If situations arise which are not considered a material breach, such issues shall be resolved as per Section 42. Without limiting the generality of the foregoing and in addition to those instances referred to as a breach, an event of default shall include the following:

a.   Corporation has not performed services as per this Agreement;

b.   Corporation has refused or failed, except in the case for which an extension of time is provided, to supply properly skilled Staff personnel;

c.   Corporation has failed to obtain the approval of the City where required by this Agreement;

d.   Corporation has refused or failed, except in the case for which an extension of time is provided, to provide the Services as defined in this Agreement.

e. The failure, refusal or other default by the City in its duty: (1) to pay the amount required to be paid to the Corporation under this Agreement within 30 days following the due date for such payment; or (2) to perform any other material obligation under this Agreement (unless such default is excused by an Force Majeure and to the extent provided herein).

f. Any representation or warranty of either party hereunder that was false or inaccurate in any material respect when made, and which materially and adversely affects the legality of this Agreement or the ability of either party to carry out its obligations hereunder.

13.2   In the event either Party fails to comply with the provisions of this Agreement, the other Party may: (1) declare the Party in default, notify defaulting party in writing, and give defaulting party fifteen (15) calendar days from receipt of notice to make substantial efforts towards curing the default. If defaulting party fails to make substantial efforts towards curing such default within fifteen (15) calendar days, such Agreement shall be terminated as per Section 12.1 and any compensation due and owing to Corporation shall be paid by City; or (2) such party may exercise such provisions under Section 42 regarding the alleged breach without waiving or being estopped from subsequently pursuing the breach as a matter of law. If Corporation is the defaulting party, the compensation to Corporation through termination shall be the prorated Compensation Amount for any completed professional services minus any damages assessed pursuant to Section 13.3. Upon termination City shall begin transition efforts and Corporation shall assist such transition, provided, however, City shall be liable for the reasonable costs for transition efforts as demonstrated by the Corporation. In the event payment has been made for professional services not completed, Corporation shall return these sums to the City within ten (10) days after receipt of notice that these sums are due. Nothing in this Article shall limit the either Party's right to terminate, at any time, pursuant to Sections 11 and 12, its right for damages under Section 13.3, and its right to assign pursuant to Section 38.

13.3   In an Event of Default by either Party, it shall be liable for all damages resulting from the default.

13.4   Subject to the dispute provisions contained in Section 42 of this Agreement, either Party may take advantage of each and every remedy specifically existing at law or in equity. Each and every remedy shall be in addition to every other remedy specifically given or otherwise existing and may be exercised from time to time as often and in such order as may be deemed expedient by the Party. The exercise or the beginning of the exercise of one remedy shall not be deemed to be a waiver of the right to exercise any other remedy. The Parties' rights and remedies as set forth in this Agreement are not exclusive and are in addition to any other rights and remedies available to either Party in law or in equity.

SECTION 14. TRANSITION

14.1   In the event of the full termination for any reason, partial termination or expiration of this Agreement, Corporation and City shall cooperate in good faith in order to effectuate a smooth and harmonious transition from Corporation to City, or to any other person or entity City may designate, and to maintain during such period of transition the same quality services otherwise afforded to the residents of the City pursuant to the terms hereof.

14.2   In the event of the full termination, partial termination or expiration of this Agreement, the City shall have the absolute right to offer employment to any of the Corporation Employees. If, upon termination for any reason other than default of the Corporation, City exercises its option to assume employment of Corporation's employees as contemplated by this Section 14.2, in addition to the Compensation Amount due to Corporation for the completed services, as prorated pursuant to Section 9.5 herein, City shall pay to Corporation as additional compensation the following as compensation to Corporation for expended funds related to employment, training, benefit packages, start-up and transition costs that Corporation would not be able to recoup:

If termination and assumption of Corporation employees occurs in the first year of this Agreement, City shall pay to Corporation the sum of: (1) 35% for staff with salaries above $100,000, and (2) 20% for staff with salaries less than $100,000. For each subsequent renewal period the percentage due for each assumed employee shall be reduced at 1/6 per year such that there is no payment at the end of the Term. The percentage amounts shall be based upon the then current salaries of the respective staff members during the contract year in which the termination takes place.

14.3   In the event of the full termination, partial termination or expiration of this Agreement, and in the further event that the City is unable to provide the same level of services at the time of such termination or expiration, the then pending term of this Agreement may be extended by the City for a period of ninety (90) days or until City is capable, in its sole discretion, of rendering such services, whichever occurs sooner. The remuneration to be paid to Corporation during the transition period shall be based upon actual cost of providing such services during the transition period plus a mutually agreed upon fee, provided, however such fee shall not exceed the Compensation Amount which would be due and owing to the Corporation for the provision of said services pursuant to the terms of this Agreement.

14.4   In the event of the full termination, partial termination, expiration of the term or non-renewal of the term, the City may either accept assignment of Corporations' current leases and/or agreements for the project or City may pay any associated buy-out or termination charges, provided, however, prior to entering into any leases or agreements after the effective date of this Agreement which contain buy-out provisions or termination charges in excess of $1,000.00, Corporation shall submit the terms of the same to the City Manager for approval in writing prior to entering into such lease or agreement. Corporation has provided City with a list of all leases and agreements entered into by Corporation and City hereby approves such.

14.5   The following terms apply to vehicles assets leased by Corporation during the term of this Agreement:

a.   Corporation will enter into a lease agreement with Automotive Rental, Inc. ("ARI") for the vehicles required for performance of the services under this Agreement for the City's benefit.

b.   Corporation will be responsible for maintaining the required insurance for the leased assets.

c.   The Compensation Amount under Section 9 has provided for reimbursement to Corporation for the monthly lease amounts.

d.   Under Corporation's lease with ARI, after the initial twelve (12) months Corporation has the option to continue to lease the vehicles on a month to month basis; return the vehicle(s) to ARI; or purchase the vehicle(s). Any time after the initial twelve (12) months, City may request to purchase the vehicle at Corporation's cost plus a transfer fee and applicable taxes, at which point Corporation will exercise its purchase option with ARI.

SECTION 15.   INDEMNIFICATION

15.1   Corporation shall indemnify, defend and hold harmless the City, its officers, agents, servants and employees from and against any and all liability, suits, actions, damages, costs, losses and expenses, including attorneys' fees, demands and claims for personal injury, bodily injury, sickness, diseases or death or damage or destruction of tangible property, to the proportionate extent arising out of any errors, omissions, willful misconduct or negligent acts of Corporation, its officials, agents, employees or subcontractors in the performance of the services of Corporation under this Agreement, from and against any orders, judgments, or decrees which may be entered thereon and from and against all costs, damages of every kind and nature, attorneys' fees, expenses and liabilities incurred in and about the defense of any such claim and investigation thereof. Corporation's indemnification, however, shall be limited to the actual amount of any liability of City and not encompass any sums for which City is exempt based upon Georgia municipal immunity Statutes.

15.2   Corporation acknowledges that specific consideration has been paid or will be paid under this Agreement for this hold harmless and indemnification provision, and further agrees with the foregoing provisions of indemnity and with the collateral obligation of insuring said indemnity as set forth In Section 16, Insurance.

15.3   To the extent allowable by Georgia law, City shall indemnify, defend and hold harmless the Corporation, its officers, agents, employees, and subcontractors from and against any and all liability, suits, actions, damages, costs, losses and expenses, including attorneys' fees, demands and claims for personal injury, bodily injury, sickness, diseases or death or damage or destruction of tangible property, to the proportionate extent arising out of any errors, omissions, willful misconduct or negligent acts of City, its officials, agents, servants, or subcontractors in the performance by the City of its obligations under this Agreement, whether from and against any orders, judgments, or decrees which may be entered thereon and from and against all costs, damages of every kind and nature, attorneys' fees, expenses and liabilities incurred in and about the defense of any such claim and investigation thereof.

15.4   In disputes between City and Corporation, in no event shall either party, its subcontractors or their officers or employees be liable to the other party for any special, indirect or consequential damages, whether such liability arises in breach of contract or warranty, tort including negligence, strict or statutory liability, or any other cause of action, provided, however, such limitation does not include any liability for which Corporation is obligated to indemnify City based upon special, indirect or consequential damages suffered by any third-parties.

15.5   In compensation for benefits conveyed to the City by this Agreement, the parties agree that Corporation's liability to the City will, in the aggregate, not exceed $3,500,000 per term of this Agreement. This provision takes precedence over all conflicting provisions of this Agreement except the Severability provision of Section 30. This limitation of liability will apply to all claims brought by the City against the Corporation, whether Corporation's liability to the City arises under breach of contract or warranty; tort, including negligence, strict liability, statutory liability; or any other cause of action, and shall include Corporation's officers, affiliated corporations, employees, and subcontractors. This subsection does not apply to claims for indemnification by the City against Corporation.

15.6   In compensation for benefits conveyed to the City by this Agreement, the parties agrees that Corporation shall be liable for fines or civil penalties to a maximum aggregate of One Hundred Fifty Thousand Dollars ($150,000) per year, which may be imposed by any federal or state department or regulatory agency that are a result of Corporation's negligent operation. City will assist Corporation to contest any such fines in administrative proceedings and/or in court prior to any payment by Corporation. Corporation shall pay the costs of contesting any such fines. Corporation shall not be liable for fines or civil penalties that result from violations that occurred prior to the effective date of this Agreement or for the effects of prior violations by the City that have contributed to the assessment of any fine or civil penalty caused by Corporation's negligent operations.

15.7   City and Corporation shall perform a condition assessment of the assets and infrastructure within sixty (60) days after the execution of this Agreement to establish the existing condition of the assets and infrastructure of the City. The City shall be responsible for the costs, claims, liabilities and expenses related to the condition of the assets up to the assessment determination. Following the date of assessment, Corporation is responsible for maintaining the assets as per this Section 4.4.1 of this Agreement.

SECTION 16. INSURANCE

16.1   Corporation shall not commence work under this contract or continue performance of the services unless and until Corporation has obtained all insurance required under this Section 16 as per the following:

16.1.1   Corporation shall provide the following insurances throughout the term of the Agreement, and shall provide to City Certificates of Insurance demonstrating compliance with this provision:

16.1.1.1   Statutory Worker's Compensation and Employers Liability Insurance as required by the State of Georgia. Such workers compensation coverage shall be as provided by O.C.G.A. § 34-9-1 et. seq

16.1.1.2   Comprehensive Automobile and Vehicle Liability Insurance with 5 Million Dollars ($5,000,000) combined single limits, covering claims for injuries to members of the public and/or damages to property of others arising from the use of Corporation owned or leased motor vehicles, including onsite and offsite operations.

16.1.1.3   Commercial General Liability Insurance with limits of 5 Million Dollars ($5,000,000) per occurrence and in the aggregate, covering claims for injuries to members of the public or damages to property of others arising out of any covered acts of the Corporation undertaken to provide services for the City as required in this Agreement or omission of Corporation or any of its employees, or subcontractors.

16.1.1.4   Professional Liability Insurance with limits of 5 Million Dollars ($5,000,000) per occurrence and in the aggregate.

16.1.1.5   Excess Liability Insurance with limits of 45 Million Dollars ($45,000,000).

16.2   City shall warrant that the following insurances are carried throughout the term of the Agreement, and shall provide Corporation with Certificates of Insurance to demonstrate compliance with this provision:

16.2.1   Property Damage Insurance for all property including City supplied vehicles and equipment for the full fair market value of such property.

16.2.2   Liability Insurance for all motor vehicles and equipment provided by City and operated by Corporation under this Agreement.

16.2.2.1   City and Corporation will insure that any and all policies of insurance procured hereunder shall provide for a waiver of subrogation against the other, and each party waives any claim against the other arising in contract or in tort which are covered by their respective insurance hereunder.

16.3   Corporation shall be responsible for maintaining this professional liability insurance for a minimum of two (2) years from the date of expiration of this Agreement. Upon request of City, Corporation shall make available for inspection copies of any claims filed or made against any policy during the policy term. Corporation shall additionally notify City, in writing, within thirty (30) calendar days, of any claims filed or made as it relates to the scope of services provided under this Agreement against any policy in excess of $25,000 during the policy term.

16.4   Certificates of insurance, reflecting evidence of the required insurance, shall be filed with the City Manager or designee prior to the commencement of the work. Policies shall be issued by companies authorized to do business under the laws of the State of Georgia, with financial ratings acceptable to the City Manager. The City shall be named as an additional insured on allowable polices obtained regarding services under this Agreement, including but not limited to the Commercial General Liability and Comprehensive Auto Liability insurance policies. Corporation agrees to furnish City with at least thirty (30) days prior written notice of any cancellation of any insurance policy required under this Agreement.

16.5   In the event the insurance certificate provided indicates that the insurance shall terminate and lapse during the period of this contract, then in that event, Corporation shall furnish, fifteen (15) days after expiration of such insurance, a renewed certificate of insurance as proof that equal and like coverage for the balance of the period of the contract and extension hereunder is in effect. Corporation shall not continue work pursuant to this Agreement unless all required insurance remains in full force and effect.

16.6   The costs of all policies of insurance required hereunder shall be the obligation of Corporation and the City shall in no way be responsible therefore.

16.7   City shall pay for and maintain its own comprehensive general liability insurance or maintain a self-insuring fund for the term of this Agreement in the amount determined by City to adequately insure the City's liability assumed herein, but in no event shall coverage be less than the amount of statutory waiver of sovereign immunity. In the event such coverage is modified, in any regard, before the expiration date of this Agreement, and unless otherwise agreed, City will provide at least thirty (30) days prior written notice to Corporation.

16.7.1   Corporation shall supply a Performance Bond on an annual basis to City in the amount of $500,000 or 10% of the Compensation Amount (whichever is less) to be supplied to City within thirty (30) days of execution of this Agreement.

SECTION 17.   CONFLICTS OF INTEREST/ COLLUSION/CONTINGENT FEES

17.1   Corporation shall not review or perform any services regarding any application made to the City by any client of Corporation, unless the services Corporation performs for such client are unrelated to the City. In such instance, Corporation shall disclose the relationship immediately to the City Manager, who may retain an alternate contractor or service provider to Corporation for those services the performance of which by the Corporation would create a perceived or real conflict of interest. If the services relate to a fixed fee service, the fees for the alternate to Corporation shall be deducted from the fixed fee paid to Corporation.

17.2 Neither Corporation nor any of its officers or employees shall have or hold any employment or contractual relationship that is antagonistic or incompatible with Corporation's loyal and conscientious exercise of judgment related to its performance under this Agreement.

17.3 Neither Corporation nor any of its directors, officers or employees shall obtain any kickbacks or benefits for itself, themselves or other clients as a result of any City purchases or transactions.

17.4 Corporation shall not collude with other City contract providers regarding City business or matters. Corporation shall not enter into any business relationships with other City contract providers regarding City business or matters, without the approval of the City Manager, which approval may be withheld at the City Manager's sole discretion.

17.5 Corporation warrants that it has not employed or retained any company or person, other than a bona fide employee working solely for Corporation, to solicit or secure this Agreement, and that it has not paid or agreed to pay any person, company, corporation, individual or firm, other than a bona fide employee working solely for Corporation, any fee, commission, percentage, gift, or other consideration contingent upon or resulting from the award or making of this Agreement. Provided however, this provision does not encompass Corporation's ability to have hired or engaged consultants to assist in preparation of the proposal and delivery of the services hereunder. For the breach or violation of this provision, the City shall have the right to terminate the Agreement without liability at its discretion, to deduct from the contract price, or otherwise recover the full amount of such fee, commission, percentage, gift or consideration.

SECTION 18. POLICY OF NON-DISCRIMINATION

Corporation shall not discriminate against any person in its operations, activities or delivery of services under this Agreement. Corporation shall affirmatively comply with all applicable provisions of federal, state and local equal employment laws and shall not engage in or commit any discriminatory practice against any person based on race, age, religion, color, gender, sexual orientation, national origin, marital status, physical or mental disability, political affiliation or any other factor which cannot be lawfully used as a basis for the provision or denial of service delivery.

SECTION 19. DRUG FREE WORKPLACE

Corporation shall maintain a Drug Free Workplace.

SECTION 20. INDEPENDENT CONTRACTOR

Corporation, for the purposes of this Service Agreement, is and shall remain an independent contractor; not an employee, agent, or servant of the City. Personal services provided by Corporation shall be by employees of Corporation and subject to supervision by Corporation, and not as officers or employees of City. Personnel policies, tax responsibilities, social security and health insurance, employee benefits, and other similar administrative procedures applicable to services rendered under this Agreement shall be those of Corporation.

SECTION 21. COSTS AND ATTORNEY'S FEES

If the either party is required to enforce the terms of this Agreement by court proceedings or otherwise due to breach of contract, whether or not formal legal action is required, the prevailing party shall recover its attorney's fees and costs incurred due to such.

SECTION 22   RIGHTS IN DATA; COPYRIGHTS; DISCLOSURE

22.1   Definition. The term "Data" as used in this Agreement includes written reports, studies, drawings, or other graphic, electronic, chemical or mechanical representation.

22.2   Rights in Data. Drawings, specifications, designs, models, photographs, computer CADD discs, reports, surveys, software, and other data developed or provided in connection with this Agreement (excluding company proprietary documents and software) shall be the property of City and City shall have the full right to use such data for any official purpose permitted under Georgia Statutes, including making it available to the general public. Such use shall be without any additional payment to or approval by Corporation. City shall have unrestricted authority to publish, disclose, distribute and otherwise use, in whole or in part, any data developed or prepared as per this Section 22.2. All software purchased by the Corporation on behalf of City shall be licensed appropriately under the name of the City. Corporation shall disclose to City Manager any anticipated proprietary documents or software before utilization under this Agreement and shall obtain City Manager approval prior to usage. To the extent the Corporation deems it necessary and with the consent of the City Manager; the Corporation may designate any additional software or proprietary information as confidential, a trade secret, or other reason under Georgia law that exempts the information from disclosure.

22.3   Copyrights. No data developed or prepared in whole or in part under this Agreement shall be subject to copyright in the United States of America or other country, except to the extent such copyright protection is available for the City. Corporation shall not include in the data any copyrighted matter unless Corporation obtains the written approval of the City Manager and provides said City Manager with written permission of the copyright owner for Corporation to use such copyrighted matter in the manner provided herein.

22.4   If this Agreement is terminated for any reason prior to completion of the work, the City may, in its discretion, use any design and documents prepared hereunder.

SECTION 23. COMPLIANCE WITH LAWS; ADVICE OF OTHER PROFESSIONALS

23.1   Corporation shall fully obey and comply with all laws, ordinances and administrative regulations duly made in accordance therewith, which are or shall become applicable to the services performed under the terms of this Agreement. Any changes in costs to perform services or comply with such laws, ordinances or administrative regulations or ability of Corporation to perform services due to change in applicable laws, ordinances, governing permits, or administrative regulations after effective date of this Agreement shall entitle Corporation to modification of this Agreement as per Section 9.2

23.2 Corporation acknowledges that the City is advised by its City Attorney and that, on all legal matters, Corporation shall abide by the advice and direction of the City Attorney in the performance of its duties as they relate to matters of the City, provided, however that should compliance with such direction require an increase in the scope of services under this Agreement, such increase shall be handled as per Section 9.2 hereof. Provided, however, in no case shall the Corporation be required to abide by the advice and direction of the City Attorney in the event that such advice would cause the Corporation to violate any of its obligations under this Agreement.

23.3 Corporation acknowledges that the City is also advised by various other professionals (including, but not limited to, engineers, traffic engineers, planners, building officials, police officers and firefighters), and that, on all matters within their respective expertise, subject to the approval of the City Manager, Corporation shall abide by their advice and direction in the performance of its duties as they relate to matters of the City, as long as such advice doesn't increase the scope of services or cost under Agreement. If such direction does increase the scope of services pursuant to this Agreement, it shall be handled as per Section 9.2.

SECTION 24. OWNERSHIP OF WORK PRODUCT DOCUMENTS

24.1 All work product prepared by Corporation exclusively for the City shall immediately become the property of the City, excluding other company proprietary documents and software as disclosed pursuant to Section 22.2.

24.2 Corporation understands and agrees that any information, document, report or any other material whatsoever which is given by the City to Corporation or which is otherwise obtained or prepared by Corporation exclusively for City under the terms of this Agreement is and shall at all times remain the property of the City.

SECTION 25. AUDIT AND INSPECTION RIGHTS

25.1 The City may, at reasonable times, and for a period of up to three (3) years following the date of final performance of Services by Corporation under this Agreement, audit, or cause to be audited, those books and records of Corporation that are related to Corporation's performance under this Agreement, excluding all financial records unless related to direct cost reimbursable expenses or other matters contemplated herein, including but not limited to buy-out provisions, unless a court of competent jurisdiction orders disclosure of such information. Corporation agrees to maintain all such books and records at its principal place of business for a period of three (3) years after final payment is made under this Agreement. Corporation shall make all necessary books and records available for audit in Fulton County, Georgia.

25.2   The City may, at reasonable times during the term hereof, inspect Corporation's facilities and perform such inspections and process reviews, as the City deems reasonably necessary, to determine whether the services required to be provided by Corporation under this Agreement conform to the terms of this Agreement. Corporation shall make available to the City all reasonable facilities and assistance to facilitate the performance of inspections by the City's representatives.

SECTION 26. WARRANTIES OF CORPORATION

Corporation hereby warrants and represents that at all times during the term of this Agreement it shall maintain in good standing all required licenses, certifications, and permits required under federal, state and local laws necessary to perform the Services.

SECTION 27. PUBLIC RECORDS

Corporation understands that the public shall have access, at all reasonable times, to all documents and information pertaining to the City, subject to the provision of O.C.G.A. §50-14-1 et seq., and agrees to allow access by the City and the public to all documents subject to disclosure under applicable law. Corporation's willful failure or refusal to comply with the provisions of this Section shall result in the immediate termination of this Agreement by the City. Corporation agrees to retain all public records in accordance with the City's records retention and disposal policies, O.C.G.A. 50-18-92 et. seq., and the Georgia Administrative Code.

SECTION 28. GOVERNING LAW; CONSENT TO JURISDICTION

This Agreement shall be construed in accordance with and governed by the laws of the State of Georgia. Subject to the arbitration requirements of Section 42, and when federal jurisdiction is permitted, the parties submit to the jurisdiction of federal court in any action or proceeding arising out of, or relating to, this Agreement. Venue of any action to enforce this Agreement shall be in Northern District Federal Court.

SECTION 29. HEADINGS

Headings are for the convenience of reference only and shall not be considered in any interpretation of this Agreement.

SECTION 30. SEVERABILITY

If any provision or subsection of any provision of this Agreement or the application thereof to any person or situation shall, to any extent, be held invalid or unenforceable, the remainder of this Agreement including the general provision of any invalid or unenforceable subsection of a provision, and the application of such provisions to persons or situations other than those as to which it shall have been held invalid or unenforceable, shall not be affected thereby, and shall continue in full force and effect, and be enforced to the fullest extent permitted by law.

SECTION 31. CONFLICT

In the event of a conflict between the terms of this Agreement and any terms or conditions contained in any attached documents, the terms in this Agreement shall prevail.

SECTION 32. SURVIVAL OF PROVISIONS

Any terms or conditions of this Agreement that require acts beyond the date of its termination shall survive the termination of this Agreement, shall remain in full force and effect unless and until the terms of conditions are completed, and shall be fully enforceable by either party.

SECTION 33. ENTIRE AGREEMENT

33.1   This Agreement and its attachments constitute the entire agreement between Corporation and City, and all negotiations and oral understandings between the parties are merged herein.

33.2   No modification, amendment or alteration in the terms or conditions of this Agreement shall be effective unless contained in a written document executed with the same formality as this Agreement.

SECTION 34. WAIVER

The waiver by either party of any failure on the part of the other party to perform in accordance with any of the terms or conditions of this Agreement shall not be construed as a waiver of any future or continuing similar or dissimilar failure.

SECTION 35. EQUIPMENT APPRAISAL AND TRANSFER

35.1   In the event of full termination, partial termination or expiration of this Agreement, City shall have the option to purchase from Corporation any piece of equipment belonging to the Corporation or purchased by the Corporation to provide the services outlined herein. The City shall also pay any unamortized costs incurred by Corporation at the time of such termination or expiration which are directly attributable to the purchase or use of such equipment.

35.2   The purchase price for such equipment shall be determined by mutual agreement of the parties as to the fair market value of such equipment.

35.3   Upon the exercise by the City of its option to possess the subject equipment and upon payment by City, Corporation shall convey within ten (10) days or upon such other mutually agreed time, all of its rights, title and interest, thereto, to the City by Bill of Sale Absolute or Certificate of Title, as applicable.

SECTION 36. AUTHORITY TO EXECUTE:
NO CONFLICT CREATED

36.1   Corporation by execution hereof does hereby represent to City that Corporation has full power and authority to make and execute this Service Agreement, to the effect that:

   a.   The making and execution hereof shall create a legal obligation upon Corporation, which shall be legally binding upon Corporation.

   b.   The same shall be enforceable by the City according and to the extent of the provisions hereof.

36.2   Nothing contained or any obligation on the part of Corporation to be performed hereunder shall in any way be contrary to or in contravention of any policy of insurance or surety bond required of Corporation pursuant to the laws of the State of Georgia.

36.3   Corporation shall perform this Agreement under the name of CH2M HILL, Inc., provided, however that CH2M HILL, Inc. may perform services under this Agreement through any wholly owned affiliates of CH2M HILL Limited and if so, such affiliates shall be bound by the terms and conditions of this Agreement to the same extent as if they had been a signatory hereof. It shall be the duty of Corporation to insure: (1) that any affiliates who conduct business for the City pursuant to this Agreement have executed all documents necessary to be legally bound to the City regarding said business; and (2) that any affiliates who conduct business for the City pursuant to this Agreement are in full compliance with the terms hereof.

36.4   The City Manager, Mayor and City Clerk, by their respective executions hereof, do each represent to Corporation that they, collectively, have full power and authority to make and execute this Service Agreement on behalf of the City, pursuant to the Resolution of the City Council of the City.

36.4.1   Nothing herein contained is intended in any way to be contrary to or in contravention of the Charter of the City and the Laws of the State of Georgia, and to the extent such conflict exists; the City and Corporation shall be mutually relieved of any obligations of such conflict.

SECTION 37. NOTICES

Whenever either party desires to give notice to the other, it must be given by written notice, sent by certified United States mail, with return receipt requested, hand delivered or by facsimile transmission with proof of receipt, addressed to the party for whom it is intended, at the place last specified, and the place for giving of notice in compliance with the provisions of this paragraph. Notice shall be deemed given upon receipt by any method of delivery authorized above. For the present, the parties designate the following as the respective places for giving of notice:

For Corporation: CH2M HILL INC.
                                9193 S. Jamaica Street, Suite 400
                                Englewood, CO 80112
                                ATTN: Catherine Lang
                                FAX: 303-740-7061

For City: (NEED TO FILL IN)

SECTION 38. ASSIGNABILITY

Either Party shall not assign any of the obligations or benefits imposed hereby or contained herein, without the written consent of the other Party. Such consent on behalf of the City Council of the City must be evidenced by a duly passed Resolution. Notice of Assignment shall be mailed via U.S. Mail, return receipt requested and any notice required hereunder shall be addressed to the party intended to receive the same at the addresses noted in Section 37. In the event that the City exercises its option to assign this agreement pursuant to this section, the City is not obligated to provide the Notice of Termination identified in Section 12 of this contract. However, Corporation shall coordinate and cooperate with the City as may be required for expeditious and efficient assignment of service pursuant to this article. In addition, Corporation shall transition this contract pursuant to this section in accordance with Section 14 of this Agreement.

SECTION 39. FORCE MAJEURE

Neither party shall be liable for damages, delays, or failure to perform its obligations under this Agreement if performance is made impractical, abnormally difficult, or abnormally costly, as a result of any unforeseen occurrence, including but not limited to fire, flood, strike, acts of God, failure of a third party to cooperate in providing services other than Corporation's second tier subcontractors as such term is defined in paragraph 2.4 of this Agreement, or other occurrences, beyond its reasonable control. The party invoking this Force Majeure clause shall notify the other party immediately by verbal communication and in writing of the nature and extent of the contingency within ten (10) working days after its occurrence, and shall take reasonable measures to mitigate any impact of Force Majeure. If the Force Majuere event shall impact schedule or increases the costs incurred by Corporation (excluding those scope of services already anticipated and detailed out in Exhibit A), such items shall be handled as per Section 9.2.

SECTION 40. NEGOTIATION

The parties acknowledge that the terms of this Agreement were jointly negotiated between the parties, that both parties were represented by attorneys and that, in the case of any dispute regarding the terms of this Agreement, the terms should not be construed in favor of or against either party.

SECTION 41. BINDING EFFECT

This agreement shall inure to the benefit of and be binding upon the respective parties' successors.

SECTION 42. DISPUTES

42.1   To facilitate the timely and effective resolution of any controversy or dispute that may arise under this Service Agreement or out of the performance of this Service Agreement, each party shall appoint one representative to serve on a Management Board. The Management Board will resolve any issues that arise from the Service Agreement that cannot be resolved from the project management level. The party believing there is a controversy or dispute shall put such notice in writing and deliver to the other party. Such demand shall be filed within a reasonable time after the dispute or claim has arisen, but in no event after the applicable statute of limitations for a legal or equitable proceeding would have run. The Management Board shall convene to discuss such notice and shall make a good faith effort to resolve any issues within a period of thirty (30) days of its receipt.

42.2   If a compromise is not negotiated within sixty (60) days of the written notice then in that event the parties shall refer the matter to non-binding mediation. If the parties can not come to an agreement after the non-binding mediation, any claim or counterclaim for less than Two Hundred Thousand Dollars ($200,000) in damages shall be decided by a single arbitrator appointed by the parties for determination as per American Arbitration Association procedures. If the parties are unable to agree on a single arbitrator, each party shall appoint one arbitrator, and the appointed arbitrators shall select a third arbitrator who shall serve as chairperson of the arbitration panel. The third arbitrator selected as chairman shall be a disinterested person of recognized competence. Such arbitration shall be non-binding. The prevailing party shall be entitled to recover its attorney's fees and costs for such arbitration or court proceeding in proportion to the percentage of the recovery. Each party shall pay 50% of the third party costs of arbitration.

42.3   Unless the parties mutually agree otherwise, rules comparable to the Commercial Industry Arbitration Rules of the American Arbitration Association then in effect shall govern the proceedings, provided that failure of the arbitrator(s) to comply with the American Arbitration Association rules shall not invalidate the decision by the arbitrator(s). Notwithstanding Section 28, *Governing Law*, the parties agree this Agreement specifically acknowledge and agree that this contract evidences a "transaction involving commerce" under the Federal Arbitration Act, and that this Agreement to arbitrate shall be governed by the Federal Arbitration Act.

42.4   In those binding arbitration situations, the prevailing party shall be entitled to recover its attorney's fees and costs for such arbitration in proportion to the percentage of the recovery. Each party shall pay 50% of the third party costs of arbitration.

42.5   Should either party seek damages for an amount over Two Hundred Thousand Dollars ($200,000), in a claim or counterclaim, either party may file for litigation as per Section 28.

42.6   Unless otherwise agreed in writing, Corporation shall continue to provide services during any dispute resolution proceedings. If Corporation continues to perform, City shall continue to make payments in accordance with this Agreement. During the period, the parties are in dispute resolution proceedings, such Agreement shall be not be deemed to be in default as per Section 13, provided, however, the election to pursue a material breach by virtue of this Section 42 dispute resolution provision shall not constitute a waiver of any breach of the Agreement.

AGREEMENT BY AND BETWEEN CORPORATION AND THE CITY OF SANDY SPRINGS FOR CONTRACT SERVICES AS SET FORTH HEREIN.

IN WITNESS WHEREOF, the parties hereto have caused their respective agents to execute this instrument on their behalf, at the times set forth below.

CH2M HILL INCORPORATED

_____   _____

By: DATE

ATTEST

_____   _____

                                     DATE

CITY OF SANDY SPRINGS

_____   _____

By: DATE
Mayor and Chair

_____   _____

By: DATE
City Manager

_____   _____

By: DATE
City Clerk

Approved as to form and legal
Sufficiency subject to execution
by the parties

_____   _____

By: DATE
City Attorney

A P P E N D I X   E

SCOPE OF SERVICES

AGREEMENT BY AND BETWEEN CORPORATION AND THE CITY OF SANDY SPRINGS

EXHIBIT "A"
RFP 1—ADMINISTRATION
SCOPE OF SERVICES

Services described in this Exhibit A will be delivered in a manner that is consistent with reasonable municipal management practices as compared with municipalities of similar size in the State of Georgia.

The Corporation will provide sufficient staff, including contractor and subcontractor personnel, to provide the services described in this Exhibit A. It is recognized that the project staffing may fluctuate due to seasonal or other conditions to meet the service demands. It is envisioned that the average annual staffing levels will be approximately fifty-two (52) full-time equivalent (FTE) positions, to deliver the intended services consistent with reasonable municipal management practices as compared with municipalities of similar size in the State of Georgia. If there are modifications to the scope of service that require significant additional staffing levels, such changes will be handled as per Section 9.2 of the Agreement. Unless otherwise noted, the Corporation is not responsible for providing security services.

The services to be provided are described in the following sections.

1.1 ADMINISTRATIVE SERVICES

Administrative services shall include the following:

1.1.1 Contract Administration

1.1.1.1 Assist in negotiating City contracts, as directed by the City Manager. The City Manager and/or Mayor shall approve final contracts and execute and bind the City to such agreements.

1.1.1.2 Advise the City Manager on the status of negotiations, as well as contract provisions and their impacts on the City.

1.1.1.3 Make recommendations on contract approval, rejection, amendment, renewal, and cancellation, as directed by the City Manager.

1.1.1.4 Provide contract administration and supervision of contracts and agreements, as directed by the City Manager. Such tasks shall include, but not be limited to, monitoring contract amendments, obtaining applicable insurance certificates, and monitoring applicable progress.

1.1.1.5 Work with the City Manager to plan and implement processes for the ongoing protection of the City's interests.

1.1.1.6 Recommend and implement policies and procedures to provide for compliance with laws related to bidding, contracting, and purchasing as set forth in the State of Georgia, by examining the applicable laws and developing procedures for bidding, contracting, and procurement processes.

1.1.1.7 Assist and coordinate necessary grant applications and submissions as directed by the City Manager.

1.1.2 Policy Implementation

1.1.2.1 Research current and likely future trends impacting the City as identified and agreed upon with the City Manager.

1.1.2.2 Prepare administrative and financial analyses related to policy decisions being considered by the City and provide recommendations of available options.

1.1.2.3 Attend City Council meetings, hearings, and agenda meetings as directed by the City Manager.

1.1.2.4   Assist the City Manager with the identification of significant policies and analyze their administrative and financial impacts.

1.1.2.5   Assist the City in the preparation of plans and procedures to implement City Council policies and directives successfully, as directed by the City Manager.

1.1.2.6   Prepare regular monthly status reports and, as required, special reports to advise the City Manager of the progress and results of public policy implementation.

1.1.2.7   This scope does not include support associated with litigation activity, including but not limited performance as expert witnesses, outside of work performance parameters for the respective employee.

1.1.3   Daily Communications

1.1.3.1   Respond and/or coordinate responses to inquires in a timely fashion and in accordance with the established communications plan and policies approved by the City.

1.1.3.2   In accordance with established communications plans and policies, prepare correspondence regarding City affairs as directed and approved by the City Manager and the City Clerk.

1.1.3.3   Assist the City with administrative compliance with Open Records and Open Meetings laws as set forth in the Official Code of Georgia Annotated Sections (O.C.G.A. §§) 50-14-1 et seq. and O.C.G.A. §§ 50-18-70 et seq..

1.1.3.4   Corporation shall provide nominal and routine assistance to input information into character generation for cable broadcast, as approved by City Manager.

1.1.3.5 This scope of services for communications does not include Public Television broadcast or Web-cast of City events or meetings.

1.1.4   Customer Service

1.1.4.1   Provide staff as opposed to voice mail during business hours as the first point of contact for incoming calls to the City. The initial first year staffing compliment will include a level of effort consistent with three (3) dedicated FTEs and three (3) backup FTEs to support this function. The backup FTEs will be drawn from other administrative functions as required. After business hours, provide answering service equipped with emergency contact information as needed.

1.1.4.2   Develop and implement response protocols and direct customers to the appropriate party.

1.1.5   Departmental Support

1.1.5.1   Provide administrative clerical support staff at a level of effort consistent with five (5) FTEs to assist City functions and departments in their respective operations, by doing such tasks as answering the phone, greeting customers, filing, and other miscellaneous clerical tasks.

1.1.6   Clerking Support

Staffing at a level of effort consistent with four (4) FTEs shall complete the following:

1.1.6.1   Record and transcribe City Council meetings, hearings, and agenda meetings.

1.1.6.2   Assist the City Clerk during City Council meetings, take attendance, record motions, record votes taken, and swear in witnesses of others presenting testimony to the Council.

1.1.6.3   Assist in the review of documents to be presented to the City Council, as directed by the City Manager.

1.1.6.4   Upon the City Clerk's absence, authenticate City documents by appropriate signatures and City Seal.

1.1.6.5   Retain public records and make them available for inspection by the public in conformance with Georgia Law.

1.1.6.6   Under the direction of the City Clerk, prepare City Council meeting agendas.

1.1.6.7   Under the direction of the City Clerk, publish appropriate public notices.

1.1.6.8   Serve the administrative needs of Boards, Authorities, or other entities established by the City for the furtherance of City objectives that can be reasonably supported by staffing at a level of effort consistent with four (4) FTEs.

1.1.6.9 Scope does not include costs to codify City Codes.

1.1.7 Records Management

1.1.7.1 At contract inception, start developing and implementing processes and procedures for manual records management in accordance with State law to facilitate creating, saving, and archiving Microsoft Word° and Excel° documents. These processes and procedures will be transitioned to a commercially available Document Management System that is leading industry technology at the time of installation. Implementation of the Document Management System will be initiated after the implementation of the computerized financial application system is complete. The estimated completion date for the implementation of the Document Management System is on or around June 30, 2007.

1.1.7.2 Facilitate employee productivity, collaboration, and document security by allowing the users to search for documents by profile information, content, person who created the document, or last person to edit the document. Users may modify a previously created document for their use if they leave the original document unmodified.

1.1.7.3 Provide up to three (3) Document Scanning Stations in City Hall so that paper documents such as signed contracts, ordinances, resolutions, and other important City documents may be imported into the Document Management System using a Document Scanning Station. Documents that will be scanned will be 8-1/2" x 11" (letter), 8-1/2" x 14" (legal), and 11" x 17".

1.1.7.4 Protect the completeness of public records in accordance with the requirements of State law by storing backups of electronic files off site on a server and hard copy documents at City Hall.

1.1.7.5 Promote the sharing of information and collaborative work between City staff by using the Document Management System, which will allow City staff to access records in an electronic format.

1.1.7.6 Provide an application server that will store and manage required data.

1.1.7.7   Provide and maintain access to data to other City contract providers as necessary.

1.1.7.8   For public records, design storage strategies and systems that are leading industry technology at the time of installation. Implement and coordinate the transfer of data, records, or other materials from Fulton County, Georgia, as necessary for the operation of the City.

1.1.8   Public Relations

1.1.8.1   Establish a public relations protocol as directed by the City Manager in order to maintain continuous dialog and communications with City residents, vendors and businesses with timely updates.

1.1.8.2   Promote City policy, programs, and achievements by providing communications staff and programs to prepare and distribute various informational data via print, media, and city website-approved messages about the City's progress.

1.1.8.3   Serve as a liaison with residents, civic groups, and other governments, as directed by the City Manager, provided, however, all such activities shall include the disclosure that the Corporation does not have the authority to commit or bind the City without, depending upon the circumstances, the approval of either the City Manager or the Mayor and Council.

1.1.8.4 Document important City events for future use in City-developed publications.

1.1.9   Annual Reports

1.1.9.1   Develop a graphical and thematic design for the Annual Report, subject to the approval by the City Manager.

1.1.9.2   Coordinate with the graphic designers, photographers, editors, and others as necessary.

1.1.9.3   Provide effective written and non-written communications to reflect the year's message and inform residents of the City's actions and achievements per the agreed upon communications plan.

1.1.9.4   Produce and print the annual reports and make available to City residents in hard copy, which may be picked up at City Hall, or electronically in PDF format, which may be downloaded from the City's website.

1.1.10   City Website

1.1.10.1   Design and host the City website, which may contain City contact information, statistics, history, departmental and facility descriptions, the City Council meeting schedule, meeting agendas, agenda packages, minutes, City Codes, notices, pictures, and multimedia. The website will be approved by the City Manager.

1.1.10.2   Update the City website as needed or on a weekly basis to post the latest agendas, packages, minutes, and notices. Redesign the website annually.

1.1.10.3   Publish City-provided geographic information system (GIS) database interface on the website.

1.1.11   City Newsletter

1.1.11.1   Provide text, pictures, graphics, maps, and exhibits as necessary for the quarterly newsletter. The quarterly newsletter will be approved by the City Manager.

1.1.11.2   Coordinate with the publishers to produce a useful, informative, timely and attractive publication.

1.1.11.3   Produce, print, and make available a quality newsletter to City residents.

1.1.12   Program Presentation

1.1.12.1   Publish studies, reports and analysis for staff and public presentation, as directed by the City Manager.

1.1.12.2   Prepare various media presentations of City programs to the staff and general public, as directed by the City Manager.

1.1.13   Information Technologies and Telephone Systems

1.1.13.1   Provide, install, and maintain computerized network system software and hardware that are leading industry technology at the time of installation and sufficient to efficiently satisfy the City's computing needs. The Corporation will develop and implement manual processes sufficient to meet the needs of the City in the Financial Scope of Services (see Section 1.2) prior to January 1, 2006. The implementation of the computerized system will be complete on or about August 31, 2006, with modules being available before then. The manual processes in support of Section 1.1.14 will also be implemented prior to January 1, 2006, while the computer system to support this function on which the module is based will be implemented on or about August 31, 2006.

1.1.13.2   Provide a domain network that is leading industry technology at the time of installation to handle future growth and technologies. The network system will have limited functions on January 1, 2006. Upon completion of the office space renovations at City Hall, a fully functional system shall be available.

1.1.13.3   Provide, install, configure, and maintain a server at City Hall and the City's offices to improve performance, mitigate against data loss, and minimize potential down time. The server will be leading industry technology at the time of installation.

1.1.13.4   Provide centralized management of network resources and a central location for the storage of the City's documents on site.

1.1.13.5   Assist with maintaining data security and preventing corruption with a nightly backup (with offsite storage) and the ability to restore from a central location.

1.1.13.6   Provide, configure, and maintain ten (10) laptop computers that are leading industry technology at the time of contract inception for the members of the City Council (7), City Manager (2), and City Clerk (1).

1.1.13.7   Provide, install, configure, and maintain up to seventy (70) computer workstations that are leading industry technology at the time of installation for contract and subcontract staff.

1.1.13.8   Provide one digital phone and remote connection for each park site with an office via data line connections that carry both data and voice signal. Provide phone service for the other five existing park sites without offices.

1.1.13.9   Maintain software and hardware uniformity and interchangeability among users.

1.1.13.10   Provide, install, and maintain sufficient network laser printers to efficiently conduct City business.

1.1.13.11   Maintain a 3-year replacement program for computers and equipment.

1.1.13.12   Provide, install, and maintain network cabling/data line system that are leading industry technology at the time of installation for communications, networking, and data sharing.

1.1.13.13   Provide, install, configure, and maintain servers in support of utility functions. Utility servers differ from domain servers in that they are specifically configured to run certain contracted applications.

1.1.13.14   Provide City and Corporation with Internet and e-mail connections on a separate server for internal and external communications and common contact lists and scheduling.

1.1.13.15   Archive e-mails in compliance with State retention requirements.

1.1.13.16   Provide, install, and maintain a telephone system that is leading industry technology at the time of installation in City facilities, with sufficient lines and features to satisfy the management needs of the City. The telephone system will have limited functions on January 1, 2006. Upon completion of the office space renovations at City Hall, a fully functional system shall be available.

1.1.14.   Databases—Municipal Management Software

1.1.14.1   Provide, install, configure, and maintain a database that is leading industry technology at the time of installation and programmed to manage the City's occupational and business license functions

1.1.14.2   Coordinate the procurement, installation, configuration, and maintenance of databases required of municipalities in the State of Georgia by governmental agencies.

1.1.15   Court Services

1.1.15.1   Provide requested aspects of court record keeping and reporting
             as required by law and reasonable, sound practices, including,
             but not limited to, the maintenance of calendars, the recording
             of sentences and dispositions, the coordination with probation
             services, and the coordination of collection of fees, fines and
             surcharges.

1.1.15.2   The Corporation will provide a level of effort consistent with one
             (1) FTE Court Clerk and three (3) FTE Assistant Court Clerks
             for court hearings. The City will provide a Clerk of the Court at
             City expense.

1.1.15.3   Oversee and maintain systems required for fee, fine, and sur-
             charge accounting, reporting and remittance.

1.1.16   Police

1.1.16   Provide contract administration for police services provided to
             the City under Inter-Governmental Agreement (IGA) by moni-
             toring and tracking such IGA. After Fulton County transition of
             services to the City on or about December 31, 2006, Corporation
             shall provide clerical and administrative support to a level consis-
             tent with two and half (2 1/2) FTE, clerks. Such services exclude
             providing services to input data into the NCIC or GCIC or a
             similar legally required database.

1.1.17   Fire

1.1.17   Provide contract administration for fire protection services pro-
             vided to the City under IGA by monitoring and tracking such
             IGA. After Fulton County transition of services to the City on
             or about December 31, 2006, Corporation shall provide clerical
             and administrative support to a level consistent with two and
             half (2 1/2) FTE, clerks.

1.1.18   Election Support

1.1.18.1   Provide clerical support to the City Clerk's office in coordinating
             municipal and special elections as required, including, but not
             limited to, addressing polling station issues, preparing frequently
             asked ballot questions, or other related issues arising from elec-
             tion clerical support, not including the preparation of ballots.

1.1.19 **Solid Waste**

1.1.19.1 Administer and coordinate franchise agreements with solid waste providers.

1.2 **FINANCIAL SERVICES**

Financial services shall include the following:

1.2.1 **Revenue Collection**

1.2.1.1 Coordinate and liaise with local, state and federal agencies charged with the collection and disbursement of taxes, assessments, fees, charges, and other impositions. To the extent databases delineate Sandy Springs' boundaries, existing tax collection processes and procedures will be used to facilitate timely collection and transfer of revenues to the City. The Corporation is not responsible for the identification and collection of additional revenues from taxpayers and incidents of taxation that are not identified in the existing databases.

1.2.1.2 Administer the existing (and future to the extent that they do not substantially effect the scope of services set out herein) processes, fees, charges, and their miscellaneous revenues pertaining to utilities, private enterprises (for example, business licenses, alcoholic beverage licenses, franchise, and other taxes and fees lawfully enacted by the City) and individuals as they interface with the City programs. This scope assumes the City will adopt the existing or substantially similar fee schedules, methodology, and regulations of Fulton County relative to business licenses, alcoholic beverage licenses, and other applicable taxes and fees.

1.2.1.3 Recommend enforcement actions to the City Manager to induce payment in accordance with City and State law and approved policies and procedures.

1.2.1.4 Prepare monthly financial reports showing revenues and expenses to date in comparison with budget projections and submit the reports to the City Manager no later than the tenth day of the following month.

1.2.1.5 Maintain the existing and future Fulton County address list and database for the City and State Departments of Revenue to assist the City with obtaining local and shared revenues.

1.2.1.6   This scope does not include the cost analysis and fee modeling required to establish and collect regulatory fees pursuant to O.C.G.A. § 48-13-7 and O.C.G.A. § 48-13-9.

1.2.2   Capital Program Administration

1.2.2.1   Coordinate the capital needs of the City with the designated City representatives. Capital Program Administration means providing coordination and recommendation to the City on an annual basis as to the capital program requirements in future years, which includes the scheduling of capital program projects. Both Parties agree that Corporation's duties under this Agreement are limited to the coordination for capital improvement programs and procurement and program management for small projects (i.e., estimated procurement contract value of under $50,000 although final decision will be based upon the complexity of said project), unless otherwise agreed upon between the Parties. Corporation's duties do not include the program management of the large or complex (those projects outside of the above definition of small projects) which would be outside the Scope of Services herein and, accordingly, handled through an additional services authorization and change to the Agreement as per Section 9.2 of this Agreement.

1.2.2.2   As directed by the City Manager, advise and assist the City in obtaining financing if necessary and maintain proper fund accounting procedures.

1.2.2.3   As directed by the City Manager, formulate recommendations and provide resources to administer and implement the City's approved capital program financing.

1.2.3   Investment Services

1.2.3.1   Assist the City in the development of investment policies and procedures pursuant to Government Finance Officers Association of America (GFOA) and State law.

1.2.3.2   Assist the City in selecting an investment firm that will invest City Funds at the direction of City Manager and in accordance with GFOA policies and State law.

1.2.3.3   Produce investment reports, including cash flow analysis and modeling stating the effectiveness of the chosen investment policy, on a quarterly basis.

1.2.4   Fund Accounting

1.2.4.1   Develop and implement a Fund Accounting System in accordance with Governmental Accounting Standards Board (GASB), the Uniform Accounting System prescribed by Department of Community Affairs, and the rules of the Georgia Department of Audits and Accounts.

1.2.4.2   Prepare reports in accordance with reasonable and customary City reporting standards for Department of Community Affairs and State Revenue Department and distribute in a format to be agreed upon between the parties.

1.2.4.3   Prepare monthly management reports and other financial reports as required by applicable law and accounting standards.

1.2.5   Accounts Payable/Receivable

1.2.5.1   Administer the purchase order system such that timely payment of invoices will be made on behalf of the City, provided the necessary funds are made available by the City.

1.2.5.2   Coordinate tax collection, franchise fees, utility taxes, and other receivables.

1.2.6   General Fixed Asset Accounting

1.2.6.1   Account for assets constructed by or donated to the City for maintenance.

1.2.6.2   Within the first twenty-four (24) months from contract execution, inventory City property in accordance with GASB and the Georgia Department of Audits and Accounts.

1.2.7   Budgeting

1.2.7.1   Prepare and submit annual budgets per GFOA standards to the City Manager.

1.2.7.2   Coordinate with and assist City departments for annual budget preparation and presentation.

1.2.7.3   Provide material for and attend required budget meetings, hearings, and agenda meetings.

1.2.7.4   Coordinate the budgeting function between City departments and other governmental entities as necessary.

1.2.7.5   Present the City approved budgetary information to appropriate parties as requested and in accordance with City approval in oral, print, multimedia, and web-based forms.

1.2.8   Forecasting

1.2.8.1   Prepare detailed financial forecasts and analysis in a format to be agreed upon between the parties.

1.2.8.2   Identify trends and analyze their impact upon the City's finances, operations, and capital and advise the City of such findings.

1.2.8.3   Provide data and assist with the development of policy and action recommendations.

1.2.8.4   Coordinate the forecasting function with and/or between City departments and other governmental entities.

1.2.8.5   Present findings in oral, print, multimedia, and web-based forms to the City.

1.2.9   Comprehensive Annual Financial Report (CAFR)

1.2.9.1   Prepare the Annual Financial Report for Units of Local Government in accordance with Generally Accepted Accounting Principles as defined by the GFOA.

1.2.10   Risk Management

1.2.10.1   Work in conjunction with City-designated insurance broker regarding claims to City's insurance policies and with recommending and advising the City of the appropriate amounts and types of insurance and work with insurance broker to procure the necessary insurance as directed by the City Manager.

1.2.10.2   Assist in the processing of claims at the direction of the City Attorney and the City-designated insurance broker.

1.2.10.3   Develop and maintain a risk management claims review procedure in coordination with the City Manager, the City Attorney, and the City-designated insurance broker.

1.2.10.4   Review insurance policies and coverage amounts of City vendors.

1.2.11   Human Resources

1.2.11.1   Maintain databases and documents to assist in the proper functioning of employment services, payroll, fringe benefit, insurance, tax, and other City-specific and general law-provided human resources functions.

1.2.11.2   Develop and implement a Code of Conduct for personnel that emphasizes the responsibility of the staff to be professional, patient, and responsive. The Code should emphasize that rudeness and impoliteness toward any person is unacceptable conduct and will not be tolerated.

1.2.11.3   Develop and implement with employees an Employee Policies and Procedures Manual, which shall include, but not be limited to, policies and procedures on carrying out duties to the City, consequences of non-compliance to policies, and functions and roles of the employees.

1.2.12   Purchasing

1.2.12.1   Recommend to the City Manager, for approval by Mayor and City Council, and assist in the implementation of, approved procurement policies and procedures consistent with State and local laws, rules, and regulations.

1.2.12.2   Consistent with approved policies and procedures, assist in selection of vendors.

1.2.12.3   Participate in county and State level purchase plans when determined to be in the best interests of the City and as directed by City Manager.

1.2.12.4   Prepare Request for Proposals to be distributed to vendors and suppliers as directed by the City Manager.

1.2.12.5   Prepare and process purchase requisitions.

1.2.13   **Health Insurance Portability and Accountability Act of 1966 (HIPAA)**

1.2.13.1   Review and make recommendations regarding City systems and procedures to meet the requirements of HIPAA.

3.2   **Facilities Maintenance, Repair and Contracts**

3.2.1   Provide a level of effort consistent with three (3) FTE personnel to maintain, repair, clean, and keep in good working order City Hall facilities commensurate with local governmental standards, which shall include, but not be limited to, such services as janitorial services, painting services, and minor repair of equipment. However, this provision shall not apply to landscaping maintenance of City rights-of-way or land. The structural, mechanical, electric, and plumbing facility maintenance for all City facilities is not included in the scope.

3.2.2   The Corporation will implement a Computerized Maintenance Management System that will allow for the generation of work orders to track and schedule maintenance activities in this scope of services. The manual procedures in support of the scheduling of maintenance will be place on January 1, 2006. Modules will be implemented in phases until June 30, 2006. Full implementation will be completed on or around June 30, 2006.

3.3   **Furniture, Fixtures, Equipment and Supplies**

3.3.1   Provide furniture, fixtures, equipment, and supplies in an amount not to exceed one hundred and fifty thousand dollars ($150,000.00) for the term of this Agreement for the reasonable operation of departments and functions of the City.

3.3.2   Title to such furniture, fixtures, equipment, and supplies shall vest in the City upon purchase by Corporation on behalf of City. All leases shall be in the name of Corporation and shall include an assignability clause to the City.

3.3.3   All software purchased by the Corporation on behalf of City shall be licensed appropriately under the name of the City.

4.0 **PURCHASING, PROCUREMENT
AND CONTRACTING**

4.1 The Corporation shall comply with applicable laws and requirements regarding purchasing and procurement as set forth by the State of Georgia. The Corporation shall comply with applicable laws and requirements regarding contracting required in the course of fulfilling the duties under this Agreement as set forth by the State of Georgia.

A P P E N D I X   F

AGREEMENT BY AND BETWEEN

CITY OF SANDY SPRINGS, GEORGIA

AND

CH2M HILL, INC

FOR PROVISION OF SERVICES FOR

PUBLIC WORKS, TRANSPORTATION, STREETS, RIGHT-OF-WAY, FACILITIES, PARKS AND RECREATION, CAPITAL IMPROVEMENTS, PLANNING AND ZONING, INSPECTIONS, CODE ENFORCEMENT, PERMITTING, PURCHASING, PROCUREMENT, AND CONTRACTING SERVICES

THIS AGREEMENT is made and entered into this _____ day of _____ _____, 200__, by and between the CITY OF SANDY SPRINGS, a Georgia municipal corporation, (the "CITY"), and CH2M HILL, Inc., a Florida corporation. ("Corporation").

WHEREAS, the City is desirous of maintaining a level of competent professional and economically feasible contract administrative, finance and community services in conjunction and harmony with its fiscal policies of sound, economical management, and

WHEREAS, Corporation has agreed to render to the City a continuing level of professional contract services and the City is desirous of contracting for such services upon the terms and conditions hereinafter set forth, and

WHEREAS, Corporation is licensed to do business within the state of Georgia as a foreign corporation, and

WHEREAS the City is desirous of providing these daily services to its constituents through a contractual relationship with Corporation,

WHEREAS the Governors Commission for the City of Sandy Springs, an entity created pursuant to O.C.G.A. § 36-31-8, followed a specific procedure, issued a request for proposals, and the proposals were reviewed by representatives of the Governor's Commission and the members of the Governor's Commission and were made available to the members of the public at large,

WHEREAS the City has the power to contract,

WHEREAS the City will have on-hand funds to pay for all obligations incurred hereunder,

NOW THEREFORE, in consideration of the sums hereinafter set forth and for other good and valuable considerations, the receipt and legal sufficiency of which are hereby acknowledged, it is hereby agreed as follows:

SECTION 1. PRIOR AGREEMENTS

As of the effective date hereof, all prior agreements between the City and Corporation are terminated and replaced by the terms hereof.

SECTION 2. GENERAL SERVICES

2.1   Corporation shall provide to City for the term hereinafter set forth, as the same may be extended in accordance with the provisions hereof, competent services as set forth herein, within and throughout the corporate limits of City to the extent and in the manner hereinafter described.

2.2   The City hereby engages Corporation to provide, and Corporation hereby agrees to provide, all of the services described herein and in the "Scope of Services," attached hereto as Exhibit A and incorporated herein by reference.

2.3   The parties recognize that this Agreement is intended to provide flexibility to the City in order to meet its evolving challenges. The Corporation reserves the right to reasonably allocate resources for the performance of services between this Agreement and the Agreement for Administrative, Financial Community Services, Motor Vehicle, Staffing, And Purchasing, Procurement And Contracting Services per the priorities agreed-to with the City Manager so long as such allocations do not adversely affect the City regarding either (1) cost of services under this Agreement, or (2) service quality to the public. Staff additions as agreed upon between the parties resulting from new services outside the Scope of Services in this contract will be considered a change to this Agreement.

2.4   Corporation agrees to provide City all services and personnel necessary to fulfill the obligations of Corporation under this contract; provided, however, that to the extent that the City must cooperate and/or perform services in conjunction with a third party excluding Corporation's second tier subcontractors which shall be defined as any individual or entity retained, employed, affiliated, or engaged by or under contract with Corporation to undertake any services performed hereunder, should the third party fail to fulfill their obligations, any additional services performed or costs reasonably incurred by the Corporation in conjunction with compensating for the failure of the third party to fulfill its obligations shall be handled as a change to this Agreement as per Section 8.2.

2.5   Except as otherwise hereinafter specifically set forth, such professional services shall encompass all those duties and functions of the type coming within the jurisdiction of and customarily rendered by municipal departments (other than those provided by other contract providers) in accordance with the Charter of the City, and the Statutes of the State of Georgia.

2.6   Corporation shall, at all times, foster and maintain harmonious relationships with the members of the City Council, all employees of the City, all employees of the City's contract services providers and all City's residents, and shall represent the City in the best light possible.

2.7 All communications to the Mayor, City Council, and press, unless otherwise authorized, shall be through the City Manager. All mass communications to residents shall be reviewed and approved by the City Manager prior to printing and dissemination.

2.8 The President or Senior Executive Officer of Corporation shall be available to meet with the City Manager at City Hall on an annual basis, date to be determined by mutual agreement and at any other times and at the request of the City Manager after reasonable notice has been provided to President or Senior Executive Officer of Corporation.

SECTION 3. ADDITIONAL SERVICES

3.1 Corporation shall provide to the City, upon the request of the City Manager and the availability of resources, such additional services as may from time to time be needed at the discretion of the City.

3.2 The cost of such additional services shall be borne by the City and shall be payable in such amounts and in such a manner as may be determined by mutual agreement, upon each occurrence in accordance with Section 8.2.

3.3 Corporation may provide management of capital improvements and engineering services (provided, however, Corporation acknowledges that it is responsible for certain engineering services encompassed in that certain Agreement for Administrative, Financial Community Services, Motor Vehicle, Staffing, And Purchasing, Procurement And Contracting Services executed contemporaneously herewith) as set out in Section 2.1.2.1 of the Scope of Services attached hereto as Exhibit A. Both Parties agree that Corporation's duties under this Agreement are limited to the coordination for capital improvement programs and procurement and program management for small projects (i.e., estimated procurement contract value of under $50,000 although final decision will be based upon the complexity of said project), unless otherwise agreed upon between the Parties. Corporation's duties do not include the program management of the large or complex projects (those projects outside of the above definition of small projects) which would be outside the Scope of Services herein and, accordingly, handled through an additional services authorization and change to the Agreement as per Section 8.2 of this Agreement. Subject to all other requirements contained herein, the parties agree that if requested to conduct program management of the operations of a capital improvement project, Corporation may provide for such services to be completed by either Corporation, an affiliate of Corporation, or second tier subcontractor.

3.4   **MAINTENANCE. REPAIR AND**
               CAPITAL IMPROVEMENTS

3.4.1   Corporation shall provide for ordinary maintenance of City assets and infrastructure in the course of its duties under this Agreement as per Exhibit A, Scope of Services. Such ordinary maintenance shall be performed to the extent of the capabilities of the project staff during normal business hours. For the purposes of this Agreement, the definition of ordinary maintenance shall be: the routine/repetitive activities required for operational continuity, safety, and performance of City assets or infrastructure.

3.4.2   Corporation shall provide for repair of City assets and infrastructure in the course of its duties under this Agreement as per Exhibit A, Scope of Services. For the purposes of this Agreement, the definition of repair shall be: the cost of non-routine/non-repetitive activities required for operational continuity, safety, and performance generally resulting from the failure or to avert a failure of the equipment, vehicle, roadway, or facility or some component thereof. The parties agree that such repair work shall be limited to $50,000 annually unless otherwise specified in the Scope of Services or unless and in the event Corporation is responsible for the needed repairs through its failure to perform routine maintenance or because of any intentional acts of the Corporation's employees. The parties further agree that Corporation is authorized pursuant to this Agreement to immediately perform emergency repair services which may fall outside of the Scope of Services hereto to address unforeseen issues of safety and welfare which may arise, provided, however, Corporation and shall notify the City Manager of the existence of, and the scope of, any such emergency repair as soon as feasible based upon the circumstances, but in no event later than within twenty-four (24) hours of receipt of notification of such emergency repairs.

3.4.3   A capital improvement is defined as, any work or materials applied to an existing asset that restores that asset or infrastructure to a "like new" condition and/or improves the performance and/or reliability levels of the asset beyond the capabilities of the original installation or performs a duty or service that was not previously provided. The Corporation's duties under this Agreement do not encompass payment for capital improvements to assets of the City unless so agreed to between the parties.

SECTION 4.   HOURS OF OPERATION

4.1   Corporation shall maintain for the purpose of City business, fully staffed business hours equal to, but not less than, the City's business hours of 8:00 a.m. to 5:00 p.m., Monday through Friday, with the exception of the following holidays:

New Year's Day
Martin Luther King Birthday
President's Day
Memorial Day
Independence Day
Labor Day
Veteran's Day
Thanksgiving Day
Day After Thanksgiving Day
Christmas

4.2   For all City related matters, Corporation shall use the address of Sandy Springs City Hall, including both incoming and outgoing mail.

SECTION 5.   CORPORATION EMPLOYEES

5.1   All personnel employed by Corporation in the performance of such services, functions and responsibilities as described and contemplated herein for the City shall be and remain Corporation employees (the "Corporation Employees").

5.2   Corporation shall be solely responsible for all compensation benefits, insurance and rights of the Corporation employees during the course or arising or accruing as a result of any employment, whether past or present, with Corporation, as well as all legal costs including attorney's fees incurred in the defense of any conflict or legal action resulting from such employment or related to the corporate amenities of such employment. Accordingly, the City shall not be called upon to assume any liability for or direct payment of any salaries, wages, contribution to pension funds, insurance premiums or payments, workers compensation benefits under O.C.G.A. §34-9-1 et seq., or any other amenities of employment to any of the Corporation Employees or any other liabilities whatsoever, unless otherwise specifically provided herein.

5.3   In conformance with standards established by City for achieving an acceptable level of customer service and delivery of municipal services to the City residents and constituents consistent with reasonable municipal management practices as compared with municipalities of similar size in the State of Georgia, Corporation shall have and maintain the responsibility for and control of the rendering of the services, the standards of performance, the discipline of the Corporation Employees and other matters incident to the performance of the services, duties and responsibilities as described and contemplated herein.

5.4   In order to perform its obligations hereunder, certain Corporation Employees will be assigned to work full-time for the City (the "Designated Employees"). Prior to assigning any Designated Employees to the City, Corporation shall subject each prospective Designated Employee to a full background check, including a driver's license review. Corporation retains the ability to discipline such Designated Employees as per Corporation's established guidelines, including termination.

5.5   The Corporation Employees shall wear attire with the logo of the City when, and only when, they are performing services for the City, except as otherwise directed by the City Manager.

5.6   The City Manager shall have the right utilizing an objective standard based upon job performance to require Corporation to transfer any of the Designated Employees out of the Cit or to a different position. Corporation agrees to transfer any of the Designated Employees immediately upon notification by the City Manager. Utilizing an objective standard based upon job performance, the City Manager shall have the right to prohibit any Corporation Employee that is not a Designated Employee from performing any work for the City, and shall also have the right to limit, in any manner, the work done for the City by any Corporation Employee that is not a Designated Employee.

5.7   Corporation shall have the discretion to transfer or reassign any personnel out of the City for the following reasons:

   a. Situations where an employee requests a transfer in order to accept a promotion or special assignment, which has been offered to him or her by Corporation upon his or her special education qualifications or career path;

   b. Disciplinary reasons;

   c. Failure of an employee to meet Corporation performance standards;

   d. At the request of the employee.

In the event Corporation transfers or reassigns any employee for the above stated reasons, Corporation shall provide the City Manager with prompt written notice of such transfer or reassignment and explain the basis of the reassignment. Corporation shall not transfer or reassign any of the Corporation Employees for any other reason unless the City Manager concurs prior to any transfer, which concurrence shall not be unreasonably withheld. Any personnel, transferred or reassigned out of the City, pursuant to this subsection, shall not occur without first filling the vacated position with a Corporation employee approved and authorized by the City Manager, which approval and authorization shall not be unreasonably withheld.

SECTION 6.   ASSISTANT CITY MANAGER AND PROGRAM DIRECTOR

6.1   The Program Director assisted by the Assistant City Manager shall, among other duties specified by the City Manager:

a. Act as liaison between the City and Corporation;

b. Attend staff meetings, City Council meetings and any agenda meetings, at which attendance by the Program Director or Assistant City Manager is deemed necessary by the City Manager. Attend other County and State agency meetings and forums as required by the City Manager;

c. Provide information to City Manager and City Council on all issues relevant and applicable to the City, its officials, its constituents or to its status as a municipal corporation;

d. Assist the City in all relations with other Contractors;

e. When so directed by the City Manager, carry out such other duties and responsibilities as are necessary to fulfill services under Exhibit A, but that are not inconsistent with Corporation's obligations under this Agreement, nor expand Corporation's obligations under this Agreement.

6.2   In the event of a vacancy in the position of the Program Director or Assistant City Manager, Corporation agrees to make such selections in good faith and in the best interest of the City. The City Manager shall have the opportunity to interview each of the candidates, and no person may be appointed Program Director or Assistant City Manager without the City Manager's consent, which may be withheld for any reason or no reason, in City Manager's sole discretion.

6.3   In the event the City Manager becomes dissatisfied with the performance of the Program Director or Assistant City Manager, utilizing an objective standard based upon job performance, the City Manager may, in its sole discretion, provide notification to Corporation. Thereafter, representatives of Corporation and the City Manager shall meet to discuss possible remedies of the problems experienced by the City. Corporation agrees to act in good faith in resolving any problems experienced by the City, including if necessary the removal of Al Crace as Assistant City Manager and Rick Hirsekorn as Program Director and Nancy Leathers as Community Development Director.

SECTION 7.   COMMUNITY DEVELOPMENT DIRECTOR

7.1   The Community Development Director shall, among other duties
               specified by the City Manager and/or Assistant City Manager:

      a.   Oversee and ensure the proper implementation and execu-
               tion of all duties set forth in Section 7.0 et seq. and 8.0 et
               seq. of Exhibit "A" hereto.

      b.   Attend all City Manager and/or Assistant City Manager
               staff meetings, council meetings and any other meetings
               deemed necessary by the City Manager and/or Assistant
               City Manager.

      c.   Act as a liaison, with City Manager and Assistant City
               Manager approval, between the City, Fulton County,
               Georgia, the Atlanta Regional Council and necessary fed-
               eral, state, and local officials and/or agencies.

7.2   In the event of a vacancy in the position of the Community
               Development Director, Corporation agrees to make such selec-
               tions in good faith and in the best interest of the City. The
               City Manager shall have the opportunity to interview each of
               the candidates, and no person may be appointed Community
               Development Director without the City Manager's consent,
               which may be withheld for any reason or no reason, in City
               Manager's sole discretion.

7.3   In the event the City Manager becomes dissatisfied with the
               performance of the Community Development Director, the
               City Manager may, in its sole discretion, provide notification
               to Corporation. Thereafter, representatives of Corporation and
               the City Manager shall meet to discuss possible remedies of the
               problems experienced by the City. Corporation agrees to act in
               good faith in resolving any problems experienced by the City,
               including if necessary the removal of Nancy Leathers.

SECTION 8.   COMPENSATION

8.1   The City shall pay to Corporation as compensation for services
               performed under this Agreement a fixed price of $18,500,000
               for the first year of this Agreement ("Compensation Amount").
               One-twelfth (1/12) of the Compensation Amount shall invoiced
               by the first of the month in which services are to be performed

and the invoice shall be due thirty (30) days from receipt. The City shall budget an additional fifteen percent (15%) of the annual Compensation Amount for new services not defined in Exhibit A, Scope of Services. Access to these funds will be controlled by the City and authorized via the defined Change Order process outlined in Section 8.2 of this Service Agreement. **The Compensation Amount does not include Sales, Use or other taxes. Such applicable taxes will be added to the monthly invoice.** Such Compensation Amount shall be adjusted on an annual basis as per Section 8.4, to take effect on January 1ˢᵗ of the new calendar year in which Corporation is performing services. Corporation shall provide to City on a monthly basis the breakdown of monthly price per overall service in a format to be agreed upon between the parties.

8.2   The City from time-to-time may request the Corporation to perform services which are not included in Exhibit A, Scope of Services ("Change Order"). Upon request by the City, the Corporation will, within a reasonable time period (generally within 5 working days) provide to the City a price for the Change Order service(s) in writing. The estimate will be provided to the City for review and approval. If approved by the City in writing, the Corporation will proceed with the Change Order services. Unless otherwise stated in the estimate, the Corporation will invoice the City on the next billing cycle after completion of Change Order service(s). If the Change Order service request generates an on-going new service or will result in an on-going new service under the Scope of Services, the Corporation will include the associated adjustment for the Change Order to the monthly Compensation Amount invoice for City consideration.

8.3   City shall pay interest at an annual rate equal to Wells Fargo Bank, N.A.'s prime rate plus one and one-half percent (1-1/2%) (said amount of interest not to exceed any limitation provided by law) on payments not paid and received within thirty (30) calendar days from date of receipt by the City of Corporation's monthly invoice, such interest being calculated from the due date of the payment, so long as said delay is not caused by Corporation. City shall pay all undisputed amounts according to the terms of this Agreement. If City disputes any invoices issued, City shall notify Corporation in writing within five (5) days of receipt of invoice detailing out the invoice charge disputed and reasons why. Corporation shall respond within five (5) days to such notification. If such issue is not resolved within fifteen (15) days after notification, such issue shall be handled as per Section 41. Valid disputes on invoices shall not accrue interest until the date of resolution, and applicable interest, if any, shall be calculated from the date of resolution of the dispute.

8.4   For the fiscal year beginning January 1, 2007, the annual fee for the services pursuant to this Agreement will be $16,096,762. For years Fiscal Year 2008 and beyond, the Compensation Amount shall be an amount as determined by the following formula:

[CPI x (45% x Baseline Compensation Amount which is the current year compensation to be adjusted)] + [ECI x (55% x Baseline Compensation Amount which is the current year compensation to be adjusted)]

CPI = Consumer Price Index for all urban consumers as published by U.S. Department of Labor, Bureau of Labor Statistics in the CPI Detailed Report for the month October of the calendar year presently operating in, (South Urban region, Atlanta, GA)

ECI = Compensation for Civilians Workers, Not Seasonally Adjusted (Employment Cost Index) for the third quarter of the calendar year presently operating in as published by U.S. Department of Labor, Bureau of Labor Statistics in the Detailed Report.

Such adjustment formula does not take into consideration significant price increases related to gasoline, power, asphalt, fuel, and other commodities or services related to force majeure events. In the event Corporation can demonstrate that significant regional price increases have occurred, that are outside the reasonable control of Corporation, the City and Corporation will engage in good faith efforts to assess the relative impact on the respective variable to the Compensation Amount.

Subject to the foregoing paragraph regarding significant price increases, in no event shall the total upward adjustment of the

Compensation Amount pursuant to this section exceed the sum of nine percent (9%) in any given annual period. Further, the Compensation Amount may not be increased in any fiscal year without the approval of the City Council. In addition, should any upward adjustment of the Compensation Amount be negotiated regarding the Agreement, City shall have a similar right to a proportional adjustment upwards of the amounts regarding Corporation's liability for costs, including but not limited to: (1) liability caps for damages and/or fines, (2) repair and maintenance costs, and (3) furniture, fixture and equipment expenditures under this Agreement, which shall all be set out in writing by way of addendum to this Agreement at the time of agreement upon any revised terms.

8.5   If, during any fiscal year, there is a reduction in the scope of services not related to default by Corporation as per Section 12, the Compensation Amount shall be reduced by an amount agreeable to the City Manager and Corporation, but in no event shall reduced Compensation Amount be an amount less than the actual cost of said services, and the allocated overhead and profit for such services. If the City elects not to assume performance of the reduced or eliminated services as contemplated herein, and therefore the equipment, materials and staff procured or hired by Corporation for the provision to the City of said reduced services results in expense to the Corporation, Corporation may recover those expenses caused by such unassumed services including any demobilization costs, unamortized costs incurred by Corporation, and any applicable termination charges assessed by vendors or suppliers retained by Corporation to provide the eliminated service. If the City Manager and Corporation are unable to agree upon an amount, the reduced Compensation Amount shall be equal to the actual cost, allocated overhead and profit, less any allowed offsets as set forth in this Section.

8.6   The parties may agree to modify the baseline compensation amount for Fiscal Year 2008, provided, however, should Corporation seek to modify such baseline amount such request must be made in writing directed to the City Manager, setting forth all costs and justifications for such modification no less than six (6) months prior to the termination date under the Agreement. Any modification of the baseline compensation amount shall be subject to approval of the City Council.

SECTION 9. TERM

As per O.C.G.A. 36-60-13, this Service Agreement is effective as of January 1, 2006 and shall be effective for one year terms ending at the close of each calendar year. This Service Agreement shall be automatically renewed as per Section 10.

SECTION 10. OPTION TO RENEW

As per O.C.G.A. 36-60-13, this Agreement shall be automatically renewed for a period of five (5) one (1) year terms at the expiration of the initial term, upon the mutual agreement between the Parties unless either party furnishes the other party written notice of its intent not to renew this Agreement not less than one hundred twenty (120) days prior to the expiration of this Agreement.

SECTION 11. TERMINATION

11.1   Corporation may terminate this Service Agreement at its discretion either with or without cause, by giving written notice thereof to City; provided, however, that such termination shall not be effective until the one hundred and eightieth (180th) day after receipt thereof by City.

11.2   City may terminate this Service Agreement in its entirety at its discretion either with or without cause, by giving written notice thereof to Corporation; provided, however, that such termination shall not be effective until the one hundred and eightieth (180th) day after receipt thereof by Corporation. City may also terminate this Service Agreement in its entirety, at its discretion with no advance notice, in the event of a vote by the Board of Directors, officers or employees to transfer of a controlling interest in Corporation (which shall be defined to mean more than 50% of the ownership interest) to a non-related entity. Corporation shall notify the City Manager immediately in the event of such a vote to so transfer of a controlling interest in Corporation.

11.3   City may partially terminate this Service Agreement as to any specific service or services provided by Corporation hereunder by giving at least sixty (60) days advance written notice thereof to Corporation specifying the specific service or services that the City desires Corporation to cease performing. Upon a partial termination, the Compensation Amount shall be reduced pursuant to Section 8.5 of this Agreement.

11.4   In the event of termination by either party, the other party shall render such aid, coordination and cooperation as might be required for an expeditious and efficient termination of service.

11.4.1 In the event of termination by City for reasons other than default as per Section 12, and if the City elects not to assume performance of some or all of the reduced services Corporation may recover costs as set forth in Section 8.5 of this Agreement.

This Service Agreement is contingent upon sufficient appropriation and authorization being made annually by the City Council, at least one hundred and twenty (120) days prior to renewal period, for the performance of the services provided in this contract. If sufficient appropriations and authorizations are not so made, this Contract shall terminate pursuant to the terms of this Section 11 upon written notice being given by the City to Corporation

SECTION 12. DEFAULT

12.1   An event of default shall mean a material breach of this Agreement. If situations arise which are not considered a material breach, such issues shall be resolved as per Section 41. Without limiting the generality of the foregoing and in addition to those instances referred to as a breach, an event of default shall include the following:

   a. Corporation has not performed services as per this Agreement;

   b. Corporation has refused or failed, except in the case for which an extension of time is provided, to supply properly skilled Staff personnel;

   c. Corporation has failed to obtain the approval of the City where required by this Agreement;

d. Corporation has refused or failed, except in the case for which an extension of time is provided, to provide the Services as defined in this Agreement.

e. The failure, refusal or other default by the City in its duty: (1) to pay the amount required to be paid to the Corporation under this Agreement within 30 days following the due date for such payment; or (2) to perform any other material obligation under this Agreement (unless such default is excused by an Force Majeure and to the extent provided herein).

f. Any representation or warranty of the City hereunder that was false or inaccurate in any material respect when made, and which materially and adversely affects the legality of this Agreement or the ability of the City to carry out its obligations hereunder.

12.2 In the event either Party fails to comply with the provisions of this Agreement, the other Party may: (1) declare the Party in default, notify defaulting party in writing, and give defaulting party fifteen (15) calendar days from receipt of notice to make substantial efforts towards curing the default. If defaulting party fails to make substantial efforts towards curing such default within fifteen (15) calendar days, such Agreement shall be terminated as per Section 11.1 and any compensation due and owing to Corporation shall be paid by City or (2) such party may exercise such provisions under Section 41 regarding the alleged breach without waiving or being estopped from subsequently pursuing the breach as a matter of law. If Corporation is the defaulting party, the compensation to Corporation through termination shall be the prorated Compensation Amount for any completed professional services minus any damages assessed pursuant to Section 12.3. Upon termination City shall begin transition efforts and Corporation shall assist such transition, provided, however, City shall be liable for the reasonable costs for transition efforts as demonstrated by the Corporation. In the event payment has been made for professional services not completed, Corporation shall return these sums to the City within ten (10) days after receipt of notice that these sums are due. Nothing in this Article shall limit the either Party's right to terminate, at any time, pursuant to Sections 10 and 11, its right for damages under Section 12.3, and its right to assign pursuant to Section 37.

12.3   In an Event of Default by either Party, it shall be liable for all damages resulting from the default.

12.4   Subject to the dispute provisions contained in Section 41 of this Agreement, either Party may take advantage of each and every remedy specifically existing at law or in equity. Each and every remedy shall be in addition to every other remedy specifically given or otherwise existing and may be exercised from time to time as often and in such order as may be deemed expedient by the Party. The exercise or the beginning of the exercise of one remedy shall not be deemed to be a waiver of the right to exercise any other remedy. The Party's rights and remedies as set forth in this Agreement are not exclusive and are in addition to any other rights and remedies available to either Party in law or in equity.

SECTION 13. TRANSITION

13.1   In the event of the full termination for any reason, partial termination or expiration of this Agreement, Corporation and City shall cooperate in good faith in order to effectuate a smooth and harmonious transition from Corporation to City, or to any other person or entity City may designate, and to maintain during such period of transition the same quality services otherwise afforded to the residents of the City pursuant to the terms hereof.

13.2   In the event of the full termination, partial termination or expiration of this Agreement, the City shall have the absolute right to offer employment to any of the Corporation Employees. If, upon termination for any reason other than default of the Corporation, City exercises its option to assume employment of Corporation's employees as contemplated by this Section 13.2, in addition to the Compensation Amount due to Corporation for the completed services, as prorated pursuant to Section 8.5 herein, City shall pay to Corporation as additional compensation the following in anticipation of compensating Corporation for expended funds related to employment, training, benefit packages, start-up and transition costs that Corporation would not be able to recoup:

If termination and assumption of Corporation employees occurs in the first year of this Agreement, City shall pay to Corporation the sum of: (1) 35% for staff with salaries above $100,000, and (2) 20% for staff with salaries less than $100,000. For each subsequent renewal period the percentage due for each assumed employee shall be reduced at 1/6 per year such that there is no payment at the end of the Term. The percentage amounts shall be based upon the then current salaries of the respective staff members during the contract year in which the termination takes place.

13.3   In the event of the full termination, partial termination or expiration of this Agreement, and in the further event that the City is unable to provide the same level of services at the time of such termination or expiration, the then pending term of this Agreement may be extended by the City for a period of ninety (90) days or until City is capable, in its sole discretion, of rendering such services, whichever occurs sooner. The remuneration to be paid to Corporation during the transition period shall be based upon actual cost of providing such services during the transition period plus a mutually agreed upon fee, provided, however such fee shall not exceed the Compensation Amount which would be due and owing to the Corporation for the provision of said services pursuant to the terms of this Agreement.

13.4   In the event of the full termination, partial termination, expiration of the term or non-renewal of the term, the City may either accept assignment of Corporations' current leases and/or agreements for the project or City may pay any associated buy-out or termination charges, provided, however, prior to entering into any leases or agreements after the effective date of this Agreement which contain buy-out provisions or termination charges in excess of $1,000.00, Corporation shall submit the terms of the same to the City Manager for approval in writing prior to entering into such lease or agreement. Corporation has provided City with a list of all leases and agreements entered into by Corporation and City hereby approves such.

13.5   The following terms apply to vehicles assets leased by Corporation during the term of this Agreement:

a. Corporation will enter into a lease agreement with Automotive Rental, Inc. ("ARI") for the vehicles required for performance of the services under this Agreement for the City's benefit.

b. Corporation will be responsible for maintaining the required insurance for the leased assets.

c. The Compensation Amount under Section 9 has provided for reimbursement to Corporation for the monthly lease amounts.

d. Under Corporation's lease with ARI, after the initial twelve (12) months Corporation has the option to continue to lease the vehicles on a month to month basis; return the vehicle(s) to ARI; or purchase the vehicle(s). Any time after the initial twelve (12) months, City may request to purchase the vehicle at Corporation's cost plus a transfer fee and applicable taxes, at which point Corporation will exercise its purchase option with ARI.

SECTION 14. INDEMNIFICATION

14.1   Corporation shall indemnify, defend and hold harmless the City, its officers, agents, servants and employees from and against any and all liability, suits, actions, damages, costs, losses and expenses, including attorneys' fees, demands and claims for personal injury, bodily injury, sickness, diseases or death or damage or destruction of tangible property, to the proportionate extent arising out of any errors, omissions, willful misconduct or negligent acts of Corporation, its officials, agents, employees or subcontractors in the performance of the services of Corporation under this Agreement, whether from and against any orders, judgments, or decrees which may be entered thereon and from and against all costs, damages of every kind and nature, attorneys' fees, expenses and liabilities incurred in and about the defense of any such claim and investigation thereof. Corporation's indemnification, however, shall be limited to the actual amount of any liability of City and not encompass any sums for which City is exempt based upon Georgia municipal immunity Statutes.

14.2   Corporation acknowledges that specific consideration has been
              paid or will be paid under this Agreement for this hold harm-
              less and indemnification provision, and further agrees with the
              foregoing provisions of indemnity and with the collateral obli-
              gation of insuring said indemnity as set forth In Section 15,
              Insurance.

14.3   To the extent allowable by Georgia law, City shall indemnify,
              defend and hold harmless the Corporation, its officers, agents,
              employees, and subcontractors from and against any and all liabil-
              ity, suits, actions, damages, costs, losses and expenses, including
              attorneys' fees, demands and claims for personal injury, bodily
              injury, sickness, diseases or death or damage or destruction of
              tangible property, to the proportionate extent arising out of any
              errors, omissions, willful misconduct or negligent acts of City,
              its officials, agents, servants, agents or subcontractors in the per-
              formance by the City of of its obligations under this Agreement,
              whether from and against any orders, judgments, or decrees
              which may be entered thereon and from and against all costs,
              damages of every kind and nature, attorneys' fees, expenses and
              liabilities incurred in and about the defense of any such claim
              and investigation thereof.

14.4   In disputes between City and Corporation, in no event shall
              either party, its subcontractors or their officers or employees be
              liable to the other party for any special, indirect or consequential
              damages, whether such liability arises in breach of contract or
              warranty, tort including negligence, strict or statutory liability,
              or any other cause of action, provided, however, such limitation
              does not include any liability for which Corporation is obligated
              to indemnify City based upon special, indirect or consequential
              damages suffered by any third-parties.

14.5   In compensation for benefits conveyed to the City by this
              Agreement, the parties agree that Corporation's liability to the
              City will, in the aggregate, not exceed $3,500,000 per term
              of this Agreement. This provision takes precedence over all
              conflicting provisions of this Agreement except the Severability
              provision of Section 29. This limitation of liability will apply to
              all claims brought by the City against the Corporation, whether
              Corporation's liability to the City arises under breach of contract

or warranty; tort, including negligence, strict liability, statutory liability; or any other cause of action, and shall include Corporation's officers, affiliated corporations, employees, and subcontractors. This subsection does not apply to claims for indemnification by the City against Corporation.

14.6   In compensation for benefits conveyed to the City by this Agreement, the parties agrees that Corporation shall be liable for fines or civil penalties to a maximum aggregate of One Hundred Fifty Thousand Dollars ($150,000) per year, which may be imposed by any federal or state department or regulatory agency that are a result of Corporation's negligent operation. City will assist Corporation to contest any such fines in administrative proceedings and/or in court prior to any payment by Corporation. Corporation shall pay the costs of contesting any such fines. Corporation shall not be liable for fines or civil penalties that result from violations that occurred prior to the effective date of this Agreement or for the effects of prior violations by the City that have contributed to the assessment of any fine or civil penalty caused by Corporation's negligent operations.

14.7.   City and Corporation shall perform a condition assessment of the assets and infrastructure within sixty (60) days after the execution of this Agreement to establish the existing condition of the assets and infrastructure of the City. The City shall be responsible for the costs, claims, liabilities and expenses related to the condition of the assets up to the assessment determination. Following the date of assessment, Corporation is responsible for maintaining the assets as per this Section 3.4.1 of this Agreement.

SECTION 15. INSURANCE

15.1   Corporation shall not commence work under this contract or continue performance of the services unless and until Corporation has obtained all insurance required under this Section 15 as per the following.

15.1.1   Corporation shall provide the following insurances throughout the term of the Agreement, and shall provide to City Certificates of Insurance demonstrating compliance with this provision:

15.1.1.1 Statutory Worker's Compensation and Employers Liability Insurance as required by the State of Georgia. Such workers compensation coverage shall be as provided by O.C.G.A. § 34-9-1 et. seq

15.1.1.2 Comprehensive Automobile and Vehicle Liability Insurance with 5 Million Dollars ($5,000,000) combined single limits, covering claims for injuries to members of the public and/or damages to property of others arising from the use of Corporation owned or leased motor vehicles, including onsite and offsite operations.

15.1.1.3 Commercial General Liability Insurance with limits of 5 Million Dollars ($5,000,000) per occurrence and in the aggregate, covering claims for injuries to members of the public or damages to property of others arising out of any covered act acts of the Corporation undertaken to provide services for the City as required in this Agreement or omission of Corporation or any of its employees, or subcontractors.

15.1.1.4 Professional Liability Insurance with limits of 5 Million Dollars ($5,000,000) per occurrence and in the aggregate.

15.1.1.5 Excess Liability Insurance with limits of 45 Million Dollars ($45,000,000).

15.1.2 City shall warrant that the following insurances are carried throughout the term of the Agreement, and shall provide Corporation with Certificates of Insurance to demonstrate compliance with this provision:

15.1.2.1 Property Damage Insurance for all property including City supplied vehicles and equipment for the full fair market value of such property.

15.1.2.2 Liability Insurance for all motor vehicles and equipment provided by City and operated by Corporation under this Agreement.

15.2 City and Corporation will insure that any and all policies of insurance procured hereunder shall provide for a waiver of subrogation against the other, and each party waives any claim against the other arising in contract or in tort which are covered by their respective insurance hereunder.

15.3   Corporation shall be responsible for maintaining this professional liability insurance for a minimum of two (2) years from the date of expiration of this Agreement. Upon request of City, Corporation shall make available for inspection copies of any claims filed or made against any policy during the policy term. Corporation shall additionally notify City, in writing, within thirty (30) calendar days, of any claims filed or made as it relates to the scope of services provided under this Agreement against any policy in excess of $25,000 during the policy term.

15.4   Certificates of insurance, reflecting evidence of the required insurance, shall be filed with the City Manager or designee prior to the commencement of the work. Policies shall be issued by companies authorized to do business under the laws of the State of Georgia, with financial ratings acceptable to the City Manager. The City shall be named as an additional insured on allowable policies obtained regarding services under this Agreement, including but not limited to the Commercial General Liability and Comprehensive Auto Liability insurance policies. Corporation agrees to furnish City with at least thirty (30) days prior written notice of any cancellation of any insurance policy required under this Agreement.

15.5   In the event the insurance certificate provided indicates that the insurance shall terminate and lapse during the period of this contract, then in that event, Corporation shall furnish, fifteen (15) days after expiration of such insurance, a renewed certificate of insurance as proof that equal and like coverage for the balance of the period of the contract and extension hereunder is in effect. Corporation shall not continue work pursuant to this Agreement unless all required insurance remains in full force and effect

15.6   The costs of all policies of insurance required hereunder shall be the obligation of Corporation and the City shall in no way be responsible therefore.

15.7   City shall pay for and maintain its own comprehensive general liability insurance or maintain a self-insuring fund for the term of this Agreement in the amount determined by City to adequately insure the City's liability assumed herein, but in no event shall coverage be less than the amount of statutory waiver of sovereign immunity. In the event such coverage is modified, in any regard, before the expiration date of this Agreement, and unless otherwise agreed, City will provide at least thirty (30) days prior written notice to Corporation.

15.8   Corporation shall supply a Performance Bond on an annual basis to City in the amount of $500,000 or 10% of the Compensation Amount (whichever is less) to be supplied to City within thirty (30) days of execution of this Agreement.

SECTION 16. CONFLICTS OF INTEREST/ COLLUSION/CONTINGENT FEES

16.1   Corporation shall not review or perform any services regarding any application made to the City by any client of Corporation, unless the services Corporation performs for such client are unrelated to the City. In such instance, Corporation shall disclose the relationship immediately to the City Manager, who may retain an alternate contractor or service provider to Corporation for those services the performance of which by the Corporation would create a perceived or real conflict of interest. If the services relate to a fixed fee service, the fees for the alternate to Corporation shall be deducted from the fixed fee paid to Corporation.

16.2   Neither Corporation nor any of its officers or employees shall have or hold any employment or contractual relationship that is antagonistic or incompatible with Corporation's loyal and conscientious exercise of judgment related to its performance under this Agreement.

16.3   Neither Corporation nor any of its directors, officers or employees shall obtain any kickbacks or benefits for itself, themselves or other clients as a result of any City purchases or transactions.

16.3.1   Corporation shall not collude with other City contract providers regarding City business or matters. Corporation shall not enter into any business relationships with other City contract providers regarding City business or matters, without the approval of the City Manager, which approval may be withheld at the City Manager's sole discretion.

16.3.2   Corporation warrants that it has not employed or retained any company or person, other than a bona fide employee working solely for Corporation, to solicit or secure this Agreement, and that it has not paid or agreed to pay any person, company, corporation, individual or firm, other than a bona fide employee working solely for Corporation, any fee, commission, percentage, gift, or other consideration contingent upon or resulting from the award or making of this Agreement. Provided however, this provision does not encompass Corporation's ability to have hired or engaged consultants to assist in preparation of the proposal and delivery of the services hereunder. For the breach or violation of this provision, the City shall have the right to terminate the Agreement without liability at its discretion, to deduct from the contract price, or otherwise recover the full amount of such fee, commission, percentage, gift or consideration.

SECTION 17. POLICY OF NON-DISCRIMINATION

Corporation shall not discriminate against any person in its operations, activities or delivery of services under this Agreement. Corporation shall affirmatively comply with all applicable provisions of federal, state and local equal employment laws and shall not engage in or commit any discriminatory practice against any person based on race, age, religion, color, gender, sexual orientation, national origin, marital status, physical or mental disability, political affiliation or any other factor which cannot be lawfully used as a basis for provision or denial of service delivery.

SECTION 18. DRUG FREE WORKPLACE

Corporation shall maintain a Drug Free Workplace.

SECTION 19. INDEPENDENT CONTRACTOR

Corporation, for the purposes of this Service Agreement, is and shall remain an independent contractor; not an employee, agent, or servant of the City. Personal services provided by Corporation shall be by employees of Corporation and subject to supervision by Corporation, and not as officers or employees of City. Personnel policies, tax responsibilities, social security and health insurance, employee benefits, and other similar administrative procedures applicable to services rendered under this Agreement shall be those of Corporation.

SECTION 20. COSTS AND ATTORNEY'S FEES

If the either party is required to enforce the terms of this Agreement by court proceedings or otherwise due to breach of contract, whether or not formal legal action is required, the prevailing party shall recover its the attorney's fees and costs incurred to such.

SECTION 21. RIGHTS IN DATA; COPYRIGHTS; DISCLOSURE

21.1   Definition. The term "Data" as used in this Agreement includes written reports, studies, drawings, or other graphic, electronic, chemical or mechanical representation.

21.2   Rights in Data. Drawings, specifications, designs, models, photographs, computer CADD discs, reports, surveys, software, and other data developed or provided in connection with this Agreement (excluding company proprietary documents and software) shall be the property of City and City shall have the full right to use such data for any official purpose permitted under Georgia Statutes, including making it available to the general public. Such use shall be without any additional payment to or approval by Corporation. City shall have unrestricted authority to publish, disclose, distribute and otherwise use, in whole or in part, any data developed or prepared as per this Section 21.2. All software purchased by the Corporation on behalf of City shall be licensed appropriately under the name of the City. Corporation shall disclose to City Manager any anticipated proprietary documents or software before utilization under this Agreement and shall obtain City Manager approval prior to usage. To the extent the Corporation deems it necessary and with the consent of the City Manager; the Corporation may designate any additional software or proprietary information as confidential, a trade secret, or other reason under Georgia law that exempts the information from disclosure.

21.3   Copyrights. No data developed or prepared in whole or in part under this Agreement shall be subject to copyright in the United States of America or other country, except to the extent such copyright protection is available for the City. Corporation shall not include in the data any copyrighted matter unless Corporation obtains the written approval of the City Manager and provides said City Manager with written permission of the copyright owner for Corporation to use such copyrighted matter in the manner provided herein.

21.4   If this Agreement is terminated for any reason prior to completion of the work, the City may, in its discretion, use any design and documents prepared hereunder.

SECTION 22. COMPLIANCE WITH LAWS; ADVICE OF OTHER PROFESSIONALS

22.1   Corporation shall fully obey and comply with all laws, ordinances and administrative regulations duly made in accordance therewith, which are or shall become applicable to the services performed under the terms of this Agreement. Any changes in costs to perform services or comply with such laws, ordinances or administrative regulations or ability of Corporation to perform services due to change in applicable laws, ordinances, governing permits, or administrative regulations after effective date of this Agreement shall entitle Corporation to modification of this Agreement as per Section 8.2.

22.2   Corporation acknowledges that the City is advised by its City Attorney and that, on all legal matters, Corporation shall abide by the advice and direction of the City Attorney in the performance of its duties as they relate to matters of the City, provided, however that should compliance with such direction require an increase in the scope of services under this Agreement, such increase shall be handled as per Section 8.2 hereof. Provided, however, in no case shall the Corporation be required to abide by the advice and direction of the City Attorney in the event that such advice would cause the Corporation to violate any of its obligations under this Agreement.

22.3   Corporation acknowledges that the City is also advised by various other professionals (including, but not limited to, engineers, traffic engineers, planners, building officials, police officers and firefighters), and that, on all matters within their respective expertise, subject to the approval of the City Manager, Corporation shall abide by their advice and direction in the performance of its duties as they relate to matters of the City, as long as such advice doesn't increase the scope of services or cost under Agreement. If such direction does increase the scope of services pursuant to this Agreement, it shall be handled as per Section 8.2.

SECTION 23. OWNERSHIP OF WORK PRODUCT DOCUMENTS

23.1   All work product prepared by Corporation exclusively for the City shall immediately become the property of the City, excluding other company proprietary documents and software as disclosed pursuant to Section 21.2.

23.2   Corporation understands and agrees that any information, docu-
              ment, report or any other material whatsoever which is given by the
              City to Corporation or which is otherwise obtained or prepared by
              Corporation exclusively for City under the terms of this Agreement
              is and shall at all times remain the property of the City.

SECTION 24. AUDIT AND INSPECTION RIGHTS

24.1   The City may, at reasonable times, and for a period of up to
              three (3) years following the date of final performance of Services
              by Corporation under this Agreement, audit, or cause to be
              audited, those books and records of Corporation that are related
              to Corporation's performance under this Agreement, excluding
              all financial records unless related to direct cost reimbursable
              expenses or other matters contemplated herein, including but not
              limited to buy-out provisions, unless a court of competent juris-
              diction orders disclosure of such information. Corporation agrees
              to maintain all such books and records at its principal place of
              business for a period of three (3) years after final payment is made
              under this Agreement. Corporation shall make all necessary books
              and records available for audit in Fulton County, Georgia.

24.2   The City may, at reasonable times during the term hereof, inspect
              Corporation's facilities and perform such inspections and process
              reviews as the City deems reasonably necessary, to determine
              whether the services required to be provided by Corporation
              under this Agreement conform to the terms of this Agreement.
              Corporation shall make available to the City all reasonable facili-
              ties and assistance to facilitate the performance of inspections by
              the City's representatives.

SECTION 25. WARRANTIES OF CORPORATION

Corporation hereby warrants and represents that at all times during the term
of this Agreement it shall maintain in good standing all required licenses,
certifications, and permits required under federal, state and local laws necessary to perform the Services.

SECTION 26. PUBLIC RECORDS

Corporation understands that the public shall have access, at all reasonable
times, to all documents and information pertaining to the City, subject to

the provision of O.C.G.A. §50-14-1 et seq., and agrees to allow access by the City and the public to all documents subject to disclosure under applicable law. Corporation's willful failure or refusal to comply with the provisions of this Section shall result in the immediate termination of this Agreement by the City. Corporation agrees to retain all public records in accordance with the City's records retention and disposal policies, O.C.G.A. 50-18-92 et. seq., and the Georgia Administrative Code.

SECTION 27. GOVERNING LAW; CONSENT TO JURISDICTION

This Agreement shall be construed in accordance with and governed by the laws of the State of Georgia. Subject to the arbitration requirements of Section 41, and when federal jurisdiction is permitted, the parties submit to the jurisdiction of federal court in any action or proceeding arising out of, or relating to, this Agreement. Venue of any action to enforce this Agreement shall be in Northern District Federal Court.

SECTION 28. HEADINGS

Headings are for the convenience of reference only and shall not be considered in any interpretation of this Agreement.

SECTION 29. SEVERABILITY

If any provision or subsection of any provision of this Agreement or the application thereof to any person or situation shall, to any extent, be held invalid or unenforceable, the remainder of this Agreement including the general provision of any invalid or unenforceable subsection of a provision, and the application of such provisions to persons or situations other than those as to which it shall have been held invalid or unenforceable, shall not be affected thereby, and shall continue in full force and effect, and be enforced to the fullest extent permitted by law.

SECTION 30. CONFLICT

In the event of a conflict between the terms of this Agreement and any terms or conditions contained in any attached documents, the terms in this Agreement shall prevail.

SECTION 31. SURVIVAL OF PROVISIONS

Any terms or conditions of this Agreement that require acts beyond the date of its termination shall survive the termination of this Agreement, shall remain in full force and effect unless and until the terms of conditions are completed, and shall be fully enforceable by either party.

SECTION 32. ENTIRE AGREEMENT

32.1   This Agreement and its attachments constitute the entire agreement between Corporation and City, and all negotiations and oral understandings between the parties are merged herein.

32.2   No modification, amendment or alteration in the terms or conditions of this Agreement shall be effective unless contained in a written document executed with the same formality as this Agreement.

SECTION 33. WAIVER

The waiver by either party of any failure on the part of the other party to perform in accordance with any of the terms or conditions of this Agreement shall not be construed as a waiver of any future or continuing similar or dissimilar failure.

SECTION 34. EQUIPMENT APPRAISAL AND TRANSFER

34.1   In the event of full termination, partial termination or expiration of this Agreement, City shall have the option to purchase from Corporation any piece of equipment belonging to the Corporation or purchased by the Corporation to provide the services outlined herein. The City shall also pay any unamortized costs incurred by Corporation at the time of such termination or expiration which are directly attributable to the purchase or use of such equipment..

34.2   The purchase price for such equipment shall be determined by mutual agreement of the parties as to the fair market value of such equipment.

34.3   Upon the exercise by the City of its option to possess the subject equipment and upon payment by the City, Corporation shall convey within ten (10) days or upon such other mutually agreed time, all of its rights, title and interest, thereto, to the City by Bill of Sale Absolute or Certificate of Title, as applicable.

SECTION 35. AUTHORITY TO EXECUTE

35.1   Corporation by execution hereof does hereby represent to City that Corporation has full power and authority to make and execute this Service Agreement, to the effect that:

a.   The making and execution hereof shall create a legal obligation upon Corporation, which shall be legally binding upon Corporation.

b.   The same shall be enforceable by the City according and to the extent of the provisions hereof.

35.2   Nothing contained or any obligation on the part of Corporation to be performed hereunder shall in any way be contrary to or in contravention of any policy of insurance or surety bond required of Corporation pursuant to the laws of the State of Georgia.

35.3   Corporation shall perform this Agreement under the name of CH2M HILL, Inc., provided, however that CH2M HILL, Inc. may perform services under this Agreement through any wholly owned affiliates of CH2M HILL Limited and if so, such affiliates shall be bound by the terms and conditions of this Agreement to the same extent as if they had been a signatory hereof. It shall be the duty of Corporation to insure: (1) that any affiliates who conduct business for the City pursuant to this Agreement have executed all documents necessary to be legally bound to the City regarding said business; and (2) that any affiliates who conduct business for the City pursuant to this Agreement are in full compliance with the terms hereof.

35.4   The City Manager, Mayor and City Clerk, by their respective executions hereof, do each represent to Corporation that they, collectively, have full power and authority to make and execute this Service Agreement on behalf of the City, pursuant to the Resolution of the City Council of the City.

35.5   Nothing herein contained is intended in any way to be contrary to or in contravention of the Charter of the City and the Laws of the State of Georgia, and to the extent such conflict exists; the City and Corporation shall be mutually relieved of any obligations of such conflict.

SECTION 36. NOTICES

Whenever either party desires to give notice to the other, it must be given by written notice, sent by certified United States mail, with return receipt requested, hand delivered or by facsimile transmission with proof of receipt, addressed to the party for whom it is intended, at the place last specified, and the place for giving of notice in compliance with the provisions of this paragraph. Notice shall be deemed given upon receipt by any method of delivery authorized above. For the present, the parties designate the following as the respective places for giving of notice:

For Corporation: CH2M HILL INC.
                                         9193 S. Jamaica Street, Suite 400
                                         Englewood, CO 80112
                                         ATTN: Catherine Lang
                                         FAX: 303-740-7061

For City: (NEED TO FILL IN)

SECTION 37. ASSIGNABILITY

Either Party shall not assign any of the obligations or benefits imposed hereby or contained herein, without the written consent of the other Party. Such consent on behalf of the City must be evidenced by a duly passed Resolution. Notice of Assignment shall be mailed via U.S. Mail, return receipt requested and any notice required hereunder shall be addressed to the party intended to receive the same at the addresses noted in Section 36. In the event that the City exercises its option to assign this agreement pursuant to this section, the City is not obligated to provide the Notice of Termination identified in Section 11 of this contract. However, Corporation shall coordinate and cooperate with the City as may be required for expeditious and efficient assignment of service pursuant to this article. In addition, Corporation shall transition this contract pursuant to this section in accordance with Section 13 of this Agreement.

SECTION 38. NEGOTIATION

The parties acknowledge that the terms of this Agreement were jointly negotiated between the parties, that both parties were represented by attorneys and that, in the case of any dispute regarding the terms of this Agreement, the terms should not be construed in favor of or against either party.

Section 39. Force Majeure

Neither party shall be liable for damages, delays, or failure to perform its obligations under this Agreement if performance is made impractical, abnormally difficult, or abnormally costly, as a result of any unforeseen occurrence, including but not limited to fire, flood, strike, acts of God, failure of a third party to cooperate in providing services other than Corporation's second tier subcontractors as such term is defined in paragraph 2.4 of this Agreement, or other occurrences, beyond its reasonable control. The party invoking this Force Majeure clause shall notify the other party immediately by verbal communication and in writing of the nature and extent of the contingency within ten (10) working days after its occurrence, and shall take reasonable measures to mitigate any impact of Force Majeure. If the Force Majuere event shall impact schedule or increases the costs incurred by Corporation (excluding those scope of services already anticipated and detailed out in Exhibit A), such items shall be handled as per Section 8.2.

SECTION 40. BINDING EFFECT

This agreement shall inure to the benefit of and be binding upon the respective parties' successors.

SECTION 41. DISPUTES

41.1   To facilitate the timely and effective resolution of any controversy or dispute that may arise under this Service Agreement or out of the performance of this Service Agreement, each party shall appoint one representative to serve on a Management Board. The Management Board will resolve any issues that arise from the Service Agreement that cannot be resolved from the project management level. The party believing there is a controversy or dispute shall put such notice in writing and deliver to the other party. Such demand shall be filed within a reasonable time after the dispute or claim has arisen, but in no event after the applicable statute of limitations for a legal or equitable proceeding would have run. The Management Board shall convene to discuss such notice and shall make a good faith effort to resolve any issues within a period of thirty (30) days of its receipt.

41.2   If a compromise is not negotiated within sixty (60) days of the written notice then in that event the parties shall refer the matter to non-binding mediation. If the parties can not come to an agreement after the non-binding mediation, any claim or counterclaim for less than Two Hundred Thousand Dollars ($200,000) in damages shall be decided by a single arbitrator appointed by the parties for determination as per American Arbitration Association procedures. If the parties are unable to agree on a single arbitrator, each party shall appoint one arbitrator, and the appointed arbitrators shall select a third arbitrator who shall serve as chairperson of the arbitration panel. The third arbitrator selected as chairman shall be a disinterested person of recognized competence. Such arbitration shall be non-binding. The prevailing party shall be entitled to recover its attorney's fees and costs for such arbitration or court proceeding in proportion to the percentage of the recovery. Each party shall pay 50% of the third party costs of arbitration.

41.3   Unless the parties mutually agree otherwise, rules comparable to the Commercial Industry Arbitration Rules of the American Arbitration Association then in effect shall govern the proceedings, provided that failure of the arbitrator(s) to comply with the American Arbitration Association rules shall not invalidate the decision by the arbitrator(s). Notwithstanding Section 27, *Governing Law*, the parties agree this Agreement specifically acknowledge and agree that this contract evidences a "transaction involving commerce" under the Federal Arbitration Act, and that this Agreement to arbitrate shall be governed by the Federal Arbitration Act.

41.4   In those binding arbitration situations, the prevailing party shall be entitled to recover its attorney's fees and costs for such arbitration in proportion to the percentage of the recovery. Each party shall pay 50% of the third party costs of arbitration.

41.5   Should either party seek damages for an amount over Two Hundred Thousand Dollars ($200,000), in a claim or counterclaim, either party may file for litigation as per Section 27.

41.6   Unless otherwise agreed in writing, Corporation shall continue to provide services during any dispute resolution proceedings. If Corporation continues to perform, City shall continue to make payments in accordance with this Agreement. During the period, the parties are in dispute resolution proceedings, such Agreement shall be not be deemed to be in default as per Section 12, provided, however, the election to pursue a material breach by virtue of this Section 41 dispute resolution provision shall not constitute a waiver of any breach of the Agreement.

AGREEMENT BY AND BETWEEN CORPORATION AND THE CITY OF SANDY SPRINGS FOR CONTRACT SERVICES AS SET FORTH HEREIN.

IN WITNESS WHEREOF, the parties hereto have caused their respective agents to execute this instrument on their behalf, at the times set forth below.

CH2M HILL INCORPORATED

_____   _____

By: DATE

ATTEST

_____   _____

                                      DATE

CITY OF SANDY SPRINGS

_____   _____

By: DATE
Mayor and Chair

_____   _____

By: DATE
City Manager

_____   _____

By: DATE
City Clerk

Approved as to form and legal
Sufficiency subject to execution
by the parties

_____   _____

By: DATE
City Attorney

APPENDIX F

SCOPE OF SERVICE

AGREEMENT BY AND BETWEEN CORPORATION AND
THE CITY OF SANDY SPRINGS

EXHIBIT "A"
RFP 2—PUBLIC WORKS
SCOPE OF SERVICES

Services described in this Exhibit A will be delivered in a manner that is consistent with reasonable municipal management practices as compared with municipalities of similar size in the State of Georgia.

The Corporation will provide sufficient staff, including contractor and subcontractor personnel, to provide the services described in this Exhibit A. It is recognized that the project staffing may fluctuate due to seasonal or other conditions to meet the service demands. It is envisioned that the average annual staffing levels will be approximately sixty-one (61) full-time equivalent (FTE) positions to deliver the intended services consistent with reasonable municipal management practices as compared with municipalities of similar size in the State of Georgia. If there are modifications to the scope of service that require significant additional staffing levels, such changes will be handled as per Section 8.2 of the Agreement. As discussed in the contract, the corporation reserves the right to rearrange such positions as appropriate to address capacity and capability issues for the services under this agreement. Per Section 2.3 of this Agreement, the Corporation has the ability to reallocate resources.

The Corporation has provided references to FTEs in this scope of services to establish a level of effort consistent with reasonable municipal management practices. The corporation shall allocate resources among the scopes of services in this document and RFP 1- Administration.

Unless otherwise noted, the Corporation is not responsible for providing security services.

The services to be provided are described in the following sections.

1.0	**PUBLIC WORKS**
1.1	Public Works services shall include staffing and maintaining the Public Works Department for the City. The areas of responsibility shall include the following:
1.1.1	**Stormwater**
1.1.1.1	Under the direction of the City, coordinate with other City personnel and/or contractors for the transfer, maintenance, storage, and retrieval of available documents and records from Fulton County, Georgia, that are necessary for the effective implementation and operation of the City's stormwater requirements under applicable, federal, state, and local laws. The City shall facilitate the transfer of records. The Corporation shall be responsible for determining the documentation necessary for transfer, as well as coordinating and implementing the physical retrieval, reproduction, and storage of the transferred records.
1.1.1.2	Provide ongoing engineering, design and maintenance for the operation of stormwater system, as needed, to meet the needs of the City per Section 3.3 of the Agreement. Scope of services is limited to daily maintenance. Other services such as master planning and design services for capital program shall be handled per Section 3.3 of the Agreement.
1.1.1.3	Develop and recommend to the City and upon approval implement the necessary policies, protocols, rules, and regulations to meet or exceed the City's stormwater requirements under applicable federal, state, and local laws, including, but not limited to, federal clean water requirements.

1.1.1.4 Integrate activities as necessary with Planning/Zoning and other departments by establishing department head planning sessions that incorporate integrated client service goals.

1.1.1.5 To accomplish the stormwater services, the Corporation will provide the following levels of effort consistent with reasonable municipal management practices:

  a. Furnish a level of effort consistent with 50 percent of one FTE position during startup and two FTEs ongoing for records transfer.

  b. Furnish a level of effort consistent with 25 percent of one FTE for stormwater design.

  c. Furnish a level of effort consistent with a crew of three FTE for stormwater maintenance.

  d. Furnish a level of effort consistent with 25 percent of one FTE for policy development.

1.1.1.6 The scope does not include water sample collection, environmental testing, or reporting.

1.1.2 **Emergency Preparedness**

1.1.2.1 Develop and recommend policies and guidelines to the City, and upon approval, coordinate, operate, and maintain the City's emergency preparedness program in accordance with applicable federal, state, and local laws, as well as prudent local government practices.

1.1.2.2 Integrate and coordinate emergency preparedness operations in conjunction with Homeland Security, Emergency 911, Federal Emergency Management Agency (FEMA), and Georgia Emergency Management Agency (GEMA).

1.1.2.3 To accomplish emergency preparedness, the Corporation will provide:

  a. Baseline safety audit during transition

  b. Recommended Emergency Preparedness Plan (EPP) policy during transition

  c. Practice exercise during transition

d. Up to $50,000 for emergency cleanup (annually).

1.1.3   **Recycling**

1.1.3.1   Prepare and recommend policies and guidelines to the City, and operate the City's recycling program or a similar recycling program, which is defined presently as the City's proportionate share of the Keep Sandy Springs/North Fulton Beautiful Recycling Center (up to $81,000 annually).

1.1.3.2   Upon adoption, coordinate implementation of program and other activities with City personnel and/or contractors.

1.1.3.3   Fulfill reporting duties as required by applicable federal, state and local laws.

1.1.3.4   This scope of service does not include the hauling or disposing of yard waste or hazardous substances.

1.1.4   **Geographic Information System (GIS)**

1.1.4.1   Coordinate with the necessary City personnel and/or contractors for the transfer, maintenance, storage, and retrieval of available documents and records from Fulton County, Georgia, that are necessary for the effective implementation and operation of the City's geographic information system (GIS) database. The Corporation shall be responsible for determining the documentation necessary for transfer, as well as coordinating and implementing the physical retrieval, reproduction, and storage of the transferred records. Core elements of the GIS database will be in place to allow City staff to store and access GIS files and data obtained from Fulton County. The full implementation of the GIS database and interfaces will be complete on or around August 31, 2006.

1.1.4.2   Service, update, and maintain GIS databases on not less than a monthly basis.

1.1.4.3   Provide GIS-related information and/or data in response to requests and needs of City personnel.

1.1.4.4   To provide GIS services, the Corporation will provide levels of effort consistent with one (1) FTE during startup and two (2) FTEs for ongoing operations.

2.0   TRANSPORTATION

2.1   At the direction of the City, the transportation services shall include establishing, staffing, and maintaining the Transportation Department for the City. The areas of responsibility shall include the following:

2.1.1   Funding and Grant Applications

2.1.1.1   Conduct activities necessary to identify, develop, and prepare submissions for federal, state or local funding and grant programs, and provide fund oversight as required by law. Coordinate those aspects of the above, as necessary with the Atlanta Regional Commission and other local governmental entities as may be necessary. To accomplish the above service, Corporation will provide a level of effort consistent with 30 percent of a Transportation Planning Manager and 30 percent of a transportation planner.

2.1.2   Traffic Engineering

2.1.2.1   Conduct operational activities (maintenance, engineering, and planning services) necessary to maintain a traffic system, including conducting necessary studies and implementing traffic control improvements. To accomplish these services, the Corporation will provide a level of effort consistent with seventeen (17) FTEs under the direction of the Transportation Director, which includes up to $850,000 for the first year (2006) of traffic system operations and improvements, which includes street striping and signage. Design services for capital program projects and consulting services for master planning are not included in this scope of services and shall be handled per Section 3.3 of the Agreement.

2.1.2.2   The scope does not include the purchase of Christmas decorations for the City.

2.1.3   Street Design

2.1.3.1   Conduct activities necessary to maintain a street system plan, including the coordination, review, and management of contracts for streets, sidewalks, and related projects. To accomplish these services, the Corporation will provide a level of effort consistent with 25 percent of one road engineer. In addition, in order to manage ongoing Capital Improvement Plan (CIP) projects, the Corporation will provide a level of effort consistent with 50 percent of one CIP manager and one CIP engineer.

2.1.4 Street Maintenance

2.1.4.1 Conduct activities necessary to maintain a roadway and bridge infrastructure system, including minor repairs, pothole repairs, cleaning, and minor repairs necessitated by storm events. At City request, Corporation may perform utility cuts to the roadway which will be repaired and inspected as per City specifications by the Corporation. Corporation may also perform, at the direction of the City, the non normal road and bridge repair (such as wash outs, sink holes and damage caused by vehicle accidents). The utility cuts and non normal repairs are not included within this Scope of Services and shall be handled as per Section 8.2 of the Agreement. In order to accomplish this service, a baseline condition of streets will need to be obtained from Fulton County and updated by the Corporation. The Corporation will then put into place a preventive and corrective maintenance system and a capital program list will be developed and prioritized for the City Council. For these services, the Corporation will provide a level of effort consistent with five (5) FTEs and maintenance sub-contractors. The scope does not include costs to procure, operate, or maintain street sweeping services or resurfacing City streets.

2.1.5 Street lights, Sidewalks, Gutters and Related Street Areas

2.1.5.1 Conduct activities necessary to maintain street lights, sidewalks, gutters, and related street areas.

3.0 STREETS, RIGHTS-OF-WAY, AND FACILITIES

3.1 General

3.1.1 Streets, rights-of-way, and facilities services shall.

3.1.1.1 Coordinate the transfer of City rights-of-way from Fulton County, Georgia. The Corporation shall be responsible for determining the documentation necessary for transfer. The City shall be responsible for facilitating this process.

3.1.1.2   Operate and oversee aspects of the City rights-of-way permitting process. Right-of-way permits are issued for curb-cuts and private use of the City-owned rights-of-way. To accomplish this process, the Corporation will provide a level of effort consistent with one (1) FTE and maintenance sub-contractors.

3.1.1.3   The Corporation shall be responsible for up to $1,000 per event and up to $10,000 per year invested in the planting and maintenance of City rights-of-way beautification.

3.1.1.4   The Corporation shall not be responsible for security at City facilities, including both staff and security apparatuses such as metal detectors.

3.1.1.5   The scope includes up to $456,000 for street light electricity. The Corporation shall not be responsible for other utility costs associated with facilities, streets, or rights-of-way, including, but not limited to, water and electricity other than noted here and in Section 4.1.1.

3.2   **Contract Administration**

3.2.1   Operate and oversee aspects of contract administration for the daily maintenance of public rights-of-way and property, including landscaping and irrigation systems, in order to provide safe and comfortable common grounds for the residents of Sandy Springs. The scope includes hiring a subcontractor, scheduling, inspecting contracted work, and reviewing and approving payment requests.

3.2.2   Operate and oversee aspects of contract administration for the construction (excluding CIP; refer to Section 3.3), operation, and maintenance of public facilities. The scope includes hiring a subcontractor, scheduling, inspecting contracted work, and reviewing and approving payment requests.

3.2.3   Operate and oversee aspects of the emergency preparedness plan for debris removal, roadway access, flood prevention, and safe, operable utilities. To accomplish this service, the Corporation will provide the elements listed in Section 1.1.2.3. The scope includes preparing the plan, setting up a practice session, distributing a contact list, and reviewing and implementing GEMA and FEMA requirements through Corporation employees and subcontractors, with local, state and federal agencies.

4.0 PARKS AND RECREATION

4.1 Parks and recreation services shall include staffing and maintaining the Parks and Recreation Department for the City. The areas of responsibility shall reasonably include the following:

4.1.1 Plan, recommend, and upon adoption, implement and coordinate staffing and contract administration for the daily maintenance and use of public parks and recreational facilities. The scope includes managing and procuring the services of subcontractors and temporary personnel on behalf of the City to administer recreation programs and manage subcontractors performing maintenance functions such as mowing, fence repair, and ballpark lining. The scope includes electrical costs of up to $240,000 for the lighting of the ballparks and associated fields.

4.1.2 Plan, recommend, and upon adoption, implement and coordinate staffing for the planning, promoting, and supervising of recreation programs and special events. Special events include festivals and parades but not field trips. The Corporation shall set up traffic barricades and provide cleanup services after an event is over, for up to two City events per year. The Corporation shall not provide security or transportation services for programs or events.

4.1.3 Plan, recommend, and upon adoption, implement and coordinate staffing for the managing, coordinating and scheduling of City athletic facilities, as needed. The Corporation shall set up traffic barricades and provide cleanup services after an event is over. The Corporation shall not provide security or transportation services for programs or events.

4.1.4 Develop and recommend to the City Manager short-, mid-, and long-range plans for capital improvements and implement the plans as directed by the City Manager. The scope does not include the development of a Park and Recreation Master Plan by the Corporation.

4.1.5 Operate and oversee aspects of emergency management procedures with local, state and federal agencies. To accomplish this service, the Corporation will provide those the elements listed in Section 1.1.2.3.

4.1.6   Conduct the activities necessary to identify, develop, and prepare submissions for federal, state or local funding and grant programs for improvements to the park and recreation system within Sandy Springs and provide fund oversight as required by law.

4.1.7   To accomplish the parks and recreation services, the Corporation will provide a level of effort consistent with three (3) FTEs, plus subcontractors, for programs and maintenance under the direction of the Parks and Recreation Director.

4.1.8   Under no circumstances shall the Corporation be directly involved in the distribution or sale of alcoholic beverages.

5.0   CAPITAL IMPROVEMENTS

5.1   Develop and recommend short-, mid-, and long-range plans for capital improvements and implement plans as directed by the City Manager. The plans should meet the requirements of the Department of Community Affairs and the Atlanta Regional Commission for adoption in the City's Comprehensive Land Use Plan. The Corporation has allotted a level of effort consistent with 10 percent of each of the following Director's positions to accomplish this service: Community Development, Public Works, Transportation, and Parks & Recreation, with support of one full-time planner and one full-time administrative assistant split between these areas. This scope of service does not include procurement services for the capital improvements, which will be handled per Section 3.3 of the Agreement.

6.0   PLANNING AND ZONING

6.1   Planning and zoning services shall include staffing as needed to meet the requirements herein and operating the Planning and Zoning Department for the City. The areas of responsibility shall include the following:

6.1.1   At the direction of the City, provide information to the general public as it relates to land development activities within the City.

6.1.2   At the direction of the City, provide information to builders and developers regarding policies and procedures related to land planning within the City.

6.1.3   Oversee the development, maintenance, and updating of land use and zoning maps as approved and required by State and local agencies.

6.1.4   Prepare and recommend policies and procedures regarding planning and zoning activities and prepare and recommend schedules and time frames for processing land development activities, including, but not limited to, zoning.

6.1.5   Provide information to the City Manager, Mayor, City Council, Planning and Zoning Boards, and other City entities needing information regarding relevant and applicable zoning and/or planning issues.

6.1.6   Develop and recommend a plan for the implementation and assessment of impact fees by the City. Upon adoption, implement the plan in coordination with City staff and/or contractors. The scope does not include an impact fee study.

6.1.7   Conduct activities necessary to maintain a planning and zoning system for the City. These include, but are not limited to, the following:

         a.   Receiving, processing, and approving building plans

         b.   Building inspection

         c.   Recommend enforcement of codes, including signs, landscape, and arborist

         d.   Preparing a comprehensive plan, including zoning ordinances

         e.   Reviewing land development plans

         f.   Inspecting land disturbances

6.1.8   Develop and recommend a plan for the issuance of certificates of use and certificates of occupancy (COs). Upon approval, implement the plan in coordination with other City staff or contractors.

6.1.9   To accomplish the planning and zoning services, the Corporation will provide a level of effort consistent with seven FTEs under the direction of one full-time Community Development Director.

7.0   INSPECTIONS, CODE ENFORCEMENT, AND PERMITTING

7.1   Inspections, code enforcement, and permitting services shall include staffing and operating the inspections, code enforcement, and permitting functions for the City. The areas of responsibility shall include the following:

7.1.1   Develop and recommend a plan for the review and inspection process for the City. Upon adoption, implement the plan in coordination with City staff or contractors.

7.1.2   Develop and recommend a plan for the building permit and inspection process for the City. Upon adoption, implement the plan in coordination with City staff or contractors.

7.1.3   Develop and recommend a plan for the code enforcement process for the City. Upon adoption, implement the plan in coordination with City staff or contractors.

7.1.4   Develop and recommend a plan for the City to conduct Soil Erosion and Sedimentation Control inspections. Upon adoption, implement the plan in coordination with City staff or contractors.

7.1.5   To accomplish the inspections, code enforcement, and permitting services, the Corporation will supply a level of effort consistent with eleven (11) FTEs in Code Enforcement and six (6) FTEs, plus sub-contracting inspection services, in Permitting and Inspections under the direction of one full-time Community Development Director.

Printed in the United States
57321LVS00003B/1-69

9 781425 954369